GREEN GIANTS

**How Smart Companies Turn Sustainability
into Billion-Dollar Businesses**

E. FREYA WILLIAMS

American Management Association

New York • Atlanta • Brussels • Chicago • Mexico City •
San Francisco • Shanghai • Tokyo • Toronto • Washington, D. C.

Bulk discounts available. For details visit:
www.amacombooks.org/go/specialsales
Or contact special sales:
Phone: 800-250-5308
Email: specialsls@amanet.org
View all the AMACOM titles at: www.amacombooks.org
American Management Association: www.amanet.org

This publication is designed to provide accurate and authoritative information in regard to the subject matter covered. It is sold with the understanding that the publisher is not engaged in rendering legal, accounting, or other professional service. If legal advice or other expert assistance is required, the services of a competent professional person should be sought.

Library of Congress Cataloging-in-Publication Data
Williams, E. Freya.
    Green giants : how smart companies turn sustainability into billion-dollar businesses / E. Freya Williams. — First Edition.
        pages cm
    Includes bibliographical references and index.
    ISBN 978-0-8144-3613-4 (hardcover) — ISBN 0-8144-3613-7 (hardcover) — ISBN 978-0-8144-3614-1 (ebook) 1. Leadership. 2. Social responsibility of business. 3. Industrial management—Environmental aspects. 4. Success in business. I. Title.
    HD57.7.W534 2015
    658.4'083—dc23   2015003047

This publication may not be reproduced, stored in a retrieval system, or transmitted in whole or in part, in any form or by any means, electronic, mechanical, photocopying, recording, or otherwise, without the prior written permission of AMACOM, a division of American Management Association, 1601 Broadway, New York, NY 10019.

The scanning, uploading, or distribution of this book via the Internet or any other means without the express permission of the publisher is illegal and punishable by law. Please purchase only authorized electronic editions of this work and do not participate in or encourage piracy of copyrighted materials, electronically or otherwise. Your support of the author's rights is appreciated.

About AMA
American Management Association (www.amanet.org) is a world leader in talent development, advancing the skills of individuals to drive business success. Our mission is to support the goals of individuals and organizations through a complete range of products and services, including classroom and virtual seminars, webcasts, webinars, podcasts, conferences, corporate and government solutions, business books, and research. AMA's approach to improving performance combines experiential learning—learning through doing—with opportunities for ongoing professional growth at every step of one's career journey.

For Tomo, Dot, and Davy

For Jamie, Dot, and Dav

CONTENTS

CONTENTS

ACKNOWLEDGMENTS

The acknowledgments are the hardest part of a book to write. I'll go in chronological order.

My journey to sustainable business began while I was in upstate New York on maternity leave with my daughter, Dot, in 2006. So, Little Green Dot, you come first. This book really started with you.

Fast forward to my friends at Ogilvy who helped me next. To Colin Mitchell, who encouraged me to go for it. To Jeremy Katz, who edited *Mainstream Green*, the inspiration for Chapter 5, as well as the essay that was the genesis of this book. He also reviewed and commented on endless versions of the proposal and helped shape the thinking. He's a mensch.

To Graceann Bennett, for sharing a brain with me in 2011. The creation of *Mainstream Green* was one of my favorite professional collaborations. Thanks also for the fun TEDx double act.

To my sustainability brains trust, who have contributed ideas, support, and encouragement along the way—Andrew Winston, Sally Uren, Jo Confino, Charlie Wilkie, Solitaire Townsend, Callum Grieve, and KoAnn Vikoren—thank you.

Thanks especially to Hunter Lovins, who insisted on reading and editing the entire book, and helped me look as though I know more than I do. Hunter, thanks for preventing me from embarrassing myself in public, and for your unwavering support (and whiskey). This book is much the better thanks to your input.

Huge thanks to my agent, Cynthia Zigmund. If you ever need someone who knows how to organize a book, work with Cynthia. It was her idea to structure the book around six common factors. To Jeremy Holden, thanks for introducing me to Cynthia.

To Stephen S. Power, my editor at AMACOM, thanks for helping me figure out how to write a half-decent chapter, and for hearing me out. The book would have been funnier had you written it. At one point, I thought you might have to. Thanks also to Michael Sivilli at AMACOM, for keeping a sense of humor throughout and for having the patience of a saint. And to copyeditor and proofreader Jacqueline Laks Gorman, who made the book better.

To the people at the study companies who helped me assemble content, reach interviewees, checked my facts, and shared their insights—thank you. Specifically, the team at GE, Chris Arnold at Chipotle, Jamie Rusby at IKEA, Jessica Sobel at Unilever, and Molly Conroy at Nike.

Thanks also to Lynn Paine at Harvard and Chris Pinney at High Meadows Institute for supporting my inclusion of their ideas.

Thanks to Jason Denner at POINT380 for the extra quantitative firepower *Green Giants* needed. Jason is a great analytics partner, should you ever find yourself in need.

Many thanks to the team at Edelman Berland including Mike Berland, Samantha Tritsch, Jeremy Guterl, and Peter Hempel, for their innovative research methodology and brilliant insights included in Chapter 5. I really enjoyed our brainstorms.

To the B+SP team at Edelman New York, thanks for your patience while I got this done. You know who you are.

Other people who helped me think include Emma Gilding, Carol Cone, Aman Singh, and Tim Maleeny. I'm sure there are many others I've missed.

Thanks also to my oldest friend, Catherine Woods, for the title to Chapter 1 and the moral support.

Thanks to my family—Mum, Dad, and Nick (and Louisa)—for your support over the years, especially during the last two holidays, on which I was next to useless.

Also to Gran, who would have loved to live long enough to see this in print.

Thank you, Davy, for being the sweetest little boy in the world, and not complaining when I wasn't around enough over the past year.

But thanks above all to Tomo who did absolutely everything so I didn't have to. Every working mother needs a Tomo. Luckily for me, I have one. Thank you, hub.

The only thing I've ever been sure I wanted to do was write a book. Now, thanks to all of you, I have.

Billion with a "B"

Over the eight years I've spent compiling evidence that brands can both maximize profit and be a force for social good, the question I've been asked most often is: "What's the business case for sustainability?"

The answer is: *a $9 burrito*.

From 2006 to 2011, revenues tripled at Chipotle, a U.S. food chain selling responsibly sourced burritos. That last year, total annual revenue reached $2.2 billion, same-store sales increased 11.2 percent, and restaurant operating margins hit 25.9 percent. In just the second quarter of 2014, revenue rose 29 percent to $1.05 billion, same-store sales rose 17.3 percent, and restaurant operating margins hit 27.3 percent, counting .03 percent losses resulting from higher food and marketing costs. As of December 2014, the company had a market value of $21.03 billion.[1] Revenues for 2014 were $3.038 billion. For reference, that's almost three times those of Burger King.[2]

In the world of business, "billion" is a magic number. Only a relative handful of brands break the billion-dollar revenue ceiling. The chances of building a company that will grow to be worth more than $1 billion is 0.00006%. The constellation is mostly studded with global super brands like Coca-Cola, McDonald's, Marlboro, and Pampers.

And now, Chipotle—doing $1 billion in revenue *each quarter*. Chipotle—which sources its meat from farmers who commit to employ more responsible practices and uses its marketing dollars to advocate for ethical, sustainable farming.

Chipotle is not an anomaly. It is one of at least nine companies globally with more than $1 billion in annual revenue directly attributable to a product, service, or line of business with sustainability or social good at its core. The other eight are GE, with its Ecomagination business line; Toyota, with the Prius hybrid car; Nike, with its Flyknit shoe; IKEA, with its line of "products for a more sustainable life at home"; as well as Whole Foods, Unilever, Tesla, and Natura.

These nine businesses represent a critical mass of success. Their combined revenues add up to more than $100 billion a year, a figure greater than the GDP of 70 percent of the world's 180 economies. (This does not refer to the total revenues of these companies. In the cases of IKEA, GE, Nike and Toyota, it refers to only the revenues from the sustainable product, service, or line of business that is the subject of this book.) The companies include Brazil's largest and most profitable beauty brand, America's second-fastest growing restaurant chain, the world's third best-selling car, and the company behind one of 2014's hottest stocks—a far cry from the hemp-wrapped feel-good products we imagine as sustainable businesses.

The companies cut across the global economy. They derive their revenue from products as diverse as burritos and beauty cream, sports shoes and sports cars, organic kale and airplane engines. They cover a spectrum of price points and spend types, from low-cost and discretionary to big-ticket, corporate purchases. They span B2B and B2C companies and include relatively new start-ups and business lines incubated within major blue chip corporations. Some are primarily national or regional, like Chipotle or Natura; others, like GE and Unilever, are global.

THE GREEN GIANTS

These nine billion dollar businesses are the Green Giants—a new generation of leaders taking over from the old.

Green Giants are businesses with a billion U.S. dollars or more in annual revenue that can be directly attributed to a product, service, or line of business with sustainability or social good at its core. The following table gives some key information about the nine Green Giant companies profiled in this book, explaining how they are more sustainable or socially responsible than their competitors and detailing the revenue their sustainable business strategies generate for them annually.

Brand	Qualification as a Green Giant	FY 2014 Revenues
Standalone Businesses		
Chipotle	100% of pork, beef, and chicken are naturally raised and a majority of dairy is pasture raised. It is the only publicly traded restaurant to have achieved these ratios and is the nation's largest restaurant purchaser of sustainable and humanely reared meats.	$4.11 billion
Unilever	Committed to doubling its sales while halving its environmental footprint by 2020. Aims to source 100% of its agricultural feedstocks from sustainable agriculture and to improve the lives of 1 billion people.	$52.37 billion

(continued on next page)

Whole Foods Market	30% of sales are organic, more than any other national retailer. The first national supermarket to have its retail operation be certified organic.	$14.19 billion[3]
Natura	The world's largest and first publicly traded B Corp. Its goal is to source one-third of ingredients sustainably from the Amazon. A pioneer of integrated reporting.	$2.65 billion[4]
Tesla	Manufactures the world's first commercially successful all-electric vehicle.	$3.2 billion[5]
Product Lines or Business Units		
IKEA Products for a More Sustainable Life at Home	Products in the line are designed to help customers use energy more efficiently, produce renewable energy, reduce waste, recycle more, and save, reuse, or purify water.	$1.13 billion[6]
GE Ecomagination	A line of products ranging from diesel locomotives to electric vehicle charging stations that are certified against a set of criteria and verified by a third party as delivering superior environmental *and* financial performance to customers.	$28 billion*
Nike Flyknit	A technology that allows athletic shoes to be woven rather than pieced together, resulting in a high performance shoe that creates up to 80% less waste than conventional athletics shoes during manufacture.	$1 billion (estimated)[7]

* 2013 figure; FY 2014 not available.

Toyota Prius	The first mass-produced hybrid vehicle, it topped the 2013 Greenest list, an automotive ranking by the American Council for an Energy-Efficient Economy.	$15.44 billion (estimated)[8]
Total		**$122.09 billion**

This book studies the Green Giants, explaining why they are so important, how they have converted sustainability or social responsibility into billion-dollar revenue streams, and how you can follow their example.*

While the Green Giants are the focus, the book also features some Next Billions—companies that display similar characteristics to the Green Giants but have not yet reached the billion-dollar benchmark, though most are well on their way. Featured Next Billions include Warby Parker, Airbnb, The Honest Company, SweetGreen, Patagonia, and Method Home.

Note that Green Giants and Next Billions are not boring, crunchy granola companies or obscure B2B suppliers. They are some of the most vibrant, sexy brands out there today.

Together, they prove that businesses predicated on sustainability and social good aren't just a viable alternative to business as usual. They are more profitable and more sustainable financially.

They aren't trying to compete with the big boys. They *are* the big boys. And they will be the big boys of the future.

---

* Full transparency: I work for marketing communications firm Edelman. Edelman's clients include GE, Natura, Unilever, and Chipotle. I identified the study companies for this book and conducted interviews with GE and Chipotle before I joined Edelman. I have also, in the past, provided some counsel to Nike. With the exception of Unilever, I do not currently advise any of these clients directly.

THE BUSINESS CASE FOR SUSTAINABILITY

Mine is not the first book to make the business case for sustainability.[9] Evidence of the positive impact of sustainability on business outcomes is now irrefutable; there are at least 54 reports that prove it, and counting.[10] Among them is a 2007 report from Goldman Sachs that found that companies that are the leaders in sustainable, social, and good governance policies have 25 percent higher stock value than their less sustainable competitors.[11] Most recently, a report by CDP (formerly called the Carbon Disclosure Project), released in September 2014, showed that companies that outperform on sustainability metrics are more profitable and return better dividends to their shareholders than those that don't.[12]

And yet the perception persists that sustainability and business are competing agendas. In 1970, economist Milton Friedman dismissed business with a "social conscience" as "unadulterated socialism." Since then, the notion that sustainability and social good are fundamentally opposed to profit has hardened into fact in the minds of the majority of business leaders, reinforced by the opinions of Wall Street analysts to whom they are beholden.

This view is changing, but by increments. Sustainable business leaders have called for a new incarnation of business that embraces sustainability and social good—not as the job of sustainability and corporate social responsibility (CSR) departments, a risk to be managed or a cause supported—but as completely integrated into business strategy and the purpose of the organization, and embraced as *the* path to profits and growth. They view sustainability and social good not just as where businesses *spend* their money but how they *earn* it.

Yet the vast majority of companies have not made this shift. Why?

It's not necessarily for the lack of will. Many business leaders believe they'll need to change and want to do so. But the sustainable business movement faces specific barriers, both perceived and real.

First, it has been hard to shift away from Friedman's legacy. Many people believe that its tenets are enshrined in law in countries including the United States. They are not, as Professor Lynn Stout comprehensively proved in her 2012 book *The Shareholder Value Myth: How Putting Shareholders First Harms Investors, Corporations, and the Public*. But Friedman's ideas are persistent and have proven remarkably hard to dislodge.

Some don't believe the need to embrace sustainable business practices is pressing. For example, Jeff Immelt, CEO of GE, was lambasted by one group for "overestimating the urgency of these threats"[13] (referring to climate change) after he launched the Ecomagination strategy in 2005. Meanwhile, Bob Lutz, at the time vice chair of GM, memorably called global warming "a crock of S%$#"[14] in a closed door meeting with journalists in 2008. (This came back to bite him when in 2012 conservative media pundits universally panned the Chevy Volt, GE's electric vehicle, causing Lutz to lament that "all the icons of conservatism are deliberately not telling the truth" about the Volt because "they assume that if it's electric it must be a product of the left-wing, Democratic enviro-political machine."[15]) In addition, there are the long-term, well-funded efforts to deny and sow doubt about climate change backed by private sector players with a heavily vested interest in preserving the status quo.

Frequent use of the future tense doesn't help. Statements such as "In the future, the most successful businesses will . . . " and "Sustainability is the business opportunity of the 21st century" are the clarion calls of the sustainable business movement. But Wall Street thinks in increments of quarters and wants results next week, not maybe some time later this century.

The biggest barrier to adoption of sustainable practices, though, is lack of knowledge of how it can be done profitably. Many businesses have tried and failed with "green" or "eco-friendly" products, and they've given up because they assume that "green doesn't sell."

That's why the Green Giants are so exciting. They prove that addressing sustainability and social good need not be in conflict with delivering shareholder value; in fact, sustainability and social good can drive it. The Green Giants bring the debate into the present tense; it's not just that it *could* be done but that it *has been* and *is being* done—here and now. These companies are growing faster than their conventional counterparts. Most command wider profit margins than their category averages. Several are darlings of the stock market. Some are even knocking stalwarts of the strip mall and titans of industry off their long-held leadership perches, as Chipotle versus Burger King and Tesla versus the U.S. and German luxury automakers attest. GE earned $28 billion from Ecomagination in 2013,[16] which is the size of a Fortune 100 company. (It's roughly the same size as Halliburton or McDonald's and nearly four times the size of Peabody Energy, the world's largest coal company.[17])

In fact, proprietary analysis conducted for this book[18] by Jason Denner of the consulting group POINT380 found that the annual returns of publicly traded Green Giant companies have averaged 11.7 percent (23.2 percent –11.5 percent) higher than their leading competitors over the past five years.[19] That means that if you had invested $1,000 in a portfolio of the Green Giants and the same amount in a similar portfolio of their direct competitors in June 2010 (after Tesla's initial public offering), today your investment in Green Giants would be worth $3,251, while the portfolio of competitors would be worth $1,9320.[20] On average, the Green Giants' stock prices have outperformed the S&P 500 by 6.8 percent per year, which the comparison companies trailed by 4.9 percent.[21]

The selected competitors are high-performing companies. On average, they returned a total of 93 percent over the period 2010-2015. Green Giants, though, returned 225 percent. Admittedly, this number is boosted by Tesla's spectacular growth; however, if you remove Tesla from the analysis, the stock values of the remaining companies still outperformed their competitors, growing 153 percent over the period.[22] Not bad for companies not guided by delivering shareholder returns.

With upside opportunity like that, who cares if you believe in climate change or the social obligation of business?

You'd be crazy not to seize it.

THE SIX FACTORS OF GREEN GIANT COMPANIES

Getting to this point has not been easy for these companies—or for business at large. Even two years ago, I could not have written this book because not enough examples of Green Giants existed. There were green brands that didn't really sell much, some flashy green ad campaigns, and a handful of Green Giant companies, but the idea that sustainable business could be about rapid and significant top-line growth, about making a billion dollars in annual revenue, was embraced by only a brave few sustainability pioneers, not by mainstream business leaders.

In the past few years—even the past few months, as I've been researching this book—much has changed. What is enabling these companies to succeed where so many others had failed? How have they overturned prevailing business wisdom? What factors, if any, do they have in common—not just the general things, but the things that distinguish them from the rest and that account for their uncommon success? In short, what has enabled these companies to become successful businesses by *any* standard—not just the standard of sustainable business?

Those are the questions this book sets out to answer and to distill into a blueprint for Green Giant success that others can follow. This book uncovers enticing stories of iconoclastic thinking, radical innovation, tenacious commitment, standout creativity, and explosive growth—instead of the earnest themes of integrity, responsibility, and altruism more commonly associated with sustainability. It isolates six key factors or traits that Green Giants share and that have directly contributed to their uncommon success. A chapter is devoted to each trait. These are:

- *Chapter 1: The Iconoclastic Leader.* In each case, the sustainability journey can be traced back to one individual who started it all. This chapter explores those leaders' stories and diagnoses the 4 Cs of Iconoclastic Leadership.

- *Chapter 2: Disruptive Innovation.* Each of the Green Giant revenue streams is not founded on a slightly greener or more socially conscious version of an existing product but on an innovation that disrupted a category. In this chapter, you'll learn how Green Giants approach sustainability-oriented innovation to deliver breakthrough business results.

- *Chapter 3: A Higher Purpose.* This chapter reveals the higher purpose that animates Green Giants and explores the paradoxical finding that businesses with a purpose beyond profit tend to outperform the competition on—you guessed it—profit.

- *Chapter 4: Built In, Not Bolted On.* For Green Giants, sustainability means business. This chapter looks at how Green Giants integrate sustainability into six core structures of their business to enable it to become a revenue driver, not a drag.

- *Chapter 5: Mainstream Appeal.* If your product targets only what I call a Super Green niche, it's hard to reach $1 billion in revenue because there simply aren't enough people who take green values seriously enough to get you there. That's where many Green 1.0 brands went wrong. This chapter reveals the strategies Green Giants have used to achieve appeal with mainstream customers or consumers.

- *Chapter 6: A New Behavioral Contract.* Transparency, responsibility, collaboration: today's business buzzwords are alive and well at the Green Giants. But it's more than talk. Corporate reputation today is built through actions, not advertising. Your behavior is your brand. This chapter shows how the Green Giants are behaving their way to billions.

Each chapter includes an analysis of the specific factor, accompanied by insights and practical strategies you can implement in the course of your work.

These companies are not 100 percent perfect. Tesla and Toyota (with its Prius) promote private ownership of automobiles rather than the use of public transport; GE is involved in the controversial practice of hydraulic fracturing, or "fracking"; and IKEA sells furniture that some consider disposable, for example. But sometimes perfection is the enemy of progress. The Green Giants are, by their own admission, at the beginning of a long journey, and as of now, they are the best thing we've got.

IN CONCLUSION

Today, many business leaders know the world has changed. They are wrestling with the new mandate to incorporate sustainability and social good into their businesses and brands. But most companies struggle to figure out how to do this while continuing to meet their quarterly sales and earnings targets. They may have tried "green marketing" and met limited success. Or they may have skeptical shareholders convinced that this is a passing fad, or one that is just for hippies and tree huggers.

Is this you? Are you trying to change your company? Then this book is for you. It will give you the ammunition you need—and a blueprint to follow.

It is also for the next generation of social entrepreneurs and marketers seeking to build brands fit for the 21st century. It will enable you to avoid the traps of your predecessors and learn from the leaders you admire most.

The UN estimates that the market for "green trade" will grow to $2.2 trillion by 2020.[23] That's trillion with a *t* in just a few short years. The Green Giants are the leaders in an inexorable business movement, seizing the market's next great billion-dollar business opportunity.

Ignore their example at your peril.

CHAPTER **1**

The Iconoclastic Leader

"These stories begin with one person saying I absolutely believe in this and I want this to happen."
—**Professor Lynda Gratton,** London Business School

In 1999, a chef named Steve Ells visited a factory farm in Iowa that supplied his nascent 16-outlet restaurant chain—Chipotle—with pork for its signature burritos. He was fresh from a trip to Niman Ranch—an operation that aims to raise livestock traditionally, humanly, and sustainably—where he'd gone to learn more about better ways to raise meat. Ells did not like what he saw in Iowa, "grim" is a word he's used to describe it. The stark contrast between Niman and the commodity farm had a profound effect on him. Ells recalls resolving then and there to pursue a new strategy. He returned home to Denver and set about sourcing as much of his chain's meat as possible from more humane, sustainable sources.

Colleagues remonstrated with Ells, fearing the substantially greater costs of this kind of meat would sink the small, vulnerable business. "I don't care," Ells is said to have replied. "It's the right thing to do."[1]

And not just the right thing by the animals. Ells believed the meat tasted better, which would be better for customers and ultimately, therefore, for business. He introduced the new and improved meat into his restaurants, implemented a price increase of a dollar per serving—taking the pork menu offering, Carnitas, from the least expensive to the most expensive dish on the menu—and waited to see how the market would respond.[2]

And that was just the beginning. Ells stuck to his commitment to use meat from humane, sustainable sources as Chipotle grew, extending it to 100 percent of the company's pork as well as to chicken, beef, and dairy. He added produce to the plan, working to source as much as possible locally when in season. It wasn't always easy: There have been two occasions when Chipotle has had to work around a shortfall in the supply of ingredients that met its standards. But in each case, the company found a way through it. Chipotle sourced imported, grass-fed beef for a short period, rather than resort to conventionally reared meat, when its usual supply fell short in 2014. The company also pulled pork from about a third of its U.S. restaurants in 2015 when a pork supplier failed to meet ethical standards. Yet, despite efforts by opponents to stir up trouble, neither situation seems to have hurt Chipotle . jut; on the contrary, customers and commentators have appreciated its refusal to compromise.

Ells's early decision, as well as his tenacity and perseverance, paid off. Today, Chipotle is both the nation's largest restaurant seller of naturally raised meats and its most profitable fast casual restaurant chain, with margins of 25.9 percent (compared to 19 percent at McDonald's) and 2014 revenues of more than $4 billion.[3] Indeed, Chipotle's commitment to "Food with Integrity" has become so recognized a contributor to its success that, rather than suggest it dilute the strategy to manage costs, analysts describe it as a reason to consider the company's stock; they even list insufficient supply of the right ingredients as a threat to future business performance.[4] (Who ever thought we'd see Wall Street analysts fretting over the living conditions of the nation's pigs?)

This story illuminates four salient facts about Ells. First, he underwent a conversion, which for him kicked off an inner journey, instilling in him a sense of *conviction* and permanently altering his view on the world. Second, he had the *courage* to stand up and change the direction of his business, setting it on a course that at the time seemed risky and counterintuitive, at odds with conventional business thinking. Third, he had the *commitment* and tenacity to stick with the course he had set, even in the face of skepticism and opposition from others within the business, rather than buckling at the first sign of opposition. And fourth, he is something of a *contrarian*, comfortable in the role of provocateur, challenger, and outsider.

Ells is an Iconoclastic Leader. Such leadership is the first of the six shared traits of Green Giants that you'll read about in this book. As you delve into these companies' stories, you'll find that the decision to either start or change course to a sustainable strategy can almost always be traced back to one specific individual—the pioneer and long-term champion of the Green Giant strategy.

Big deal, you may say. All strong organizations have strong leaders. But the Iconoclastic Leaders of Green Giants are different. In addition to requiring the traits of all strong business leaders (because building a billion-dollar business of *any* sort requires that), these Iconoclastic Leaders tend to share a unique combination of additional characteristics: the 4 Cs.

1. They are fueled by an inner sense of *conviction* that they need to take things on, often resulting from a personal conversion.

2. They have the *courage* to stand up and change things, often in a way that seems counterintuitive or risky to colleagues or shareholders.

19

3. They have the *commitment* and tenacity to stick with the idea through thick and thin, through objections and obstacles, to see it to fruition.

4. They are *contrarian*, happy to live with the role of outsider, espousing a different view from everyone else; indeed, they thrive on it. Crucially, though, they are constructive contrarians, not contrary for the sake of it.

These characteristics are the 4 Cs of Iconoclastic Leadership.

In this chapter, you'll meet the Iconoclastic Leader at each of the nine Green Giants under study, taking a look at what each did and why. You'll delve into the 4Cs of Iconoclastic Leadership. And finally, you'll explore how you can become an Iconoclastic Leader, no matter your background or role within your company.

MEET THE ICONOCLASTIC LEADERS

The following table provides information on the nine Iconoclastic Leaders studied in this book.

Company	Leader	Title
Nike	Hannah Jones	CSO
Background: Corporate responsibility background as director for Nike of EMEA 1998–2004. Before that, a reporter and social action campaigner.		
Unilever	Paul Polman	CEO
Background: CFO at Nestlé and P&G. Became CEO of Unilever in 2009.		

GE	Jeffrey Immelt	Chair & CEO
Background: Long-time GE executive. Joined GE in 1982. Became CEO in 2001.		

IKEA	Steve Howard	CSO
Background: Climate activist; formerly CEO of The Climate Group. Joined IKEA in 2010.		

Natura	Antônio Luiz da Cunha Seabra	CEO
Background: Entrepreneur who founded Natura in his garage in 1969.		

Whole Foods	John Mackey	Cofounder & Co-CEO
Background: Entrepreneur who cofounded Whole Foods in Austin, Texas, in 1980.		

Chipotle	Steve Ells	Founder and Co-CEO
Background: Classically trained chef who founded Chipotle in 1993 in Denver, Colorado.		

Tesla Motors	Elon Musk	CEO & Chief Product Architect
Background: Engineer. Founder of PayPal. CEO and CTO of SpaceX. Chair of SolarCity.		

Toyota	Takeshi Uchiyamada	Chairman of the Board
Background: Test engineering and technical administration at Toyota. Formerly chief engineer of the Prius.		

THE 4Cs AND THE C-SUITE

As you peruse the job titles of the Iconoclastic Leaders, notice that for a group selected on the basis of their success leading a sustainable business strategy, surprisingly few of them have "sustainability" in their title. Instead, the majority—seven out of the nine—are chair and/or chief executive officer.

It's important to emphasize that the CEOs didn't make this list simply because success was achieved on their watch. Instead, these people are the individuals who envisioned, shaped, owned, and drove through the Green Giant strategy at their respective companies. In the words of Professor Lynda Gratton of the London Business School, who has studied sustainable business leadership extensively, they are the ones who stood up, said "I absolutely believe in this and I want this to happen," and saw it through from inception to execution.

Antônio Luiz da Cunha Seabra and John Mackey built businesses with sustainability at their core—a more natural beauty brand, on the one hand, and a natural, organic grocer, on the other. As far back as the garage in Brazil where Seabra started Natura in 1969, or the natural foods store Mackey and his girlfriend opened in Austin, Texas, in 1980, sustainability was integral to the concept. Meanwhile, Elon Musk joined Tesla in 2004, seven months after its incorporation. A serial Silicon Valley entrepreneur with successes at PayPal and other start-ups under his belt, he quickly became the driving force, both spiritually and financially, of the electric vehicle company that would almost certainly have failed without him.

At the multinationals on our list, GE and Unilever, Jeff Immelt and Paul Polman didn't just give their approval to plans dreamed up by their teams. Ecomagination at GE and the Unilever Sustainable Living Plan were (and are) invented and personally led by them (as we'll learn in this chapter). In both cases, the stakes were high. Both men put their reputation and position in the balance to achieve success, and they are viewed by the outside world and by their teams as the unequivocal leaders of these strategies.

At Toyota, the story was slightly different. The agenda that resulted in the development of the Prius was initially set by then-chair Eiji Toyoda and was propelled forward by other very senior executives including the subsequent president, Hiroshi Okuda. But today, the man appointed as chief engineer on the project, Takeshi Uchiyamada—the one who figured out how to crack the code on a hybrid powertrain—is viewed as the father of the Prius. And today, he is Toyota's chairman of the board.

What does this tell us? In sustainability discussions, it's common to hear people say "leadership has to come from the top." This is usually taken to mean that the CEO has to be engaged and lending his or her support. The Green Giants suggest we take the sentiment literally.

But *why* is an Iconoclastic Leader in the CEO (or other major) role a key ingredient to success in building a Green Giant business?

In the coming chapters, we'll explore how Green Giants are different from other companies. They've developed innovations that overturned the way things were done in their categories, investing millions, sometimes billions, of dollars into things like R&D and supply chain reengineering to create products and services they didn't make before—that no one's made before. They have oriented their organizations around a purpose beyond profit, rethinking the business model and taking on decades of established business ideology to prove there's a new way of doing things. They've made sustainability not the job of a separate department or team trying to sprinkle a little sustainability where they can, but they've embedded it right at the heart of the structures of their business, into the guts and sinews of their organizations. They're reengineering the value proposition to the customer and are forging a New Behavioral Contract with their key stakeholders. In the process, they're building a new kind of company.

Sometimes there was a strong legacy of sustainability or corporate responsibility (CR) at the companies before the Iconoclastic Leaders' times. This could be said of Nike, GE, and Unilever, for example. Typically, though, the Iconoclastic Leader put things into hyperdrive, shifting gears from a *sustainability strategy*, which was primarily about reducing the company's environmental footprint and managing risk, to a *business strategy*, which was about transformation and growth.

And that's the crucial point. The Green Giant strategies explored in this book are not sustainability strategies, with a goal of, say, reducing energy and water consumption or waste (though those are critically important and are being addressed by the Green Giants). Instead, they are *business strategies*, with a goal of transforming the organization and the way it makes money. These companies have shifted sustainability or social good from where they spend or save money to how they earn it.

The stories in this chapter illustrate why, to make this kind of change happen, you often have to be the boss. You need to be the anointed owner of the strategy of the business, with license to initiate a transformation agenda. You need the power to direct resources at scale and to remove roadblocks when they arise. You need a veto right, the power to overrule colleagues should it become necessary. You need the big picture view of the organization. And you need enough personal capital and authority for employees, board members, shareholders, and customers to go along with you when you inevitably find yourself saying, "I know this sounds weird, but you have to trust me."

It's hard enough to drive this kind of change through an organization when you're the boss. It's nearly impossible when you're not.

What, then, of those who are not? Two of the Iconoclastic Leaders on our list are not CEOs but CSOs, or chief sustainability officers.

They are no ordinary CSOs. The Iconoclastic Leaders at Nike and IKEA, Hannah Jones and Steve Howard, represent a new breed of CSO. They are change agents, empowered to drive the Green Giant strategy through the organization. Both report directly to the CEO and are on their respective executive teams, while the majority of CSOs are not. They break the mold of the job description, going beyond efficiency and compliance—the heartland territories of the CSO—to innovation and transformation. Both stay extremely close to their CEOs. Both also had the added advantage of inheriting a conducive environment. As we'll learn later, IKEA has had a social purpose and a culture of efficiency since the 1970s, while pioneers had opened the door to the changes Jones has since driven at Nike, including board member Jill Ker Conway and other CR leaders including Maria Eitel and Sarah Severn. And Howard and Jones embody the 4 Cs. This combination of unique position, company legacy, and personal character has allowed them to function as the Iconoclastic Leaders in their respective domains, even though they don't sit in the very top spot.

Perhaps surprisingly, though, deep sustainability chops are not a prerequisite for becoming an Iconoclastic Leader that drives a Green Giant strategy forward. In fact, the only one of the nine who comes close to fitting the image of a traditional tree hugger is John Mackey of Whole Foods. Naturally, sustainability and corporate responsibility loom large on the resumes of Jones and Howard. But Paul Polman and Jeff Immelt are blue chip corporate to the core; one used to be a CFO, the other a business unit leader. Elon Musk is a Silicon Valley whiz kid, Steve Ells is a chef, and Takeshi Uchiyamada is a career engineer.

No, besides that all-important C-suite title, the characteristics that most distinguish the Iconoclastic Leaders from their peers can't be found in the pages of their resumes. They are intangible. They are the 4 Cs.

ANATOMY OF AN ICONOCLASTIC LEADER: THE 4 Cs

As previously stated, the 4 Cs are conviction, courage, commitment, and being contrarian. Let's explore them in depth.

Conviction

On January 1, 2009, Paul Polman became chief executive officer and executive director of the multinational consumer goods company Unilever. Owner of well-loved household staples like Hellmann's mayonnaise, Suave shampoo, and Breyers ice cream, Unilever was at the time the 60th-largest company in the world by market capitalization, valued at more than $100 billion. Polman was the first CEO in the company's 125-year history to be hired from outside the company, but with a packaged goods pedigree honed at Procter & Gamble and Nestlé Foods, he seemed a solid and uncontroversial choice.

Then, on his first day on the job, Polman announced that Unilever would no longer be providing guidance to Wall Street, deeming it "inappropriate," and would be eliminating quarterly reporting altogether. To Wall Street, the gesture was like waving a red flag at a bull. Unilever's share price plummeted 8 percent in response to the news, and a further 12 percent over the next several months. The media weighed in, declaring, "Unilever could use some guidance."[5]

Polman didn't flinch. "I figured they couldn't fire me if I did it on my first day," he said, and he set about undertaking a wholesale transformation of the company.

His day one move was certainly unexpected, but it was merely the first taste of what Polman had up his sleeve. Unilever had been through a decade of low or no growth, so when the new CEO declared that the company would double its revenues by 2020, people sat up. His strategy for getting there was unorthodox, to say the least. Formalized in 2010 as the Unilever Sustainable Living Plan,[6] his vision was to create a more "inclusive" style of growth, setting the company up to prosper by being part of the solution to the social problems he observed, such as deforestation, food security, poverty, and environmental degradation. His overarching vision was "to double the size of the business, whilst reducing our environmental footprint and increasing our positive social impact." "The essence of the plan," Polman said, "is to put society and the challenges facing society smack in the middle of the business."[7] (The USLP is outlined in more detail in Chapter 4.) He gleefully admitted he had no idea how Unilever would deliver on its goals, but he began restructuring the company to deliver.

The ideological battle with Wall Street continued. Polman said achieving his goals would be impossible in a system addicted to looking at only the short term. He began actively courting longer-term investors while suggesting that short-term investors take their money elsewhere. He achieved notoriety at the annual meeting of the World Economic Forum in Davos, Switzerland, in 2011, where he railed against the hedge fund community. "They would sell their grandmother if they could make money. They are not people who are there in the long-term interests of the company," he said, a statement he later said he regretted, although he still declines to give presentations to hedge fund managers. "He is the chief executive of a multinational corporation, but Paul Polman sometimes sounds more like a spokesman for Occupy Wall Street," *The Economist* intoned in 2012.[8] Polman's unorthodox style took its toll at Unilever. Huge swaths of the senior ranks changed guard—as many as a third, by one estimate.

Then something strange began to happen. By the end of 2011, operating profits were up 26 percent to €5.4 billion ($8.34 billion) on turnover up 11 percent to €37.8 billion ($58.36 billion).[9] Unilever's stock rebounded; by late 2012, its price was more than 50 percent above where it had been when Polman started. As the research conducted for this book by Jason Denner at POINT380 revealed, Unilever has outperformed Procter & Gamble by 3.5 percentage over the past five years. And Unilever has emerged as the unquestioned leader in sustainable business, having achieved that accolade for four consecutive years in one global study.[10]

Polman credits much of the company's success to the move to long-term thinking, saying it has freed executives up to make better decisions. They no longer postpone launches or other capital investments to a less opportune moment simply to make quarterly numbers, as they might have done in the past. The move has also freed up time and resources previously spent preparing for quarterly reports. And it has reignited employee motivation and productivity.[11] Unilever is now the third most sought-after employer, behind Google and Apple.[12]

What on earth possessed Paul Polman to launch into this wildly ambitious project, to take on the global financial establishment and assume such enormous responsibility, on his first day on the job?

It seems he just became convinced it was the right thing to do.

As with Steve Ells's story about Chipotle at the beginning of this chapter, the conviction of this Iconoclastic Leader was the impetus to embark on the Green Giant strategy. I use the word *conviction* because Iconoclastic Leaders do not embark on this journey lightly. They are not just trying something on for size. They seem to believe in what they are doing with every ounce of their being.

And they accept the need to do it as simple fact. Indeed, when challenged on his strategy, Polman often responds with the facts, like this: "The fact is, it's unsustainable to have 15 percent of the world's population using 50 percent of the resources."[13] He speaks of leaders who don't see a need to change the way they do business as being "in denial." He says he sees no alternative. When asked what the business case is for sustainability (the question with which I opened the Introduction to this book), he responds, "I always turn that question around: How would you make the case that not doing this could help society and mankind?" (He is channeling Ray Anderson, late CEO of Interface Inc. and sustainable business pioneer, whose favorite answer to the same question was "What's the business case for ending life on earth?")

What brings a leader to accept the need to pursue a Green Giant strategy as fact? Sometimes the conviction is born of a conversion—a "damascene moment," as Jo Confino, executive editor of the *Guardian* and chair and editorial director of Guardian Sustainable Business (a section of the *Guardian* web platform), calls it. This is when the scales seem to fall from the leaders' eyes and they see the world anew. For Ells, it was the moment on the supplier's farm when he saw the poor conditions in which the pigs were raised. Luiz Seabra, of the Brazilian beauty company Natura, recalls reading the Roman philosopher Plotinus as a teenager. He couldn't get Plotinus's ideas—such as "the one is in the whole, the whole is in the one"—out of his head, and he directly translated them into the philosophy that has guided Natura from the beginning: Bem Estar Bem, or well-being/being well.[14] *

---

* My personal conversion happened in the toilet paper aisle of a small supermarket in rural Pennsylvania when I was on maternity leave with my first child. I couldn't find recycled toilet paper. That, and the responsibility to my new baby, somehow triggered a radicalization of my inner environmentalist. I cooked up the idea of starting a dedicated sustainability division within my employer, the ad agency Ogilvy, and never looked back. I cofounded a business unit that became known as OgilvyEarth. We had the opportunity to advise clients including Coca-Cola,

But not all epiphanies have such a spiritual quality or can be pinpointed as directly to a conversion moment.

Polman's conviction grew in part from sound business reasoning. As he said on one occasion: "We thought about some of the megatrends in the world, like the shift east in terms of population growth and the growing demand for the world's resources. And we said, 'Why don't we develop a business model aimed at contributing to society and the environment instead of taking from them?' "

But there is definitely a sense of commitment to a higher purpose. As Polman has said: "All of us need to be net contributors to society. We must offer more than we take. We cannot afford any more global warming. We cannot let people go hungry. And, we cannot allow people to work for abysmally low fees. Capitalism needs to evolve." This is a sentiment he has expressed in varying ways many times over the past five years to anyone who listens.

On the question of whether there was a more personal side to the conversion behind his conviction, Polman has said surprisingly little. He once told Jo Confino that he looked into his children's eyes and decided he would be failing them if he did not do all he could to ensure their future well-being.[15] No one else has been able to draw him out on this point. For this book, his team told me it's simply the way he wants to lead.

Either way, Polman's conviction is fueling the reinvigoration of a great company. So far, results are proving it well-founded. But for all

---

on their PlantBottle branding, and Hellmann's on their switch to free-range eggs. We also advised the United Nations, on behalf of whom we developed the award-winning Hopenhagen campaign around the crucial 2009 COP15 climate change conference in Copenhagen. The campaign recruited 6 million supporters in 60 days, 70 percent of whom had never joined a climate movement before. OgilvyEarth grew to 20 markets globally and millions (though not billions) of dollars in revenue.

Polman's certainty, the doubt still occasionally creeps in. "I do worry that if, in any six-month period, our results are not good, the cynics and critics will come out. We need to be strong enough to work our way through that if it happens," he has said—which brings us to the next of the 4 Cs.

Courage

On September 7, 2001, Jeff Immelt inherited the role of chair and CEO of General Electric from "Neutron" Jack Welch, the man who had been named Manager of the Century by *Fortune* magazine. During his 20-year tenure, Immelt's predecessor Welch had grown GE's annual sales from $25 billion to $170 billion, and its market valuation from $14 billion to nearly $500 billion. (He also made the company the environmentalists' public enemy number one by spending a reported $122 million to block efforts by the Environmental Protection Agency and others demanding that GE clean up the 1.3 million pounds of toxic chemicals—PCBs—it was alleged to have discharged into the Hudson River between 1947 and 1977.)

As Immelt began his tenure, the dot-com bubble had just burst. Then, 9/11 occurred during his first week on the job. Immelt watched as, over the next two years, GE's stock price tumbled from $54 to $24 per share, its market valuation plunged more than $200 billion, and the company lost fully 40 percent of its value.[16]

What Immelt did next nobody saw coming. Rather than hunker down and go on the defensive, he went out into the market and spent time listening to customers, assessing the market realities GE was facing. He heard from customers, particularly the big utilities and railroads, that were hungry for solutions to help them meet new emissions regulations, deliver better fuel efficiency, and enhance their reputations as environmentally friendly companies. Significant numbers of them were based in Europe and Japan, where environmental regulations were more stringent than in the United States. Signals suggested that China and even India would soon begin focusing more on cleaner technologies, in response to domestic pollution and sky-rocketing fuel prices.

Sensing an opportunity, Immelt began making significant investments in renewable energy and energy efficiency technologies. In 2002, GE purchased the biggest wind-turbine producer in the United States, and in 2004, the largest solar producer. Immelt also invested in an early form of carbon capture and storage, the technology that lies behind the contentious concept of "clean coal."[17]

In internal business reviews, he noticed that solutions to the problems he'd been hearing about from customers were already bubbling up across the organization. Teams from different business units had independently created what together amounted to a significant portfolio of products that were "competitively advantaged on environmental factors like fuel efficiency and emissions."[18] They included hybrid diesel-electric locomotives, fuel-efficient jet engines, and energy-saving dishwashers and refrigerators. None of the teams was aware of the work other teams were doing until Immelt began to connect the dots.

Immelt did his homework. He spent his 2004 summer vacation reading the most recent National Academy of Sciences report on climate change cover to cover. He came to the conclusion that what he was reading about was fact, that climate change was occurring and was driven by human activities like power generation—activities in which GE was heavily involved. He returned to work convinced there was an opportunity to unite GE's disparate products into a cohesive strategy and accelerate the commitment to developing more. He presented his idea to his management team.

Others in the senior ranks weren't immediately convinced. Gary Sheffer, vice president of communications and public affairs and a key figure in the early development of the Ecomagination strategy, told me:

> To be quite honest, internally this wasn't a big hit at first. There was concern about getting out in front of your customers, and even embarrassing them—as a B2B company, that's always your first consideration. Then there was concern from people, including myself, because we have some big legacy issues as a 100-year-old industrial company. We had a negative reputation. How much credibility would we have if we launch something like Ecomagination? How much fire will we take from people who care passionately about the Hudson River?[19]

Competitive precedent did nothing to reassure. GE had watched other companies struggle at similar efforts, either taking a reputational hit or simply failing to commercialize. Moreover, Immelt was advocating for GE to take a stand on climate change and to publicly endorse both carbon pricing and a strong U.S. climate policy. Both were considered politically combustible topics with clients "who might have a different view," as Sheffer put it. GE's government relations department worried about the policy implications.[20]

Immelt decided to gather more data points and tasked senior leaders—including his chief collaborator in the strategy, Chief Marketing Officer Beth Comstock, and Sheffer—with pressure-testing the concept in the market. They spent a year talking with NGOs, government groups, employees, and customers "to get it right and to make sure it wouldn't land with a thud in the marketplace—or the *New York Times*," Sheffer joked. Immelt personally conducted many of the conversations. Sheffer recalls "getting laughed out of people's offices" at first. But the conversations were mostly encouraging, even those GE had feared would be the most negative. "We found that when we said we wanted to invest in environmentally advantaged technology products, and our goal was to make money doing it, we found unanimously resounding support to say if GE says it's investing in this, then we're in," Sheffer told me.

Buoyed by the positive feedback, Immelt put his plan to a vote with the top 35 executives in the company. Only five or six went with him; the rest went against.[21] "In the beginning, he was a constituency of one," Sheffer admitted.

Immelt acknowledged the concerns of his management team, with whom he had by now spent years building trust and support. But he let them know he planned to proceed anyway. "There's about five times a year with that group that I say, 'Hey guys, here's where we're going, get in line.' If you did it six times, they would leave. And if you did it three times, there'd be anarchy," Immelt said at the time.[22] He directed the team to prepare for a 2005 launch.

The team went full-steam ahead. The strategy got a name: Ecomagination, inspired by the company's tagline, "Imagination at Work." GE hired a third-party consultant, Green Order, to develop an "iron clad" set of criteria and a scorecard to determine which products would qualify to carry the Ecomagination moniker. It was agreed that products must have quantifiable benefits to the customer on both environmental and financial measures.[23] Seventeen products made the cut to be part of the initial launch, including a jet engine that delivered 22 percent fuel economy, saving airline customers $350,000 per plane per year, and a hybrid diesel-electric locomotive that offered 15 percent fuel savings and a 50 percent emissions reduction over conventional models.[24]

Comstock oversaw the development of a major advertising campaign, headlined by a TV commercial memorably featuring an elephant dancing to "Singing in the Rain." The EH&S (environment, health, and safety) and innovation teams weighed in on a series of binding, public-facing goals: to more than double R&D investments in clean technologies from $700 million in 2004 to $1.5 billion in 2010; to double revenues from green technologies within five years, from $10 billion in 2004 to $20 billion in 2010; and to improve energy efficiency in GE operations by 30 percent and create an absolute reduction in greenhouse gas emissions of 1 percent by 2012. (The latter may not sound like much, but GE would have seen a 25 percent increase in greenhouse gas emissions under the business-as-usual scenario.)

Immelt spent time speaking to fossil fuel customers, letting them know the company planned to take a position on clean energy and energy policy. He agreed to clean up the Hudson River. He honed his narrative, saying, "My environmental agenda is not about being trendy or moral. It's about accelerating economic growth."[25] Jonathan Lash, CEO of the World Resources Institute, a highly respected sustainable business NGO, was drafted to share the stage with Immelt at the launch of Ecomagination. At the launch, at George Washington University in Washington, D.C., Immelt announced Ecomagination to a packed room of press and key opinion formers.

In the end, Ecomagination overwhelmingly went Immelt's way. The program earned plaudits from NGOs, the media, customers, and policy makers alike. To date, Ecomagination has generated revenues in excess of $180 billion for GE. Since the launch, GE has seen a 32 percent reduction in greenhouse gas emissions, which has saved the company $300 million.[26] Walmart's then-CEO Lee Scott described Immelt as "the Pied Piper of sustainability."

Immelt's idea had brought GE a long way from those dark first days of his tenure. It's not an exaggeration to say that all that stood between success and oblivion for this engine of value creation for GE was Immelt's conviction, courage, and sheer force of will. As Sheffer says:

> The opposition was overcome by a leader, Jeff Immelt, who acted like a leader and said, this is what we're going to do. It wasn't easy. It took a lot of courage both internally and externally for Jeff to take this position, but he was convinced it was the right thing to do for our share-owners and the right thing to do for society, so he carried it across the finish line.

Sustainable business expert Hunter Lovins (whose credentials are covered toward the end of this chapter is fond of saying, "Immelt was smart. Jack Welch was the guy who saved the company. So what could Immelt do? He had to save the world."

Leaders setting out to build a Green Giant strategy may have ambitions as grand as saving the world, or not, but either way, the obstacles Immelt faced are par for the course. As with Paul Polman at Unilever, it was the courage of Immelt's convictions that brought the Green Giant strategy to fruition. Courage is an essential ingredient to the success of the Iconoclastic Leaders.

Commitment

Today, with Tesla's stock riding high and its CEO Elon Musk seemingly unable to put a foot wrong, it's easy to forget that in 2008, bloggers had Tesla on death watch. Musk had burned through his entire PayPal fortune, down to his last $3 million—which he ended up using to make Tesla's payroll.

When Musk had joined Tesla in 2004, he must have had some idea of what he was taking on. The big auto makers were walking away from the electric vehicle (explored in more depth in Chapter 2), and Tesla itself was tiny. The company consisted of original founders Martin Eberhard and Marc Tarpenning, an unfunded business plan, and a dream. There was a basic corporation in place, but the name had not yet been registered or trademarked and the business had no formal offices or assets.

Musk joined as chair and led a Series A round of funding in 2004. Of the initial closing of $6.5 million, 98 percent of it ($6.35 percent) came from Musk. What followed was a roller coaster ride of funding rounds, delayed production schedules, personnel problems, elated and then disappointed customers, and, overwhelmingly, money woes.

After that initial Series A, Musk led Tesla's Series B investment round in February 2005, adding $13 million to the funds, and then another investment round, adding $40 million in May 2006. This third round included investment from prominent entrepreneurs such as Google cofounders Sergey Brin and Larry Page and former eBay President Jeff Skoll.[27] The fourth round, in May 2007, added another $45 million, bringing the total to more than $105 million of private financing. But Tesla was a voracious consumer of capital, and it never seemed to be enough.

Bringing a car to market seemed impossible. Tesla unveiled its first model in 2006, but by the end of 2007, the company still hadn't delivered a single vehicle to customers. By 2008, Musk had sunk $70 million of his own money into the company. "Personal bankruptcy was a daily conversation," his brother told an interviewer.[28] A series of personnel issues swirled. Cofounder Martin Eberhard had become Tesla's CEO when Musk joined, but Eberhard was voted out of the company in 2007. A spat of public mudslinging ensued, resulting in a high-profile lawsuit. While Eberhard eventually lost, the lawsuit took its toll. The company went through another CEO and had to fire 10 percent of the workforce "to reduce burn rate." In October 2008, Musk himself took over as CEO. (He was already the CEO at SpaceX.)

The year 2008 continued to be hard. In the midst of the economic crisis, further capital was hard to come by. A documentary *Revenge of the Electric Car* follows Musk through this desperate time. For most of the film, he looks pale and shell-shocked, a far cry from the assured, upbeat character we see today. One especially tense scene finds Musk and a few of his closest staffers sitting in an unprepossessing office cubicle trying to figure out how they'll make payroll. In another scene, Musk faces a room full of angry customers who've just learned he's raising the price on their wait-listed Roadsters, on which delivery dates had already been pushed back. In yet another scene, he speaks to the camera about how little he's looking forward to a party that evening where his job will be "to sell cars for five hours." Despite his obvious exhaustion, he does it anyway. "It's like eating glass every bloody day," he says.

Increasingly desperate to win confidence and raise additional capital, Musk announced the Tesla Model S in a press release on June 30, 2008.[29] The naysayers circled, declaring the Model S "pure vaporware." (Sure enough, behind-the-scenes footage in *Revenge of the Electric Car* shows a prototype Model S being built. What appears to be battery acid is being mixed in a plastic bucket next to a naked chassis.) "Elon is totally going to lose his shirt," one commentator crowed. "Elon has to learn that he can't just imagine a new world and will it into being," said another. Musk had problems in his private life, too, in the form of a very public divorce from his first wife, the mother of his five small boys. On December 22, 2008, he reached the brink of a nervous breakdown. "2008 was the worst year of my life," he told reporters.

Then, miraculously, things started to turn a corner. By April 2009, 320 Roadsters had been delivered to delighted customers.[30] In June 2009, Tesla was approved to receive $465 million in interest-bearing loans from the U.S. Department of Energy. In September 2009, Tesla announced it had raised $82.5 million from private equity investors to accelerate its retail expansion. On June 29, 2010, Tesla launched its initial public offering on NASDAQ, raising $226 million for the company and becoming the first U.S. carmaker to go public since the Ford Motor Company in 1956. General Motors Chair Bob Lutz applauded Musk, telling the *The New Yorker*, "How come some tiny little California start-up, run by guys who know nothing about the car business, can do this, and we can't?"[31]

But Tesla wasn't quite out of the woods. The Model S, due to launch at retail in 2010, was pushed back to 2012. Several factories the company had hoped to acquire fell through. News of the delay rekindled media skepticism.

"When it comes to Tesla, it is difficult to see where the riches are, or whether they'll arrive, at what continues to be a small, experimental venture," mused the *New York Times*.[32] "We genuinely want to see this ultra-idealistic company succeed. But so far, Tesla has only proven adept at making big promises," added *Fast Company*, scoffing at Tesla's personnel "soap opera" and plans to build a full range of electric vehicles (EVs) when "it only sells 10 cars a week."[33]

Even Mitt Romney had something to say, branding Tesla "a loser company" during his ultimately unsuccessful 2012 presidential campaign.[34] Others raised eyebrows at Tesla's receipt of federal funds.

Analysts suggested the company lower its sights, either by remaining a niche sports car company or by concentrating on electric powertrains and partnering with a big automaker to produce the cars. Tesla could succeed only as a subsidiary of a larger company, they said.

Oh, ye of little faith.

The first 10 customers received their Model S autos at Tesla's Fremont, California, factory on June 22, 2012. By December of that year, the factory was producing 400 cars a week. Sales continued apace throughout 2013. Tesla unexpectedly repaid its federal loan in May 2013, the first car company to have fully repaid the government, ahead of Ford and Nissan and 10 years early (a first for Tesla). That same year, the company passed $1 billion in revenue and also turned a profit. By the end of 2013, Tesla's stock was the top performer on the NASDAQ. The media changed its tune, calling the Model S "the most important car of the last 20 years."[35]

The next year, 2014, was an equally blockbuster time. Tesla could hardly make cars fast enough to meet demand. Now, analysts have begun speculating as to whether "Tesla can top GM's market cap." Since Tesla currently stands at around $35 billion to GM's $55 billion on 2014 sales of less than 10,000 vehicles to GM's 9.7 million, it doesn't seem entirely out of the question.[36] Meanwhile, Musk's personal net worth is now estimated at $8.4 billion.[37]

Throughout this whole riches-to-rags-to-riches saga, there was one person who never gave up: Musk himself. Musk admitted he'd badly underestimated how difficult and expensive it would be to establish an EV manufacturer, but that didn't stop him. "Imagine a new world and will it into being" is a great description of exactly what Musk *did* do. His determination, incredible tolerance for risk, unrelenting hard work, and dogged commitment are without doubt what propelled Tesla to the position it holds today—that, and Musk's personal fortune. But even that fortune proved insufficient to the task. It's hard to imagine remaining committed to anything in the face of such obstacles, but Musk did.

"My hat's off to them," Bill Ford, Ford Motors executive chair, said at his company's annual meeting recently. "It's really hard to start a company, particularly in the auto business, and be successful."[38]

How did Musk do it? Colleagues cite his "eternal optimism," "brilliance," "insane work ethic, "unbounded ambition," and, less generously, "strong reality distortion field." Clearly, Musk is an exceptional guy.

And yet, the stories of other Iconoclastic Leaders contain variants of the same nail-biting drama, some still ongoing. This is not a job for the faint of heart. Bringing a sustainable business idea to market is inherently fraught with obstacles. You are swimming against the tide of conventional business theory and practice, and since it's never been done before, there's really no way to be sure that it can be done. All you have is your idea, your conviction, and your courage—and the guts to commit and stay the course.

Contrarian

In 2011, my colleague Graceann Bennett and I conducted a study of diverse Americans to understand why so many of them would say in research that they wanted to live a more sustainable life but failed to follow through in reality. Our research took us to the homes of soccer moms in the Chicago suburbs, green enthusiasts in San Francisco, and Millennials in Brooklyn. The results were depressingly uniform and surprisingly mundane: Most respondents weren't going green because they just didn't want to be different. They liked the idea of recycling and buying green products, but when they did so, their neighbors would start looking at them funny, saying they were crunchy hippies who didn't wash often enough or shave their legs. In the end, it was easier for them to just ditch the green and fit in.

The exception to this were the brave few, the ones we called the Super Greens, who embraced greener behaviors in spite of the judgment of their neighbors. They weren't afraid to be a little different; in fact, they kind of liked it. But it did sometimes come at a personal cost. Being the only Super Green on your block (or the only vegan at the barbeque, in the case of one of our subjects) can be lonely. (Our research is explored in depth in Chapter 5.)

Iconoclastic Leaders are the Super Greens of the business world. In a sea of people embracing conventional business thinking, they are not afraid to go against the flow even though it would be easier not to. They embrace contrariness.

Hannah Jones has worked in corporate responsibility at Nike since 1998, beginning in Europe before moving to the United States in 2004. But she didn't start her career in the private sector and has said she never intended to end up there. Before joining Nike, Jones did stints on BBC radio, worked on social action campaigns, and was at an NGO focused on social issues like racism and HIV/AIDS. She figured she'd spend her career working in social justice.

While mailing corporations from the NGO to ask for funding, Jones received a rejection letter that got her wondering "what you could do if you were in a corporation with the reach and potential influence that these companies have across the world."[39] She describes that rejection letter as her epiphany moment, the moment she began wondering whether it was "more effective to shout from the outside or work from the inside." It was the opposite angle from the Polman and Immelt conversions, which started with business and worked out. Jones went from the outside in. Perhaps this outsider status accounts for her contrarian streak. She always was a Super Green; her challenge was to not succumb to the temptation to lose that edge and get cozy with the status quo. (So far, there's certainly no sign of that.)

In 2004, Jones took on the role of VP of Corporate Responsibilities. One of her first roles was to produce Nike's CR report for the year. The company was still working to rebound from a scandal around labor conditions in its supply chain (detailed in Chapter 6) that had battered its reputation. Jones recalls going in front of the board to recommend they disclose the location of every factory in their supply chain. She says:

> Disclosing these things was absolutely counterintuitive, because it was deemed a competitive advantage to remain secret about your supply chain. I remember this vividly, because our vice president for sourcing and I went to Phil Knight and the board and said: "Listen, if we do this, we have an opportunity to get the ball rolling on creating overall transparency about supply chains. Are you willing to take the risk?"[40]

Incredibly, they agreed, and so began Jones's streak of transformation.

As I mentioned earlier, Jones is different from some sustainability professionals in large corporations who seem to see their primary role as pulling together an overview of what's going on around the company and collating it into a report. Jones is remaking the way Nike operates with her bare hands. She didn't invent corporate responsibility or sustainability at Nike; significant strides had been made before her time. And she isn't doing it alone; she has the support of a large team and is acting on a mandate from leadership. But Jones helped Nike pivot from seeing sustainability through the lens of risk and reputation management to a lens of innovation. This pivot has allowed Nike to realize the business opportunity in sustainability, as demonstrated by the invention of the Flyknit technology. This billion-dollar-plus business line, which qualifies Nike for inclusion in this book, (Note: Nike does not report on Flyknit as an individual revenue stream; this number is an estimate) is a shoe that is "knit" and produces up to 80 percent less waste than a standard athletics shoe. (The full story of the shoe—now a technology being applied across Nike's portfolio—is told in Chapter 2, and the story of how Jones has worked with the larger Nike team to integrate sustainability into the heart of innovation in the organization is told in Chapter 4.)

The other initiatives Nike has undertaken on her watch include:

- Publishing an interactive map showing all its supplier factories and locations

- Developing the Considered Design program, a company-wide standard that helps designers incorporate sustainability considerations into their designs

- Developing the GreenXchange, an open-source platform for sharing sustainability-related intellectual property

- Creating the MAKING App to help clothing designers across the industry make more sustainable choices

- Producing the Nike Materials Sustainability Index and the Sustainable Manufacturing & Sourcing Index, which put sustainability and labor considerations on equal footing with quality, cost, and delivery in supplier selection

- Becoming a founding member of the Sustainable Apparel Coalition, an organization with a goal of transforming the apparel industry

- Forming LAUNCH, an incubator for sustainability ideas, with NASA, the U.S. Agency for International Development (USAID), and the U.S. State Department[41]

To understand how Jones operates, consider the example of Bangladesh. Nike's production team and the Sustainable Business and Innovation (SB&I) team, led by Jones, faced a dilemma. Over course of the previous decade, Bangladesh had exploded as a low-cost garment production center, so the production team were curious about opportunities to expand Nike's supplier footprint there. The downturn of 2008 sharpened the appeal; margins were under pressure, and Nike was being undercut on price by competitors. The competitors' secret? Bangladesh.

But Nike had been cautious about the market. Bangladesh didn't have a great reputation for worker safety, and after the labor debacle Nike had faced in the late 1990s regarding workers in Pakistani factories, executives were rightly circumspect. Jones and her team were developing a Manufacturing Index, a system for ranking suppliers on the basis of worker safety and environmental standards. It included a Risk Index to help the manufacturer easily identify countries with a poor track record on those issues.[42] Not surprisingly the Risk Index raised red flags about Bangladesh.

But that was the way the industry was going. Garment exports from Bangladesh doubled between 2008 and 2013, to more than $20 billion. Nike was facing shrinking margins. The pressure was on.

For Jones, the issue was clear-cut. Unwilling to allow Nike ever to find itself with supply chain risks again, and based on the evidence of the Risk Index, she believed the decision had to be "no." The production team agreed to evaluate the situation at first hand. It was decided that they would visit Bangladesh in 2013 to evaluate the situation.

Once there, the Nike staff quickly discovered sealed windows and fabric strewn across floors—both fire hazards. They returned to the United States with a decision aligned with Jones's original view that Nike should not expand its business in Bangladesh.

A few weeks later, a factory called Rana Plaza in Bangladesh collapsed, killing more than 1,100 garment workers and injuring 2,500 more. The list of brands implicated in the disaster included JCPenney, Walmart, Benetton, and H&M.[43] Nike was notable for its absence.

Jones did not make this happen alone. Nike's CEO Mark Parker is the executive sponsor and champion of the company's sustainable business strategy. But with such a strong cost argument against her, I wonder whether the team would have gone as far as to visit the factory in person had Jones not been there to push the agenda.

This dilemma is not unusual on the road to sustainable business: Take the risk and save money now, or forgo margin to do the right thing and preempt problems down the line. "Did we pass up on margin because of that? Absolutely," Jones said.[44] But it was the right thing to do.

It takes a committed contrarian to push back in a situation when margin is in the balance. This story is a microcosm of how the Iconoclastic Leader's job often looks day to day—being the burr in the fur of colleagues for whom sustainability and responsibility are not the Number 1 priority. But while Jones is a contrarian, she's an eminently constructive one. This is a crucial point. The contrarianism of Iconoclastic Leaders is in service to a better outcome. Jones doesn't just point out problems; she solves them. And she does not necessarily arrive at the outcome that's the easiest or most obvious.

As sustainable and socially responsible business becomes more mainstream, contrarian is the C that could—indeed, should—recede from relevance. As business results at the Green Giants and Next Billions increasingly vindicate their Iconoclastic Leaders's strategy, they will no longer be swimming against the tide. Instead, the tide will turn in their favor. John Mackey at Whole Foods (who, not content with being the resident contrarian of the grocery business, is seeking to reinvent capitalism) puts it like this: "Some of my ideas seem contrarian now, but capitalism is very dynamic. Eventually, businesses that focus strictly on profits will be voted out."[45]

Amen to that. But until then, change agents are required—characters hungry for change, willing to take on decades of received business thinking and stick to their guns to make change happen.

TECHNIQUES FOR WINNING WITH THE 4 Cs

You can cultivate the 4 Cs. Iconoclastic Leaders develop strategies to live the 4 Cs every day. Here are some suggestions to get your strategy off the ground and stay the course.

- *Build your case.* For the best chance of selling a sustainable business strategy to other businesspeople, more than anything, you need a robust business case. People will doubt there's one to be made, so assume you're facing a skeptical crowd and overcompensate accordingly. Jeff Immelt spent 12 months assembling the necessary information to reassure himself and persuade his board, management team, and customers to trust him on the Ecomagination strategy. He made sure he had the Holy Grail of arguments: *Our customers want it.* Hannah Jones's Manufacturing Index was a way to fight fire with fire. The case for setting up operations in Bangladesh was compelling—an easy way to grow margin. To stand any chance of pushing back, she needed to make sure that the case against it had a data set that was just as strong.

  There are facts and figures peppered throughout this book: the combined $110 billion in annual revenue these companies represent; the 11.7 percent per year superior returns they've delivered; the Purpose Paradox, proving purpose-driven brands are more profitable (we'll encounter this in Chapter 3); and the various data points on superior margins, faster growth, and consumer preference. Use them. You'll be asked time and again for evidence that what you are doing or proposing to do is right, and you should consider yourself in a perpetual state of persuasion.

- *Recruit advisers.* Building a Green Giant–style business is hard, and it is also new. You may not have time to learn everything from scratch, but nor do you need to. In Chapter 4, we'll look at the advisory boards Green Giants have built and the kinds of problems they've helped to solve. But the time to create such a group is now—right at the beginning. They can help you shape and refine your ideas. They can provide expert guidance. Their presence also carries weight and they can prove invaluable allies in the C-suite. It's way better than going it alone.

  There is a group of leaders who have devoted their careers to this topic. This includes people like Andrew Winston, author of *Green to Gold* and adviser to many of America's sustainable business leaders; Hunter Lovins, founder of Natural Capitalism Solutions and adviser to everyone from the North American CEO of Unilever to the King of Bhutan; and Mindy Lubber, CEO of the NGO Ceres, which supports businesses in the transition to sustainability. Two of them advise me and contributed thinking to this book. They also advise the Green Giants. (For more on advice from such leaders, see Chapter 4.)

- *Partner for credibility and feedback.* GE hired the consulting firm GreenOrder to develop its Ecomagination scorecard and (as previously mentioned) asked Jonathan Lash of the World Resources Institute (WRI) to join Jeff Immelt on stage for the Ecomagination launch. Unilever worked with Forum for the Future's Jonathon Porritt and many others on the development of the Unilever Sustainable Living Plan. Many of Nike's most innovative ideas involve third-party collaborators. The terrain of sustainability is way too complex to navigate without a trusted Sherpa guide. And unless you're a start-up with a blank-slate reputation, the objectivity that comes with a third-party endorsement is almost essential to building early credibility. Of GE's partnership with Lash and WRI, Gary Sheffer says: "Jonathan Lash was just really terrific. He gave us really tough, hard advice, helped us to build our network, stood with us. The value of having good, smart partners and having an environmentalist on our side cannot be overstated. When Jeff gave his launch speech, he said, 'The idea that I'd be standing here with the WRI—I never thought that would happen just a few years ago.' We had really good partners and great, honest, unvarnished feedback."[46] So partner early and partner well.

- *Find a support group.* Being the only Super Green in the boardroom can be incredibly rewarding, but it is also hard. Build a network of kindred spirits with whom you can share tales of battle, celebrate victories, and compare notes. People who are already on the path will likely be only too happy to have company. "A leader who looks over his shoulder and doesn't see anybody behind him is not very comfortable," Paul Polman has said.[47] There are plenty of networking events where those looking to build Green Giant–like brands can be found—Sustainable Brands, BSR, the Aspen Ideas Festival in Colorado, the World Economic Forum annual meeting at Davos, Switzerland. While these are primarily opportunities to share ideas and theories, they are also safe havens for the survivors of combat, a chance to network with people who share battle scars. For the Green Giant–curious or the more advanced, these events are a good place to find inspiration and affirmation.

As this chapter has shown, the billion-dollar business strategy at each of the Green Giants began with a single individual.

Change has to start somewhere.

Why not with you?

CHAPTER 2

Disruptive Innovation

"[The CEO] thinks Tesla could be a big disrupter if we're not careful. History is littered with big companies that ignored innovation that was coming their way because you didn't know where you could be disrupted."

—GM spokesperson[1]

For Green Giants, sustainability is the springboard to innovation. These companies are not introducing incremental improvement or a greener, more ethical, socially responsible variation on the status quo. Instead, they are implementing some of the most disruptive and successful business innovations of the past decade. It's the kind of innovation that has made all of the Green Giants regulars on the *Fast Company* or *Forbes* lists of the World's Most Innovative Companies over the past four years.

It's a surprising change from the early days of green marketing, when many manufacturers created products that were often less sophisticated and less effective than standard product lines, called them "eco_____," and packaged them in burlap. No wonder that when many people think of green products, they envision bathroom cleaner that doesn't clean, deodorant that doesn't deodorize, and toilet paper that is the hair shirt to Cottonelle's cashmere. To them "sustainable" has come to mean primitive, rudimentary, unsophisticated, and low-tech.

Green Giant products are the polar opposite of primitive. Each of the companies is founded on innovation that disrupted a category, and innovation pervades their cultures.

Disruptive Innovation, then, is the second characteristic of Green Giants. They embrace sustainability as a spur to develop radically better products and services, reinvent categories, unlock new sources of revenue, and in the process leapfrog less innovative incumbents. The Green Giants have disrupted the fast food, automotive, supermarket, infrastructure, apparel, and beauty industries, while the Next Billions are taking on eyewear, cleaning products, ice cream, yogurt, and hospitality. This type of innovation isn't just about product. It's about supply chains, technology, business models—and entire systems.

DEFINING DISRUPTIVE

First things first: What exactly is Disruptive Innovation?

In my pre-sustainability days, early in my career, I worked with Kodak. The company had a small division devoted to digital photography—indeed, one if its engineers had allegedly invented the digital camera. But the rest of the company preferred to sweep that under the carpet and focus on film and prints.

In one conversation with a client in the marketing department, I suggested we keep a close eye on Apple, which had recently launched the photo software iPhoto. It was great—easy to organize your photos and really easy to order prints. My client gave me a scornful look. "People talk about Apple, but our market cap is at least 200 times what theirs is. You have to remember they're tiny," she said dismissively. The year was 2002.

Today, Apple is the world's most valuable company with a market cap more than 700 times the size of Kodak's. (Indeed, Kodak declared bankruptcy and had to be bought out.) Not so tiny any more.

Apple is a serial disruptive innovator. It changes the rules of a category in a way that incumbents either don't see coming or completely underestimate. It challenges not just the technology but the business model upon which the category operates—a distinction defined by Harvard Business School Professor Clayton Christensen, the world expert on Disruptive Innovation. The traditional players are then forced to follow or risk obsolescence.

Sustainability has this kind of disruptive potential across multiple categories—as the Green Giants prove. Each of them is founded on an innovation—a product, service, supply chain, technology, or systems innovation—that has disrupted the category it entered. The innovation changes the dominant technology and, in some cases, alters the business model of the category. Each of the Green Giants has successfully overturned prevailing business wisdom and in the process brought us new ways to eat, dress, drive, shop, power the world, and define beauty.

This is what I mean by Disruptive Innovation. The table below details the Disruptive Innovation of each of the Green Giants.

Green Giant	Disruptive Innovation
Chipotle	Turned the fast food category business model (cheapest possible ingredients, cheapest possible products) on its head by building a restaurant chain on the back of more expensive ethically and environmentally responsible ingredients.
Natura	Proved the prevailing beauty industry wisdom (that you have to choose between efficacious and natural when it comes to beauty products) to be a myth.

(continues on next page)

Whole Foods	In an industry ruled by low prices, proved that the segment of U.S. consumers prepared to pay more for local, responsible, organic, fresh, or natural grocery products is much more than a niche when there's a perceived personal benefit.
Tesla	Floored the German luxury car incumbents by commercializing an incredibly high-performance electric vehicle just seven years after the documentary *Who Killed the Electric Car?* declared the technology defunct.
Nike Flyknit	Reinvented the way shoes are made, going from multiple materials cut and sewn together to knit strands of yarn that form a nearly seamless upper, dramatically decreasing waste while enabling increased athletic performance.
GE Ecomagination	Created a highly profitable and fast-growing portfolio of environmentally superior products and services at a time when industry wisdom held that sustainability could not equal profitability, and in spite of the absence of global regulation that would have favored the adoption of these products.
Toyota Prius	Proved to be the first vehicle in the world not built on the internal combustion engine to achieve mainstream adoption, independent of gas prices and even in the United States—the land of the SUV.
Unilever	Moving to decouple economic growth from carbon growth across its entire business via the Sustainable Living Plan. Individual brands are contributing to the overall goal in differing ways. Refused to report quarterly to Wall Street analysts, thus challenging the orthodoxy of managing on a 90-day payback period.

IKEA	Originally disrupted the furniture category by making stylish furniture affordable to all. Today, applies the same philosophy to more sustainable products like solar panels and LED bulbs to create the billion-dollar line of Products for a More Sustainable Life at Home.

DELIVERING DISRUPTIVE INNOVATION

Where do these Disruptive Innovations come from, and how have the Green Giants managed to make them so successful? Five principles build the kind of Disruptive Innovation that powers a Green Giant:

1. Make it better, not just greener

2. Embrace the counterintuitive

3. Bet on yourself

4. Engage the problem solvers

5. Cultivate pervasive innovation

1. Make It Better, Not Just Greener

In the summer of 2012, thousands of athletes from all over the world converged on London to compete for a chance to win Olympic gold. As 5 billion people tuned in to the Games on TV, British men's distance runner Mo Farah streaked across the finish line to take first place in the men's 5000 meters. While Farah's performance was breathtaking, the media seemed more concerned with what was on his feet. Farah was sporting neon yellow spikes featuring Nike's brand-new sneaker technology, Flyknit.

In a stunt hailed as a marketing coup, Nike, which is not an official Olympic sponsor, launched Flyknit on the feet of 400 athletes at the Games. Rather than giving each athlete a shoe color-matched to his or her uniform as it usually does, Nike blanket-clad all athletes' feet in the same distinctive neon yellow it calls Volt. The result was a guerilla takeover that stole headlines and caused the shoe, launched in stores simultaneously, to instantly sell out.

But what was so great about the shoe? (Note that in this book I refer to Flyknit as both "a shoe" and "a way to make shoes." That's because at launch, people referred to Flyknit as a model of shoe, but the woven technology is now being applied across a wide variety of Nike's shoe designs.) I decided to place it in this book because of the Flyknit's impeccable sustainability credentials. Unlike normal uppers that are made by gluing and stitching multiple pieces of different material together, the Flyknit upper, inspired by a tube sock, is woven from one continuous thread into a lightweight, streamlined shoe that can be steamed to fit your foot. In a conventional sneaker, each piece has to be cut from a larger cloth, leaving a pile of off-cuts on the factory floor. Sometimes the work-in-progress shoe is flown around the world as different pieces are added in different countries. Flyknit eliminates all of that. The simple idea of weaving the upper reduces waste by up to a staggering 80 percent.

But it's also possibly the highest performance shoe Nike has ever created. The impetus to design Flyknit was not a desire to help the environment—at least, not the sole impetus. It was the brand's athletes, demanding a shoe that felt like they weren't wearing one. To achieve this, Nike's designers had to completely rethink the way they made shoes. Designers literally started with tube socks attached to rubber soles. A team of programmers, engineers, and athletes joined the designers to figure it out. "There was no technology in the world available to do this for footwear," recalls Ben Shaffer, who at the time was director of Nike's Innovation Kitchen, Nike's notoriously secretive R&D center. They had to invent new machinery and software before they could get started. They went through a "seemingly endless" stream of prototypes—195, according to one report[2]—over the course of four years until they cracked it.

The result was a shoe 19 percent lighter than Nike's next-lightest long-distance model. Over the course of running a marathon, that saves the runner from carrying a ton, equivalent to the weight of a car,[3] which is clearly a very big deal. Trying the shoe for the first time, runner Abdi Abdirahman, who placed third in the 2012 U.S. Olympic Marathon Trials, reportedly kept looking at his feet to make sure he still had shoes on.[4]

Flyknit was such a success at the Olympics that Nike has since applied the technology to its most prestigious shoe lines, including the Mercurial Superfly IV soccer shoe, launched by soccer megastar Cristiano Ronaldo ahead of the 2014 World Cup in Brazil. Looking more like a futuristic ankle sock with cleats than a soccer shoe, with a woven Flyknit upper, the shoe—according to Nike's claims—helps players perform better by reducing material between the foot and the ball to enhance touch. In addition, designers were able to incorporate cables that propel the player forward for greater speed. Any player worth his salt wore the Superfly in the matches in Brazil. Basketball legend Kobe Bryant has also launched his latest shoe, the Kobe 9, with Flyknit built in.

And then there's the street style. Style has always been a factor in the success of Nike's most iconic designs, and Flyknit is no exception. Flyknit allows for all kinds of interesting weaves. Nike CEO Mark

Parker, who is a designer by background, says designing Flyknit is like designing in 4-D. Not surprising, then, that the Flyknit was apparently the "it" shoe at the menswear fashion shows in Paris and Milan during the 2012 season.

In fact, if the phrase "eco-friendly shoe" conjures images of Birkenstocks and other hemp-adorned footwear, then Flyknit—with its space-age shapes, eye-popping colors, and high-tech claims—is about as far away from that as a shoe can get. In terms of the innovation the Flyknit technology makes possible, Nike designers say they are just getting started.

In short, Flyknit is not just a slightly more eco-friendly shoe. It's a new way to *make* shoes—a first in 40 years of sneaker history.

One of the most common errors companies make as they attempt to build a Green Giant–like brand is to think that sustainable business is about creating a slightly greener version of something that already exists, or sprinkling a little "social good" fairy dust over their brand. This vastly underestimates the scale of both the challenge and the opportunity. Flyknit typifies a Green Giant innovation because it's not just greener, it's better. And that is what makes the billion-dollar difference.

Each of the Green Giants makes a product, service, or business idea more sustainable or socially responsible—and then goes further, making it radically better across multiple dimensions.

The Toyota Prius provides another example. It isn't just a slightly more fuel-efficient or eco-friendly car. It is, in the words of CNN, "the first vehicle to provide a serious alternative to the internal combustion engine since the Stanley Steamer ran out of steam in 1924."[5] Similarly, the Tesla Model S may be the world's first successful luxury electric sedan, but it also received the highest score of any car in history from Consumer Reports and set a new record for safety in a battery of tests conducted by the National Highway Traffic Safety Administration. Plus, it is just drop dead sexy and, according to one of its designers, "there is absolutely no car . . . that will beat you from 0 to 30."[6] It's no exaggeration to say that it may be the best sports car ever made.

Had these products just been greener or more socially responsible, but not better, they simply would not have yielded the same stellar business results. Think about it: Can you name one product that has? Research by Harvard Business School Professors Robert G. Eccles and George Serafeim supports this. Their analysis of sustainable innovation at more than 3,000 companies found a direct link between the scale of the innovation and the financial benefit to the business; indeed, minor sustainability-oriented innovations tended to be a *drag* on the business. Major ones were a boost.

Eccles and Serafeim explain: "While minor innovations, such as efficiency improvements, can nudge a downward-sloping performance frontier up a bit, only major innovations in products, processes, or business models can shift the slope from descending to ascending."[7]

There is a win-win element to this. On the one hand, sustainability advocates say that the world needs Disruptive Innovation. As Nike's 2013 sustainability report says, "The scale of today's challenges requires *breakthrough innovations* such as entirely new materials and ways to make products" (emphasis added). At the same time, the data prove that breakthrough innovation is what drives billion-dollar business results. So, the more good you do, the more money you make. What's not to love?

There are many reasons why making products better, not just greener, drives better business outcomes. Better and greener products drive mainstream, not just niche, appeal to create larger markets (as

Chapter 5 describes). They eliminate many of the barriers to adoption of traditional green products, like a trade-off in performance or quality.

But perhaps the biggest reason is that sometimes it's just time for something new. Human beings are hardwired to seek progress. And, like the gas-guzzling automobiles the Prius challenged, many of the technologies of the 20th century are ready for retirement. Some of them have barely changed since the Industrial Revolution. (The fluorescent lightbulb was essentially unchanged over the century-plus that elapsed between Thomas Edison lighting a lamp in 1879 and the advent of the CFC—and now the LED.) A candidate for reinvention may lurk inside your brand's category or even your business. Seize the leadership opportunity. Green Giants view sustainability as a call to arms to invent the technologies of the 21st century—not just greener, but better.

2. Embrace the Counterintuitive

On July 24, 2002, a procession of odd-shaped cars, headed by a lone bagpiper, snaked its way around the Hollywood Forever Cemetery on Santa Monica Boulevard in Los Angeles. This solemn parade was a funeral for a car: the EV1, the electric vehicle (EV) designed by General Motors.

Launched to much fanfare at the LA Auto Show in 1996 in a moment hailed by news outlets as "automotive history in the making," the EV1 was a Jetson-esque two-seater available for lease at around $500 a month. GM initially seemed gung ho for the car, whose advent was inspired in part by the Clean Air Act in California. The act stipulated that 10 percent of all car sales in California should come from zero-emission vehicles by 2003. GM backed the launch of the EV1 with a multimillion-dollar ad budget. Drivers responded, with EV1 owners becoming fierce advocates, creating members clubs and organizing rallies.

But the EV1 quickly found itself at the center of a legal battle pitting the car industry against the state of California. In what seemed like schizophrenia, GM lobbied *against* the Clean Air Act quotas, dooming its own vehicle. When the lawsuit was successful, GM immediately issued a mandatory recall of the EV1, citing lack of consumer demand, too high per-unit costs to make the business case work, and insurmountable issues with battery life and vehicle range, resulting in an inability to commercialize the vehicle. EV1s were rounded up, disabled, shipped off, and crushed—often in the face of fierce opposition from their lessees (GM had never made the vehicles available to purchase, only to lease).

EV1 owners were outraged, and conspiracy theories about GM's motivations began to swirl. Pictures emerged of the cars piled up in the desert, either crushed or awaiting their fate. There was something fishy about the way GM insisted that no car be left in working order and that EV1s could not even be recycled but had to be destroyed. (In fact, there's just one intact EV1 left on the planet, at the Smithsonian Institution in Washington D.C., because the Smithsonian accepts artifacts only if they are in full working order.) Had GM deliberately sabotaged its own product line in an elaborate ruse to prove the EV business model nonviable and thus protect its legacy business? Was it part of a larger conspiracy in which Big Auto was in cahoots with Big Oil to keep California's drivers addicted to gas? Or was the EV really just a nonstarter?

We may never know whether such headwinds were benign or more sinister. Either way, there appeared to be serious, even impossible, obstacles facing the electric vehicle experiment. The ersatz Hollywood mock funeral seemed to signal the death knell not just of the EV1 but of the electric vehicle, period.

So imagine for a moment that it's 2004. You're an extremely successful, 30-something Silicon Valley engineer and, having successfully sold one of your first start-ups, you're on the hunt for a new place to put your time and your millions. You've long harbored a dream to commercialize the electric vehicle, but the EV1 is in its sandy grave. A film crew is at work documenting the ill-fated vehicle's demise and finalizing their movie *Who Killed the Electric Car?* And you have absolutely zero auto industry experience.

Do you (a) run, not walk, in the opposite direction, or (b) sink your reputation, millions of dollars of your own personal fortune, significant venture capital funds, and a huge loan from the government into a tiny start-up on a mission to commercialize a high-end electric sports car?

If you picked (a), you're a normal human being. If you went for (b), you're probably Elon Musk, the now-billionaire CEO of SpaceX, and Tesla Motors—and possibly the only person with a sufficiently high tolerance for the counterintuitive to make that kind of risky decision. (Musk's motivation are explored in Chapter 3.)

Incredibly, four years after making this profoundly counterintuitive decision and six years after the EV1 was laid to rest, Musk brought his first electric vehicle, the Roadster, to market. At the time of writing (January 2015), Tesla had launched its third vehicle, the Model X, and announced its fourth, the Model 3. It had also surpassed $3 billion in revenue in 2014 and become the fastest growing automotive stock in at least two decades.[8]

Tesla's success also paved the way for Nissan to bring to market its wildly successful and much more affordable Leaf. Competitors from GM to BMW are scrambling to play catch-up. Musk singlehandedly transformed an entire sector of one of the most entrenched industries in the world.

Musk would probably get along well with Sally Uren, the CEO of Forum for the Future, the UK-based nonprofit sustainability think tank. Uren advises many CEOs on their sustainable business strategies as part of long-term partnerships. She likes her clients to feel uncomfortable—really uncomfortable. In fact, as they develop ideas together, she asks each CEO to apply the counterintuitive test. "If it doesn't feel really counterintuitive, it probably isn't radical enough," she says.

As they approach their innovation strategies, Green Giants like Tesla embrace the counterintuitive. Indeed, passing the counterintuitive test is key to each of their Disruptive Innovations. Consider these other examples:

- As we saw in Chapter 1, GE became a vocal advocate of a business built on clean energy at a time when it risked alienating the fossil fuel industry that constituted a substantial part of its client base. It was also at a time when the absence of a price on carbon was widely regarded as a barrier to success for a business built around clean energy.

- Chipotle decided to commit to ingredients that can cost significantly more than the products of factory farming. The business model of traditional fast food players is built on ingredients priced as low as possible, passed along to consumers in the form of the cheapest possible products. It assumes that suppliers should be chosen based on low price, and that consumers will buy based only on price. And yet in 2014 Chipotle managed to command profit margins of 12.1 percent, against a fast food industry average that one estimate puts at 4.6 percent[9] (though the margins at McDonald's were significantly higher at 16.6 percent.[10]) Revenue grew 27.8 percent (for reference, the

2013 fast food category average was 3 percent). (Note: Chipotle is technically classified as "fast casual," a subset of fast food. Since this is a concept Chipotle more or less invented, I think it fair to draw the comparison, and I have done so throughout the book.)

Pretty counterintuitive.

The examples go on. Each of these innovations felt profoundly counterintuitive at launch but have since proved right on the money.

But *why* is being counterintuitive an input to billion-dollar, Green Giant innovation?

Green Giants are not counterintuitive for the sake of being counterintuitive. They engage in calculated counterintuition. Green Giants recognize (and accept) that many of the assumptions upon which modern business is built are being overturned. For example, things that conventional business relies upon to be free or cheap—water, labor, emitting carbon dioxide—are becoming more expensive. Things that today are still relatively abundant—food, land, natural resources—are becoming scarce (and therefore also more expensive). Things people once considered weird—like sharing cars and bikes instead of owning them, or choosing a bar of soap based on its moral compass as much as its efficacy—are fast becoming normal and even aspirational. And business is increasingly *profiting* by doing good, instead of *paying* for it. As the rules of business are turned on their head, assumptions and instincts honed in the old era cannot be relied upon. Green Giants have had the prescience and courage to build their businesses on these new rules.

And Green Giants don't just plow ahead with little more than gut and hubris—certainly the big ones don't. Before Sally Uren and her clients settle on a counterintuitive strategy, they engage in extensive, data-driven scenario planning to define the possible future realities in which the company may find itself operating.

The scenarios provide inputs to designing and developing Disruptive Innovations. For example, Uren's scenario planning with iconic fashion brand Levi's uncovered the fact that water was going to be a real constraint on both the business and the lives of its millions of customers in the future. "That insight was fed into the R&D pipeline, and out popped Water<Less jeans," Uren told me.[11] In another example, peeking into the future with major UK DIY retailer Kingfisher PLC revealed a potential future-state in which people will share rather than buy power tools. The company has embarked on an experiment renting power tools to customers—pretty heretical given that the entire business is built on selling those same items. But Uren helps her partners understand that future realities will disrupt legacy businesses and undermine legacy revenue streams. "Many future trends, from climate change to civil unrest, will spell increased volatility for global supply chains," she says. They're already doing so. Planning for the future and getting ahead of it via Disruptive Innovation affords a company more control, rather than being forced to play catch-up when competitors, price structures, and regulations change.

And the world is changing fast. To return to Tesla for a moment, so taken aback was General Motors by Tesla's success that the company that killed its own electric car formed a task force in 2013 to study Tesla.

Smart move. By one estimate, the price of running an EV per mile in 2017 will be the equivalent of running a regular car if gasoline cost $1.60 a gallon, or $25 a barrel. While gas prices at the time of writing (January 2015) were almost this low, this is regarded as a blip, rather than a consistently reliable state of play, and as of now, Tesla's sales have been unharmed.

It seems likely that Musk's new reality will completely invert the economics of the auto industry. At the time I was writing this chapter, 2017 was two years away. Tesla felt counterintuitive in 2004. In 2015, it looks all kinds of smart. Green Giants embrace the calculatedly counterintuitive because they know it's what the future feels like.

3. Bet on Yourself

Green Giants are not afraid to invest serious money in their Disruptive Innovations. It's part of a mindset that is looking to sustainability as a spur to innovation that builds business, that is the legitimate future direction of your company rather than merely an "eco-friendly" version of your traditional product. If you're serious about it, you'll invest as much in a sustainability-oriented innovation as you would in a conventional one.

Toyota invested about $1 billion to bring the Prius to market. While this sounds like a lot (and it took Toyota more than a decade to recoup the initial investment), it is actually about average for development of a new product at Toyota. Indeed, given how different the Prius was from what had gone before at Toyota, it's a wonder the investment wasn't greater. And the Prius turned out to be Toyota's most successful product launch of all time, a result few, including Toyota's leadership, predicted.

Likewise, GE made an initial commitment to invest $1.5 billion annually (a fifth of its total annual R&D budget) in R&D as part of Ecomagination, focused on research into cleaner technologies. The money has been used to invent everything from low-emission aircraft engines to energy-efficient heavy-haul locomotives to Energy Star (certified energy efficient) dishwashers and CFL lightbulbs, several of which are helping GE beat out competitors in high-growth markets. In 2012, it invested close to $2 billion but got back $25 billion in revenue, a staggering ROI. (By 2015, GE will have invested a total of $15 billion in R&D for Ecomagination and earned more than $180 billion in revenue.) GE's initial commitment was important not just from a practical standpoint but also from a reputational one. If skeptics thought GE was merely greenwashing to cover up past mistakes (greenwash is defined by the Oxford English Dictionary as "disinformation disseminated by an organization so as to present an environmentally responsible public image"[12]), $1.5 billion signaled sincerity; GE was putting its money where its mouth was. This gave GE license to lead and the endorsement of opinion formers it needed to be succeed.

As documented in Chapter 1, Elon Musk invested big bucks too. He put $160 million of his own fortune into Tesla, along with the federal loan of $465 million[13] and several rounds of venture capital (VC) funding.

Few of us have Musk's money. Fortunately, there are other ways to raise capital to invest in a Disruptive Innovation. At the opposite end of the spectrum, in 1993, Steve Ells, at the age of 28, opened his first Chipotle restaurant on Evans Avenue in Denver, with an $85,000 loan from his dad. He estimated the store would need to sell around 100 burritos a day to become profitable. Within a few months it was selling more than 1,000. A second location was funded out of cash flow and a third with a government-backed SBA (Small Business Administration) loan. Ready to go bigger, Ells borrowed another $1.5 million from his dad and raised $1.8 million more on his own.[14]

In 1997—five years, 16 branches, and annual revenues estimated at between $14 million and $18 million later—Ells realized he'd need more cash if he wanted to scale. Hearing that McDonald's was interested in making its first purchase of an outside restaurant chain, Ells sent the fast food titan a business plan. Seeing an opportunity to find new ways to reach customers and offer its restaurant operators a new franchise, McDonald's took a minority stake in the business.

It was a risky deal for both sides: It was the first time McDonald's had backed a company outside its corporate entity, and it was unclear whether Chipotle—a chain committed to "delicious food made with the finest ingredients"—could survive a relationship with the fast food giant.

Against the odds, the partnership flourished, and by 2002, McDonald's owned more than 90 percent of Chipotle's stock.[15] Ells is quick to point out that McDonald's left Chipotle mostly well alone, freeing him up to grow the business in line with his vision and able to leverage things like the McDonald's distribution network as Chipotle scaled.

But eventually, differences mounted. McDonald's decided to sell its noncore businesses to focus on its original restaurant chain, and Ells felt the cultural differences were holding Chipotle back. In January 2006, McDonald's took Chipotle to an IPO,[16] In its first day as a public company, the stock rose exactly 100 percent. It was the best U.S.-based IPO in six years and the second-best IPO for a restaurant after Boston Market. McDonald's walked away with approximately $1.5 billion on the back of an initial investment of $360 million.[17] The partnership had taken Chipotle to more than 500 restaurants. The successful IPO capital was then used to fund Chipotle's future growth.

Chipotle says it doesn't regret the McDonald's years. Some, however, question whether selling out was the right decision for McDonald's. Its 90 percent stake in Chipotle would today be valued at more than $15 billion, or about 15 percent of McDonald's' current market value.

The point is that there are many ways to find the funding to build a Green Giant business—but you do need funds. Fortunately, sources of funding are more forthcoming today than they once were. Buoyed by the success of Green Giants like Chipotle and Tesla, there is now an arms race among the VC community to identify and back the next generation of lookalikes, or Next Billions. Warby Parker, a hipster eyewear brand that gives a pair of glasses to someone in need for every pair that you purchase, has raised more than $50 million in venture capital funding from firms including Tiger Global Management and Menlo Ventures.

Several of the Green Giants are even becoming venture capitalists to Next Billions themselves. Nike has created its own R&D arm to invest in sustainable start-ups and hired two high-profile venture capitalists to run it. Unilever announced the formation of the Unilever Foundry to connect with and commit to start-ups that can help it advance its Sustainable Living Plan. And GE has run several Ecomagination Challenges in partnership with some of these VC firms. As described in Chapter 6, the 2010 Ecomagination Challenge offered hundreds of millions of dollars to start-ups dedicated to "improving our energy future." Clearly, GE believes the billion-dollar business potential is there.

A group called We Mean Business released a 2014 report featuring the killer data point that sustainable business leaders now see an ROI of 27 percent, and sometimes as much as 80 percent, on their low carbon investments.[18] The Green Giants punch even harder than that. But if you don't put skin in the game and bet on yourself, you will never see the billion-dollar rewards that could accrue.

4. Engage the Problem Solvers

There is nothing really smart, talented designers or engineers like more than a problem that ostensibly can't be solved. The more people say it can't be done, the more they set out to prove them wrong.

As you research and work with Green Giants, you hear a lot of sentences like this one written about the work of JB Straubel in 2008: "The rap on electric cars to date has been that they could deliver neither the range nor the performance of a combustion-engine vehicle. Tesla set out to disprove that."[19]

Straubel is Tesla's chief technology officer. Every piece of what's under a Tesla car's hood—which is what produces the Tesla difference—has been created by his team. Unlike the engineering teams at more or less every other car company in the world, Straubel's team is made up exclusively of electrical rather than mechanical engineers hired from the top electrical engineering program in the world at Stanford University, Straubel's alma mater.

It's a crucial difference. Among the myriad barriers to commercializing the EV, the most elementary problems were electrical engineering ones. Problems with the battery resulted in EV performance that did not measure up to that of conventional cars. And if you couldn't crack that, you would never get past go. A car has to be able to be driven.

Under Straubel's leadership, Tesla built a team with the skills to take this on. Until Tesla, electric cars had been made using large-cell batteries that were heavy and expensive. Straubel and his team figured out a way to use cheap laptop batteries, which reduced price and enhanced performance. The batteries had a habit, however, of overheating and catching fire. Straubel's team then figured out how to get coolant to flow between the batteries to keep them functioning.

Charging time was also a huge barrier to adoption. So Straubel's team invented a super-charger and a battery pack for the car that can be charged fully twice as fast as that of other EVs. And when fires developed in a couple of cars that had driven over objects in the road, thrilling media vultures who thought they'd found a chink in Tesla's armor, Straubel and his team didn't miss a beat. Overnight, they pushed out a software patch to every Tesla Model S to raise the height at which the cars travel on the highway. Not one Tesla fire has been reported since. This was possible because in the early days, Tesla personnel had the foresight to make the cars digitally and wirelessly controlled so they could be upgraded without the need to visit a dealership. No other company has done this.

These are just a handful of the problems Tesla's talented team was able to troubleshoot. If Elon Musk is Tesla's Iconoclastic Leader, Straubel and his team are its secret sauce: tenacious, brilliant, technically skilled minds, motivated by the challenge of solving seemingly impossible problems.

It may seem self-evident that to build the world's best electric car, you need to assemble the world's best team of electrical engineers, but it hadn't been tried before. To make a Green Giant Disruptive Innovation happen, you need a team like Tesla's. Because a Disruptive Innovation is profound, not superficial, it simply can't be achieved without the right team working on the right problem. It can't be a side project, and it can't be dreamed up solely by your marketing or PR department. Nor can your sustainability department do it alone. And yet, until now, this is the way many companies have approached sustainability-oriented innovation.

Guess what? That approach doesn't work. To invent a Disruptive Innovation with billion-dollar potential requires the focus, creativity, tenacity, and (depending on your sector) technical ability of a dedicated team of brilliant professional problem solvers.

Toyota is perhaps the most extreme demonstration of this. A decade before Tesla's team cracked the code on the EV, Toyota was facing a similarly steep challenge with the hybrid. The story of the Prius began when then-chair Eiji Toyoda, the incumbent leader from Toyota's founding family, expressed anxiety about the future of the car. A visionary leader, he saw the trends of rising emissions and a future of limited oil. These developments, he believed, threatened the very society that supported his family's business.

There are many players in the story that comes next. Two of Toyoda's chief lieutenants—Yoshiro Kimbara, the head of R&D, and Katsuaki Watanabe, then the head of corporate strategy—decided to address their leader's concerns. They initiated a top-secret project, codenamed C21, to develop the vehicle of the future. The goal was fairly blue sky, but fuel efficiency was a given, with a target gas mileage of a 50 percent improvement over their most popular small car, the Corolla. They handed responsibility for the project to Executive Vice President Akihiro Wada, who assigned it to a promising engineer, Takeshi Uchiyamada. (As we saw in Chapter 1, Uchiyamada is now Toyota's chairman of the board.)

Uchiyamada set about forming his team, including representatives from a range of specific engineering disciplines: powertrain and chassis components production engineering, vehicle production technology, vehicle engineering, body engineering, engine engineering, and drive train engineering. About a year into their work, Wada dropped a number of bombshells: The fuel efficiency goal was to be raised to 100 percent; the team had to factor in hybrid powertrain technology that was being tried, with limited success, by the company's minivan engineering team; and they had 12 months to develop a concept car for presentation at the 1995 Tokyo Motor Show.

At this point, the process went into hyperdrive. It seems to have gobbled up most of Toyota's top engineering talent. The cast of characters brought in to crack the nut on designing the hybrid car is astounding; their story fills a 387-page book, *The Prius That Shook the World*, by Hideshi Itazaki. At one point, Uchiyamada had a team of more than 1,000 engineers working around the clock on the project.

The process they went through would have defeated lesser men and women. A seven-days-a-week, 24-hours-a-day testing schedule was announced. The team went through 80 iterations of the hybrid engine, then narrowed that to four. More experienced in mechanical problems, they grappled to solve the electrical issues presented by the battery technology, many of which didn't present themselves until the process was well under way. Since electrical engineering was not their forte, many of the engineers had to add studying books and case studies to their already full plates. In echoes of the Tesla story, the Toyota team also found the batteries to be extremely temperamental. The batteries didn't like high altitudes or warm climates and shut down if they got a little too hot or too cold. It was a challenge to find a semi-conductor that could handle transmitting the voltage of the battery to the electric motor (solved by a unit modeled on that of Japan's famous bullet train). Longevity of the battery was also a problem, with batteries wearing out significantly faster than the seven to 10 years they'd need to last. The solution was to create a system whereby the batteries would remain between 40 percent and 60 percent charged at all times.

There were other problems as well. At one point, the engine whined horribly. (Because of the midnight test-drives and secrecy of the project, this resulted in other Toyota staffers believing a ghost had begun haunting the test-drive building.) During demonstration drives to reveal an early model of the vehicle to Toyota executives, a team member had to sit in the passenger seat with a laptop to monitor the temperature of the battery to prevent it from bursting into flames. During a media showcase that came later, test-drives were limited to two laps of a race track because the batteries weren't up to more.

But management members refused to lower their ambition; in fact, they elevated it again, insisting that a production-ready model be available for 1997. Uchiyamada had no idea how he would meet the deadline. "I thought he demanded too much," Uchiyamada said of Wada at the time.[20]

The engineering team in Tokyo stuck doggedly to the schedule, figuring out how to add a radiator to the battery to manage overheating, redesigning semiconductors, overcoming design errors in the transaxle, finding a company that could mass-produce motors (which are different from the engines conventional cars contain), working around limited availability of the right steel for the motor's semiconductors, and always, always chipping away at the fuel efficiency. Chassis designers in America were engaged and given just two or three weeks to develop designs for the car's exterior, versus a standard two to three months. All teams went to extraordinary lengths, leaving home to live in company dormitories and working around the clock and on holidays. They restructured Toyota's hallowed design and production processes to speed things up.

Of course, in such a high-pressure environment, mistakes were made and conflicts arose. Given the careful orchestration of multiple teams' deliverables the project required, some people became frustrated when their own work was held up because other teams' deliverables (usually the battery team's) were not ready on time. But leadership attention and the project's secrecy lent the project a prestige and significance that carried them through. The addition of an intranet helped teams communicate better and find more empathy for each other's plights. There was so little time that at several crisis points, teams put finger-pointing aside to focus on simply solving the problem. Morale remained intact despite the odds.

And then suddenly, the teams achieved the goal they'd been charged with—developing a fully functioning vehicle with fuel consumption of 66 miles per gallon, with 100 percent mileage improvement—two months ahead of schedule. The Prius went on to succeed in a way project leaders admitted they never dreamed of.

This degree of Disruptive Innovation could not have been achieved without the large, skilled, and incredibly tenacious team dedicated to the task for the duration of the project. The same themes of a crack team swarming a problem and prevailing despite the odds emerge at Nike, GE, and IKEA. You'll recall that the beginning of the chapter noted that some people view sustainability as primitive. These stories prove how wrongheaded that perception is. These are not simple problems but rather seemingly impossible ones to solve. Disruptive Innovations that combine sustainability and billion-dollar business potential are breaking new ground. Because there is little in the way of precedent, practitioners are effectively making it up as they go along. Unless you understand and respect these facts, you will fail to take the innovation challenge sufficiently seriously, and you will fail to assemble a team of sufficiently high caliber to furnish you with a Disruptive Innovation. This is what the Green Giants got right.

Low-Tech Teams
Of course, not all Green Giants are in the business of technological breakthroughs. At Whole Foods and Chipotle, much of the innovation comes from the supply chain. Local, organic, or artisanal suppliers are to these Green Giants as engineers and designers are to Tesla, Toyota, and Nike. These types of Green Giants rely on suppliers for their Disruptive Innovation, and their relationship with their suppliers reflects this importance.

At Whole Foods, the Disruptive Innovation was to build a business around supremely high-quality, local, artisanal products. The typical supermarket/supplier relationship is a transactional affair. The supermarket buyer holds almost all the cards and treats the supplier accordingly. The supplier is often commoditized, competing on the basis of price and national scale.

Things are different at Whole Foods. Whole Foods depends in large part for its success on suppliers that are specialized, not commoditized. Whole Foods' competitors have jumped on the organic/local/artisanal bandwagon with gusto. In the face of this onslaught, Whole Foods' ability to discover and cultivate the most intriguing and innovative suppliers before somebody else does is what now stands between retaining and losing its billion-dollar edge.

To identify and cultivate new supplier talent, Whole Foods employs a team of what are called Local Foragers. Part trendspotter, part buyer, part foodie, and part micro-lender, the Foragers trawl the country in search of the products of the next hot country farm, urban bakery, and so on to bring to Whole Foods' shelves. If suppliers show promise but need a little help to purchase new equipment or transition to organic methods, they can apply for a Whole Foods Local Producer Loan (the company makes up to $10 million a year available for these loans).

Whole Foods discovered the Harlem, New York–based social enterprise Hot Bread Kitchen (HBK) in 2010. The bakery's wondrous breads range from the familiar (challah, sourdough, focaccia, etc.) to the exotic (Persian nan-e barbari, Moroccan m'smen, and Armenian lavash crackers) and contain a secret ingredient: They are baked by foreign-born and low-income men and women who previously struggled to find work but have exceptional bread-baking skills, honed in their home countries. In exchange for working in the bakery, candidates are offered a living wage, language lessons, and training in commercial baking and management skills. After a year, HBK supports them in finding professional baking jobs. HBK also has an incubator for local foods brands; food start-ups can rent affordable space from HBK and access crucial business resources to get themselves off the ground.

The Whole Foods relationship began when Whole Foods started stocking HBK loaves at one or two locations. Today, Whole Foods is HBK's largest retail account, and Whole Foods employs several HBK graduates in its bakery departments—an achievement of which one graduate whom I heard speak is rightly proud. Whole Foods has also picked up six other small brands from HBK's incubator. HBK founder and CEO Jessamyn Rodriguez told me:

> It's much more than a vendor relationship. We've found them to be unique in their buying practices in the grocery business. They are very proactive in trying to find the latest up-and-coming food businesses. You can be working at a tiny scale but they'll take you on and help you scale. It has been game changing. No other single company has invested in our mission the way that Whole Foods has.[21]

Rodriguez also told me that buyers from across different Whole Foods departments and regions host regular pitch nights with her incubator members as they hunt for the newest and best ideas.

There is nothing accidental about this relationship from Whole Foods' perspective. In his book *Conscious Capitalism: Liberating the Heroic Spirit of Business*, Whole Foods co-CEO John Mackey devotes a whole chapter to the importance of treating your suppliers right. This is not new age fluff but more like enlightened (mutual) self-interest. The revenue potential of Whole Foods' suppliers is directly tied to their uniqueness and originality, and collectively they represent a wealth of skills, knowledge, and passion that cannot easily be replicated. Whole Foods knows this and looks to them as its extended team of problem solvers.

Shai Agassi, a successful serial entrepreneur who pioneered an ultimately unsuccessful electric vehicle infrastructure model called Better Place, recently advised Tesla wannabes: "Challenge the designers to build greatness; ask them to build a better car than any they have ever designed."[22] He might have been speaking to all would-be Green Giants. When sustainability is left to the marketing—or even the sustainability—teams alone, Disruptive Innovation does not result. It comes only when the designers, scientists, engineers, farmers, and artisans are engaged, equipped, and invited to build greatness.

5. Cultivate Pervasive Innovation

Green Giants might begin with a signature Disruptive Innovation, but they don't end there. The spirit of innovation pervades every aspect of their culture and their business, and they constantly seek out new areas to improve.

This pursuit of perfection in all aspects of business is a characteristic of Green Giants and is a major reason they sustain their success from an entrepreneurial start-up or new venture to a billion-dollar business. It is not a characteristic unique to Green Giants, but it is one common to them.

At Chipotle, Steve Ells is always fine-tuning the raw ingredients and perfecting the process. Many column inches have been devoted to his fanaticism in pursuit of fast food nirvana. For example, he is said to have insisted his team go back to hand-chopping onions days after the company rolled out (extremely expensive) automated chopping machines across the business because the taste of machine-chopped onions was inferior. Ells is also obsessed with incremental improvements like inventing the perfect tortilla warmer or a better way to dry and fluff oregano before chopping it. He says: "If you do a hundred things like this, [customers] can tell the difference. In 10 years we will be selling better food because of hundreds of improvements like that." The same rigor and attention to detail applies to everything from the temperature in the restaurants to how employees are hired and compensated.

Similarly, in his book *The Responsible Company*, Yvon Chouinard, the CEO of the outdoor clothing and gear company and Next Billion Patagonia, describes how he and his colleagues have systematically examined every aspect of their business for opportunities to become more sustainable and responsible. One of Patagonia's earliest innovations was to shift from pitons to aluminum chocks for rock climbing when the founders realized the pitons were taking a toll on nature's rock faces. Next came the switch to organic cotton, when they learned that cotton is the world's second most toxic crop. Then they turned their attention to conditions for factory workers, then to a service to repair Patagonia clothes, then to the Footprint Chronicles (an initiative to offer the world visibility into the carbon impact of every piece of Patagonia merchandise), and then to the formation of the Sustainable Apparel Coalition (with Nike, among others). In 2011, Patagonia went right for the elephant in the room with its "Don't buy this jacket" ad, which encouraged people not to buy a new jacket unless they absolutely needed one. It launched a debate around consumption itself and a retail channel through which Patagonia customers could resell their used Patagonia merchandise. In 2014, the brand was at it again, focusing on sustainable down and giving away the patents to Yulex, its plant-based alternative to neoprene for wetsuits.

Patagonia may have begun life as a way to earn a living for a bunch of laid-back surfers from Ventura, but today a spirit of divine discontent inhabits the company, compelling its people to leave no stone unturned in pursuit of a better business. It would be easy to mistake Patagonia's business philosophy for the fanciful notion of the hippies its founders were when they started out. But make no mistake. Patagonia is one of the fastest growing companies in the apparel industry with annual growth of 27 percent in 2011 and 2012,[23] compared to an industry average closer to 4 percent.[24] Chouinard has found no conflict between doing the right thing for people and the environment and for the business. "I know it sounds crazy, but every time I have made a decision that is best for the planet, I have made money," he says.[25] Patagonia's 2013 revenues stood at about $600 million.[26]

How do you cultivate pervasive innovation to build a Green Giant brand? One word: culture. The initial innovation may come from the vision of the Iconoclastic Leader, but pervasive innovation relies on every employee in the organization doing his or her part. From the retailers that are utterly dependent on their store staff to deliver the right experience to customers, to the manufacturers that rely on the ingenuity of the professional problem solvers, employee engagement is paramount.

It may be easier when you're founder-owned and have hand-picked every employee for attitude and philosophical alignment with your purpose from the start. Corporations have to work harder to rally their professional problem solvers to the purpose and embrace the innovation challenge. They may have to overcome pockets of resistance. To get there, they work hard to develop strong cultures. They develop robust training programs and cultivate an environment of collaboration and camaraderie.

Consider Method Home Products, a Next Billion and maker of eco- and human-friendly household products in sculptural bottles, juicy colors, and mouth-watering scents. Founded in 2001 by childhood friends Adam Lowry, a marketer, and Eric Ryan, a chemist, Method worked hard to build a distinctive, entrepreneurial culture from the start. Retaining this as it grew (AKA "keeping Method weird") became a focus when Method began to feel it was losing its edge. Today, everything from Astroturf-lined table tennis rooms, to beer and cereal in the kitchen, to self-selected wacky job titles (such as chief greenkeeper and, for the CFO, big spender) are designed to keep a spirit of innovation and inspiration alive—and to keep the innovative ideas that are the company's bread and butter flowing.

Pursuit of perfection is a characteristic of the most innovative companies in any sphere, so it's not surprising it should also be true of Green Giants. One thing's for sure: As the acceleration of sustainability-oriented innovation increases, Green Giants will widen the gap between themselves and the laggards—which is the definition of first mover advantage . . . .

A Word on Being First

It may seem obvious that one of the reasons the Green Giants have had such success with their Disruptive Innovations is that they got there first. This is not entirely true. Toyota and Tesla were beaten to the market by competitors who did not have it all figured out. The brands that hit it big brought the absolutely right combination of elements to market (the components described in this book).

However, getting there first, or at least very early, enables you to set the terms of the category and get so far out in front of competitors that they find it hard to catch up. Toyota still commands more than a 50 percent share of the U.S. hybrid market 14 years after the Prius's

U.S. launch,[27] while Tesla's more traditional luxury car competitors are now scrambling to catch up. Both the Prius and Tesla's EVs have defined a category in the same way Apple did with its iPods and iPads.

For sustainability-inspired innovation, the window is still open. Relatively few businesses have truly embraced sustainability as a source of innovation opportunity. Indeed, they may view it as quite the opposite, so they aren't actively searching for a sustainability-fueled breakthrough with billion-dollar potential in the same way, say, Nike was (and still is). Green Giants have been able to turn their competitors' blind spots to their advantage. By moving first, moving fast, and moving smart, maybe you can too.

HOW TO DO IT: THE FIVE STAGES OF DISRUPTIVE INNOVATION

How do you develop your own billion-dollar, Green Giant-esque Disruptive Innovation? I divide the process into five stages:

1. Formalization

2. Inspiration

3. Generation

4. Evaluation

5. Realization

1. Formalization

Discovering, launching, and scaling a Disruptive Innovation is hard work. But by understanding that sustainability can yield such an innovation and formally committing your organization to find it, you can put yourself ahead of most other companies, since the majority are still focused on sustainability as a driver of operational efficiency or incremental product enhancements. (These are foundational good housekeeping measures that every company should be doing, but they are not likely to yield a Disruptive Innovation with billion-dollar potential.)

Take a lead from Toyota: Assign a small, crack team to lead the initiative, with accountability to deliver. Include a combustible mix of mindsets and skill sets; the sustainability team must be at the table, as must whoever in your business are the equivalent of Tesla's and Toyota's engineers, Nike's designers, and Whole Foods' Local Foragers. Include a wild card or two. I worked on a project for Unilever where the most valuable team member was the Walmart liaison because she understood what the everyday American shopper was up against. Operations and finance also should be considered. Identify a strategically selected group of external sustainability experts and retain or invite them to consult at key moments on the journey.

Set an objective. A broad objective is appropriate at this stage; it can be as simple as "Identify a Disruptive Innovation with the potential to become a Green Giant business for Company X." Agree on a deadline. Implement a governance structure and institute a clear reporting process.

Then get jazzed about it. Infect the organization with enthusiasm and urgency. Innovation opportunities this big don't come along often, and time is of the essence to beat your competition to the punch. Innovation ideas sometimes seem to be in the ether, with similar ideas surfacing simultaneously at several companies. Adidas launched its challenger to the Flyknit mere weeks after Nike. Nike was able to delay the Adidas rollout by bringing a patent infringement case against its competitors, but the Adidas Primeknit line is now ramping up globally. Time will tell how well it competes.

2. Inspiration

This phase is about assembling inspiration and information, the base of knowledge you need to understand where you are today and the spectrum of opportunity. This early phase is quite open: It's about casting a wide net for a problem to solve or an opportunity to exploit. The opportunity may be obvious—there may be a glaring need for a more sustainable way of doing something in the category in which you operate—but more likely it is not.

You might structure your inspiration inquiry around the classic Cs of marketing—company, customer/consumer, competition, category, and culture. Here are some triggers to help spur your inspiration-seeking:

- *Company.* What are your material issues—that is to say, the issues upon which your business has a significant impact? What are the greatest impacts and future risk factors in your current business model? What have you already begun that has potential? What are your unique assets? Depending on how much work has already been done in your company or industry to understand things like lifecycle impacts, material issues, and consumer concerns, you may need to embark upon a major research exercise to gain clarity, as Unilever did prior to developing the Sustainable Living Plan.

- *Customer/Consumer.* How are consumer needs, perceptions, and expectations of your business and your category changing? Are there unmet needs that exist today or will emerge tomorrow? What core consumer needs are ever-green? Could you meet the same needs in new, more sustainable ways? What role will you need consumers to play; for example, will behavior changes be required? Toyota got ahead of consumer demand for a fuel-efficient vehicle so it was ready when gas prices rose.

- *Competition.* What are your competitors doing? Are there successes or failures you can learn from? Is there white-space to be exploited? What are their blind spots? Just because a competitor has succeeded in one way, another innovation avenue may be possible—Tesla's EVs and the Prius both represent ways to disrupt the automobile category, just differently.

- *Category.* What category are you in, and how might that change in the future? For example, Toyota thinks of itself as a mobility company rather than a car company. That changes the aperture of what's possible. Even if you are in a large company, try thinking like an entrepreneur, or rather, an intrapreneur—an entrepreneur within a large corporation. What would a start-up do in this category if it could approach the situation as a blank slate? Would it build the category the way it has been built or would it do it differently? What are entrepreneurs already doing in your category? Is there an idea you could imitate or improve upon, given your unique expertise or resources? Entrepreneurial ideas may seem niche, but if the new billion-dollar companies prove anything, it's how fast things can change. Looking at the Green Giants, could their paradigm be adapted to your category? For example, could Chipotle's success be replicated with a different kind of food? Could a tech company build a device that is to computing as Tesla is to automobiles? There are several major sustainable innovation paradigms that could potentially be applied to any business to yield a new idea—including collaborative consumption, cleantech, sustainable sourcing, and local production. Could they transform your business?

- *Culture.* "Culture" is used here as catchall term to describe the operating environment. Explore trends and changing realities in dimensions like resource availability and price, regulation, infrastructure, climate, and the economic environment that might impact your business, changing the playing field and rewriting the rules for success. What are the major social and environmental issues that intersect with your business? Look for major cultural trends you can and should get ahead of. For example, Whole Foods has seen its success cemented as the major cultural trend toward local, traceable, and organic foods continues its march into the mainstream.

Use any and all sources to get at the salient information—interviews inside the company, desk research, etc. If necessary, commission market research. Some of the biggest leaps in my thinking have come from interviews with thought leaders in government, industry organizations, and NGOs. What do they see as the salient issues and major opportunities?

Once you have your Cs, use them as inputs to scenario planning. Bring the team and advisers together to develop a range of potential future scenarios. Name them. Then assess how they might overturn the assumptions your current business model is based on, making a counterintuitive alternative suddenly make sense. This approach is the most powerful way of managing in uncertain times.

3. Generation

Now that you understand the context, shift gears and begin generating ideas. This phase is still in open mode. The objective is to generate a range of potential avenues to explore; refining down to the most promising comes later. From all of the material you have generated, you will be able to isolate themes and a subset of potential problems to be solved or opportunities to be exploited. It can be useful to categorize these into buckets:

- Manufacturing problems: the impacts of making what you make

- Supply-chain problems: supply issues you need to address now or challenges you'll face in the future (for example, to get ahead of a water-constrained future, Levi's is designing jeans that use 26 percent less water to manufacture than regular jeans)

- Consumer use problems

- Disposal and end-of-life problems

Ideally, get each of these down to a tight problem or opportunity statement. If you have too many, filter them to a subset with the biggest potential.

Then move into idea generation. There are many ways to do this. I favor workshops. Structure a workshop or series of workshops to generate ideas against the identified problem statements and scenarios. These should be conducted in bright, airy environments with a dynamic moderator. Prepare provocative materials as stimulus. Get people offsite. Bring in outside thinkers. Construct the session so that different perspectives can come together. Generate as many ideas as you can. Exhaust all avenues. Make sure the idea isn't hiding in plain sight. This phase is possibly the most fun, so let your team's creativity, ingenuity, and passion lead you wherever it will.

You won't leave this stage with the idea solved; that will take hard work by the professional problem solvers. But you should have the germs of some brilliant potential ideas.

4. Evaluation

Move from possibilities to a plan. The ideas generated should be evaluated and separated into winners and losers. Depending on your situation—whether you are a small start-up with power over your own destiny or a major multinational with shareholders and a board of directors to answer to, whether your solution relies on technology and/or materials that already exist or ones that need to be invented, and whether the solution lies within your operational control or depends on third-party provision or participation—the evaluation phase can be swift and largely intuitive or much longer and more quantitative in nature. Remember, GE went through a year-long process to determine that Ecomagination was the right path forward, and the company already had several billion dollars in revenue from products that became the foundation of the portfolio, giving a strong indication of business viability.

Regardless of your size, the following set of criteria can prove useful. Each idea should be evaluated against them:

- Does this idea align with and enable you to deliver your purpose?

- Is it truly disruptive? Does it have the potential to over-turn the dominant technology or business model in the category?

- Is it not just greener but better? Does it represent a total upgrade on products or services already on the market?

- Does it feel counterintuitive but calculatedly so, given the information yielded in the scenario planning phase?

- Does it integrate business and sustainability in one agenda; that is, does it have the ability to deliver sustainability and business outcomes simultaneously? Can you quantify both?

- Does it, or could it, have mainstream appeal?

Depending on your business, this stage may also involve prototyping and other viability testing. You need to explore the business case. Only ideas that meet most or all of these criteria should be considered strong enough to move forward.

5. Realization

There is clearly no one path to realizing your Disruptive Innovation. The paths to success are as varied as the companies that realize them. However, there are some themes from Green Giants that are instructive. Two of them are outlined in this chapter: engage the problem solvers and cultivate pervasive innovation. Create a tight definition of the problem you need your team to solve. Assemble the right mix of professional problem solvers, with a clear leader and accountability to the CEO. Figure out the knowledge and skill set gaps and how to plug them: Do you need to invite your sustainability team to collaborate with your engineers or designers (your equivalent of Nike's Considered Design team)? Or do you need to hire an entirely new breed of technician, as Tesla did with its Silicon Valley-esque electrical engineers? Make it the team's day job, its members' sole job, and consider tying the team's performance evaluation and compensation to a successful outcome.

As you decide how the team is structured, you need to ask some tough questions. Is your organization structured to allow sustainable innovation to happen? Can the team survive and be successful within the existing paradigm of your business, or do you need to create a separate "pirate" entity with freedom and a mandate to disrupt? Or is acquisition more your speed? Note, though, that none of the Green Giants got there through acquisition alone. Unilever acquired the ice cream company Ben & Jerry's in 2001, and although Ben & Jerry's inherently disruptive culture undoubtedly contributed to Unilever's success, each of the Green Giants built their Disruptive Innovation in-house.

Set ambitious but realistic time frames with regular review periods. Resource the project appropriately; invest the R&D dollars. Scale up external support if necessary. Tap the wealth of external resources that now exist, whether in carbon measurement, sustainable sourcing, sustainable business models, industry-specific coalitions, green building, sustainable design and branding, and much more. Then get to work. Stay committed, maintain momentum, and stick with it through thick and thin until you have cracked your innovation.

For entrepreneurs, a few additional thoughts: This phase very likely involves finding investment, either from venture capital firms or from a corporate investor. Recall that Chipotle took investment from McDonald's for the critical years that saw it grow from a handful of restaurants to a national chain, and Next Billions like Warby Parker and Method have relied on VC money for their success. Competition for VC money today is tough, but there are investors with a history of backing Green Giant–style brands. They include Tiger Global Management, First Round Capital, Menlo Ventures, and Thrive Capital. It helps if you meet them prepared with answers to the criteria from the evaluation stage, as well as a business plan and evidence of existing revenue.

Developing a Disruptive Innovation will be one of the most engaging, confounding, frustrating, and ultimately rewarding jobs you have ever done. Invite your team to build greatness, then hold on tight.

CHAPTER **3**

A Higher Purpose

"If you want to be competitive in the long term, your business needs to have discovered its higher purpose."
—**John Mackey,** Whole Foods founder and CEO

Let's play a game. Here are the mission statements of some Fortune 500 companies. Guess which company they belong to. As you read them, think about how these missions make you *feel*. Do they feel like something you believe in? Are they something you want to be part of, *as a customer?* Would they get you out of bed in the morning *as an employee?*

1. To build shareholder value by delivering pharmaceutical and healthcare products, services, and solutions in innovative and cost-effective ways.

2. To maximize long-term stockholder value, while adhering to the laws of the jurisdictions in which we operate and at all times observing the highest ethical standards.

3. Our goal is to be a superior investment for our shareholders through the production, transmission, and distribution of electricity, natural gas, and natural gas liquids to customers in the United States.

4. Create value for shareholders through the energy business.

5. The purpose of the X Company is to earn money for its shareholders and increase the value of their investment.

We will do that through growing the company, controlling assets, and properly structuring the balance sheet, thereby increasing EPS, cash flow, and return on invested capital.

I don't know about you, but as an employee I can't wait to go properly structure a balance sheet. That's what really brings me alive. Any guesses as to which companies these mission statements belong to? It's tricky, isn't it?

Here's a second set:

1. To create a better everyday life for the many people.

2. To bring inspiration and innovation to every athlete in the world . . . If you have a body, you are an athlete.

3. To make people feel good about themselves, about others, and about the natural environment and the whole of which we are part.

4. To help expedite the move from a mine-and-burn hydrocarbon economy toward a solar electric economy.

5. To make sustainable living commonplace.

Which set of statements seems stronger? The first set are traditional corporate mission statements chosen from a list of the Fortune 500 companies.[1] They are from (1) the pharmaceutical distributor AmerisourceBergen, (2) the food and beverage company Dean Foods, (3) the energy company Dynamic Energy, (4) the energy company Kerr-McGee (which has now been acquired by another company), and (5) the tire business Cooper Tire and Rubber Company. These statements suggest that the central purpose, the raison d'être, of the business is to generate shareholder returns.

The second set of statements are from Green Giants: (1) IKEA, (2) Nike, (3) Natura, (4) Tesla, and (5) Unilever. These statements outline a purpose for the business beyond profit—and not just any purpose, but a *social* purpose, one that sees the business as part of society, with the potential to be a positive force in the world.

This is the third shared trait of Green Giants: They are motivated by a purpose beyond profit. It's not that they don't care about profit; on the contrary, they do. But they regard profit as an outcome of achieving their purpose, not the reason they exist. And a mounting body of evidence suggests that this philosophy is part of what enables them to *outperform* their profit-oriented counterparts on multiple measures including—you guessed it—profitability. This is a phenomena I call the Purpose Paradox.

This chapter explores the purpose at the heart of the Green Giants and diagnoses how it has contributed to their business success. It uncovers the evidence behind the Purpose Paradox. It explores the history of purpose in business and why it is more than a passing fad. And it provides pointers to finding a purpose for your business—with the power to unlock billion-dollar potential.

WHY DOES BUSINESS EXIST?

My work with companies committed to change has driven an exploration of how the business world uses the term "purpose." Often, the term functions as a catchall for anything that could be classified as good, whether a campaign marketing a cause, corporate philanthropy, a citizenship program, a CSR program, or not-for-profit branding. "Purpose" has become the latest business buzzword. One study shows that 88 percent of current business leaders and 90 percent of future leaders believe business should have a social purpose, while another study shows that 81 percent of business leaders see purpose as a business opportunity.[2]

But what is this mythical purpose? Is it really any different from a vision or mission statement, things business leaders have been creating forever?

Since there's no universally agreed upon definition of the term, here's mine: Purpose-driven business envisions business as a force for good, a force with the power to change the world around it and to deliver tangible improvement to human life and the environment. It delivers profit, as it delivers value to all of a company's stakeholders—not just shareholders. And it understands purpose as not just where the company spends its money but how it earns it.

The Green Giants provide excellent examples of this type of purpose, as shown in the table below.

Company	Purpose
Unilever	"To make sustainable living commonplace."
IKEA	"To create a better everyday life for the many people."
Chipotle	"Food with Integrity"
GE	"To invent and build things that power the world."
Natura	"To make people feel good about themselves, about others, and about the natural environment and the whole of which we are part."
Nike	"To bring inspiration and innovation to every athlete in the world . . . . If you have a body, you are an athlete."

Toyota	"Contribute to the economic growth of the country in which it is located (external stakeholders).
	Contribute to the stability and well-being of team members (internal stakeholders).
	Contribute to the overall growth of Toyota."
Tesla	"To help expedite the move from a mine-and-burn hydrocarbon economy toward a solar electric economy."
Whole Foods	"With great courage, integrity, and love, we embrace our responsibility to co-create a world where each of us, our communities, and our planet can flourish—all the while, celebrating the sheer love and joy of food."

Unilever doesn't exist to make its shareholders rich, nor to make great soap and laundry detergent, although it does both. Likewise, Chipotle doesn't exist to be the highest returning fast food stock in a generation, nor to make great burritos, although it does both too. These companies exist to make sustainable living commonplace and create Food with Integrity, respectively.

Natura explains how it differs from most other companies in this regard:

For most companies, profit is the salient goal. At Natura, our pursuit is greater well-being for all. The goal is to cultivate healthy, transparent, positive relationships—between the company and its stakeholders, between those individual stakeholders, between individuals and the whole. Everything is interdependent. We do everything we can as a company to behave accordingly.

Note that this is not corporate social responsibility. Whatever was intended by the founders and advocates of CSR, as practiced today, CSR is too often about how companies *spend* (or donate) the money they've earned elsewhere in their business. Nor is it a passing management fad. By orienting their businesses around a social purpose, the Green Giants are looking at purpose as the way they *earn* their money, the primary reason they exist. And more than the purpose of their own companies, these companies are challenging our fundamental beliefs about the purpose of business *as an institution*. They are asking: Why does business exist?

This is a question to which Green Giants offer answers that challenge the dominant management theory of the past three decades: that the sole purpose of business is to increase profits and maximize shareholder value.

A BATTLE FOR THE SOUL OF BUSINESS

On December 20, 1976, about 30 years after he founded IKEA, Swedish businessman Ingvar Kamprad published *The Testament of a Furniture Dealer*. In the 14-page document, Kamprad committed to paper his company's purpose: "To create a better everyday life for the many people by offering a wide range of well-designed, functional home furnishing products at prices so low that as many people as possible will be able to afford them."

He goes on to declare that IKEA has "decided once and for all to side with the many people," in contrast to his competitors, who reserve their "fine designs and new ideas . . . for a small circle of the affluent."

Peppered with language like "democratization," "protest," and "mortal sin," and with exhortations to "contribute to the process of democratization," the *Testament* reads more like a political manifesto crossed with a religious tome than a private sector strategy document. The word "responsibility" appears 18 times. Nowhere is found dry financial concepts or business jargon. Instead, Kamprad boasts proudly, "A well-known Swedish industrialist-politician has said that IKEA has meant more for the process of democratization than many political measures put together."

It's fascinating to look at the business through Kamprad's eyes. To many of today's business leaders, the advancement of democratization probably seems an unlikely way to measure business success. Yet Kamprad doesn't view IKEA's purpose as driving profits or indeed building great, low-cost furniture. Instead, he sees the business as a vehicle for achieving far-reaching social change—as well as self-actualization for himself and his employees.

As you read this, I'm guessing you find yourself in one of two camps. Half of you are thinking, "This noble vision of business is exhilarating. This is something I want to be a part of. It's much more compelling than maximizing shareholder returns."

The rest of you are thinking: "Socialist."

If you're in the latter camp, you have Nobel Prize–winning economist Milton Friedman to thank for it. "Socialist" is the word he used in his subtly titled 1970 essay "The Social Responsibility of Business Is to Increase its Profits" to describe people who advocate for the social responsibility of business. Published six years earlier than Kamprad's *Testament*, Friedman's essay declared, as the title says, that the exclusive purpose of business is to increase its returns to shareholders and that employees should engage exclusively "in activities designed to increase its profits." It dismissed the notion that business has any other social responsibility as "a fundamentally subversive doctrine."[3]

The publication of Friedman's essay is regarded as the moment at which the belief that social responsibility and profits are competing agendas hardened into fact in the minds of the business community. His legacy casts a long shadow. Today, growing profits and maximizing shareholder returns are (erroneously) taught as *the* purpose of the corporation in almost every leading business and law school in America (and to a lesser degree in Europe and beyond). Surveys show that after completing B-school, students are even more likely to see shareholder value as the most important goal of the corporation.[4] This has become our dominant business ideology.

But what if Friedman was wrong?

The business world increasingly seems to believe he was, and Kamprad certainly appears to think so. Kamprad is very pro-profit; "profit is a wonderful word!" he writes. But in his worldview, profit is not created for its own sake but rather to enable IKEA to better pursue its purpose. "A better everyday life for the many people! To achieve our aim, we must have resources," writes Kamprad in the profit section of his *Testament*, which is titled "Profit gives us resources."

For Kamprad, profits and purpose are mutually reinforcing. It's a virtuous cycle in which the purpose creates profits, which enable further pursuit of the purpose, which generates more profits, and so on. (Note that the Green Giant business line in this book is IKEA's line of Products for a More Sustainable Life at Home, a line that in some countries includes solar panels for domestic use, LED lights, storage solutions to reduce food waste, and energy-efficient appliances, all designed to "make sustainability affordable and attractive to millions of people," Jamie Rusby, manager of Climate Engagement

& Sustainability Reporting at IKEA Group, told me. While this specific strategy was not in place when the *Testament* was written, Rusby describes it as being "in line with our vision. A better everyday life includes a more sustainable life at home," he says.)

How has this "socialist" philosophy served Kamprad? In 2012, he was estimated to be the richest person in Europe and the fifth richest in the world. (This has since been revised to the 495th richest, according to an IKEA spokesperson, because Kamprad created two foundations that now own the company groups—Inter IKEA Group and the IKEA Group—and foundation statutes bar him and his family from benefiting from their funds.) That must make him one of the most successful businessmen of all time. Take that, Professor Friedman.

Philosophically, the Green Giants are in Kamprad's camp, seeing a purpose for business beyond profit. In fact, not satisfied with orienting their own businesses around a social purpose, several of them are engaged in efforts to redefine the purpose of business in society. Paul Polman of Unilever and Guilherme Leal of Natura are members of a not-so-secret society of global leaders called The B Team. Launched at the World Economic Forum in Davos in 2013, The B Team outlines its vision for the future as one "in which the purpose of business is to be a driving force for social, environmental and economic benefit." Other members of The B Team include Virgin Group founder Sir Richard Branson, Indian business leader Ratan Tata, and media star Arianna Huffington. They have made explicit commitments to "catalyze a better way of doing business for the well-being of people and the planet."[5]

In December 2014, Natura officially became certified as a B Corp, a new form of corporate entity that aims to make business as accountable for social and environmental performance as for financial performance. B Corps are certified by the U.S.-based nonprofit B Lab.

To qualify, companies must have an explicit social or environmental purpose, and performance against it is verified by a third party. B Corps have a fiduciary responsibility to take into account the interests of workers, the community, and the environment, not just shareholders.[6] Certification is not necessarily legally binding, but in more than 20 U.S. states, including Maryland and California, it now is. In those states, shareholders of a company registered as a "benefit corporation" can sue the directors for not carrying out the company's social mission, just as they might sue directors of traditional companies for violation of their regular fiduciary duties. Worldwide, there are now more than 1,000 Certified B Corps from 33 countries and more than 60 industries. Natura is the largest in terms of revenue; other B Corps include Ben & Jerry's (which is a subsidiary of Unilever) and Next Billions Warby Parker, Honest Company, and Patagonia.

Natura apparently applied for B Corp certification because it was already observing the principles of a B Corp business. Natura's shareholders seem to have agreed, raising no objection to the change. Meanwhile, at the World Economic Forum meeting in Davos in January 2015, Paul Polman of Unilever announced his desire to make Unilever the world's largest publicly traded B Corp. He envisages a long process toward certification given the complexity of a business that operates in so many geographic areas but seems determined to forge ahead nevertheless. Why does Polman want to do this? He told Guardian Sustainable Business that "becoming a B Corp would send a powerful signal that the purpose of business is not just profit, but to have a positive impact on society and the environment."[7]

John Mackey at Whole Foods outlines his vision for a new type of capitalism. In his book *Conscious Capitalism*, he explains how, through Whole Foods, he is exploring alternatives to almost every aspect of how business is typically done, including management style, accounting, remuneration, employee engagement, and even hiring and firing. His idea of conscious capitalism would have Milton Friedman spinning in his grave. Mackey writes of a business "built on love and care . . . that enriches the world by its existence and brings joy, fulfillment, and a sense of meaning to all who are touched by it." But his ideas are broadly consistent with those of The B Team. "Having a purpose beyond profit" is one of four key tenets of *Conscious Capitalism*. In a bid to propagate his philosophy and spark a movement, Mackey has written a book, formed a coalition, and hosts annual conferences where speakers have included—guess who?—Green Giant CEOs Paul Polman of Unilever and Steve Ells of Chipotle.

Non–Green Giants are also experimenting with these ideas. Indra Nooyi, CEO of PepsiCo, says her business operates under a mission called "Performance with Purpose." She sums it up perfectly: "When we articulated this notion of Performance with Purpose, people said, 'Oh, this is corporate social responsibility.' Wrong. This is not about how we spend the money we make. The focus needs to be on how we make the money." After a long period of slow growth, PepsiCo's stock has rebounded to nearly double rival Coca-Cola's over the past two years under this new concept.

Even the world's most valuable company is getting in on the action. Early in 2014, Apple CEO Tim Cook declared that Apple was committed to "advancing humanity" and told shareholders who raised questions about his sustainability initiatives, "If you want me to make decisions that have a clear ROI, then you should get out of the stock." In September 2014, he took the stage at New York's Morgan Library and Museum on the opening day of Climate Week to discuss his philosophy on business and climate change with the UN's lead climate change negotiator, Christiana Figueres. Apple is taking steps to address climate change because it's "the right thing to do for the planet and the right thing to do for the business," Cook told Figueres and a rapt audience of business and policy leaders. IKEA's current CEO, Peter Agnefjäll, was also on that stage and made similar points. He is still in Kamprad's camp.

These characters are not antibusiness or anticapitalist. They're CEOs of some of the world's largest engines of capitalism. And yet they're converging around the idea that purpose matters.

That's not to say that everyone's on board. Over the course of several years, the National Center for Public Policy Research pressured GE to "not undertake any energy saving or sustainability project solely to address the issue of climate change." The NCPPR is a conservative think tank that denies there is scientific consensus on climate change[8] and is a member of the Cooler Heads Coalition, which describes its objective as "dispelling the myths of global warming." The NCPPR was also the group that challenged Tim Cook on his sustainability spending in 2014.[9] Also that year, the group declared victory regarding GE, crowing, "Now, GE shareholders have confirmation that the company's strategies will henceforth be led by true market forces and not by blind adherence to global warming zealotry."[10] To this day, GE is still unclear what battle the NCPPR thought it had won. GE's Ecomagination strategy was always about delivering shareholder value and has done an extraordinary job of it. Since its inception, Ecomagination has grown at twice the rate of the rest of the business and generated enough revenue that it would qualify as a Fortune 100 if it were a standalone company. How any self-respecting shareholder could object to that is a mystery. But then, perhaps it's not the advocates of sustainable business who are adhering to blind zealotry in this scenario.

These campaigns against Apple and GE expose the tired belief (following Milton Friedman) that purpose and profit are at odds. In fact, the converse is true. That is what Ecomagination proves. And that is at the heart of the Purpose Paradox.

THE PURPOSE PARADOX

As described above, an increasing body of evidence suggests that GE's and Apple's "activist" shareholders may be cutting off their noses to spite their faces. That's where what I call the Purpose Paradox comes in.

New ideas take time to gain acceptance, but part of the reason conventional business leaders, and certainly conventional Wall Street analysts, have a hard time believing in purpose as a guiding business principle is the touchy-feely new-age language that sometimes (but not always) accompanies it. How could something as hippy-dippy as "to make people feel good about the world of which they are part" or "cocreating a world where we can flourish" possibly drive the performance of a billion-dollar company?

Yet the facts speak for themselves. Natura is Brazil's largest beauty brand with a profit margin north of 10 percent, while Whole Foods' purpose has spawned the 12th largest food retailer in the United States, with a share price that has outperformed those of Walmart, Costco, the British retailer Tesco, or the British grocery chain Sainsbury's.

This is the Purpose Paradox: the surprising fact, proven by a mounting body of evidence, that purpose-driven businesses actually *outperform* their profit-oriented counterparts on multiple measures including—you guessed it—profitability. For example:

- A joint team of researchers at Harvard and the London Business School found that, over an 18-year period, "high-sustainability" companies outperformed "low-sustainability" companies by an average of 4.8 percent.[11]

- Goldman Sachs has shown that companies that are leaders in environmental, social, and good governance (ESG) policy have 25 percent higher stock value.[12] (ESG is defined by the *Financial Times* as "the generic term used in capital markets and used by investors to evaluate corporate behaviour and to determine the future financial performance of companies".)

- WPP's 2012 BrandZ study demonstrated that businesses with a purpose beyond pure profit were growing at double the rate of other brands.

- In their book *Built to Last*, Jim Collins and Jerry Porras documented that organizations driven by purpose and values outperformed the market 15:1 and outperformed comparison companies 6:1.

- Fully 80 percent of sources analyzed in a meta-analysis of ESG data conducted by the University of Oxford and Arabesque Asset Management showed that the stock price performance of companies is positively influenced by good sustainability practices.[13]

- Natural Capitalism Solutions' report *Sustainability Pays* analyzed 40 (out of 54 now collected) studies all showing in one respect or another that sustainability leaders are financially outperforming sustainability laggards.[14]

Paradoxical though it may seem, this research and the performance of the Green Giants reveals there's a wildly pragmatic side to purpose: It makes business more profitable than pursuing profit alone. Their adherence to this philosophy is one of the six factors that have enabled Green Giants to unlock billion-dollar business success.

PURPOSE IN ACTION

To understand the power of purpose in action, compare two companies. On the surface, they're similar. Both produce high-end, high-design electric sports cars, one a pure EV, one a plug-in hybrid; both launched around the same time (the 2009–2011 time frame); and their vehicles launched at a similar price point ($102,000 to $109,000 for the base model).

One of these companies describes its mission as: "To lead the automotive industry into the next-generation of automobiles with high-end design expertise and eco-friendly powertrain technology." The other says its purpose is: "To help expedite the move from a mine-and-burn hydrocarbon economy toward a solar electric economy."

Today, one of the companies has a market cap of $28.35 billion; the other declared bankruptcy in 2013. Which statement fuels the success story and which the failure?

You might assume that a mission to lead the auto industry with design expertise and powertrain technology is a decent mission for an electric car company. But that's the one that led its owner, Finnish company Fisker, to bankruptcy. By the time it went bankrupt, the company, founded by respected car designer Henrik Fisker in 2007, had burned through $1.4 billion in funds from backers as diverse as the Hollywood actor Leonardo DiCaprio and VC firm Kleiner Perkins. This makes Fisker the exact opposite, then, of the companies in this book, selected for their ability to make a billion dollars—not lose it.

The second company whose purpose is given above is Tesla. Tesla's purpose is an example of the type of purpose this chapter is about. It envisages business as a positive force in society—in this case, a tool for weaning the global economy off carbon-emitting fossil fuels and building a viable alternative in their place. It's what's led Tesla to stock market success.

Of course, there are various reasons Tesla's and Fisker's fates diverged, foremost among them issues with Fisker's technology. Fisker seems to have focused on form over function with its flagship Karma auto, resulting in a sluggish ride and a battery that failed at many crucial moments, including during a Consumer Reports test-drive. (The testers couldn't resist posting a review entitled "Bad Karma."[15]). But many of the reasons tie back to purpose, specifically social purpose, and the presence or lack thereof.

Dissecting the differences helps explain the power of purpose as a driver of profit and illustrates the hallmarks of a great purpose.

Take a Stand

A purpose cannot be bland or pedestrian. You must take sides, take a stand, express a point of view, and be prepared to defend it. Your purpose is your battle cry. Name your enemy. Tesla clearly set up an enemy in its purpose statement: the "mine-and-burn hydrocarbon economy." This purpose was clear in a blog post penned by Elon Musk on August 2, 2006, entitled the "Secret Tesla Motors Master Plan." Here is the full first paragraph from that post:

> As you know, the initial product of Tesla Motors is a high performance electric sports car called the Tesla Roadster. However, some readers may not be aware of the fact that our long term plan is to build a wide range of models, including affordably priced family

cars. This is because the overarching purpose of Tesla Motors (and the reason I am funding the company) is to help expedite the move from a mine-and-burn hydrocarbon economy towards a solar electric economy, which I believe to be the primary, but not exclusive, sustainable solution.

For Musk, this runs way deeper than making a car. He's on a mission to transform the global economy, and he will stop at nothing. "My goal is to accelerate the advent of the electric car by whatever means necessary," he later said.

I'm sure Henrik Fisker felt passionately about his vehicle, but he didn't present it to his stakeholders as a tool in the struggle to win an ideological war quite the way Tesla's purpose does. Indeed, Fisker seems to have lacked the sense of crusade altogether. There are hints of ego in the story of Fisker's downfall; he flew to Monaco to hobnob with sheiks, for example, as precious funds dwindled. He refused to accept changes to his original designs, even when it became clear they were fundamentally flawed and would add millions in costs to the car design.

Musk picked up on this and criticized Fisker for it. He told *Automobile Magazine* in 2012 that Fisker:

> . . . thinks the most important thing in the world—or the only important thing in the world—is design. He is a designer or stylist . . . . . he thinks the reason we don't have electric cars is for lack of styling. This is not the reason. It's fundamentally a technology problem . . . just making something look like an electric car does not make it an electric car.[16]

In the same interview, Musk reiterated that he is motivated by "the tragedy of the commons" and his desire to fix it by whatever means he could.[17] Across the Green Giants, there are similar overtones of the epic struggle. The phrase from IKEA's *Testament* springs to mind here: "We have decided once and for all to side with the many."

In the absence of a higher purpose, Fisker missed the opportunity to galvanize employees, shareholders, customers, and commentators to not just buy his product but join his cause. Take a stand, and hopefully one day you'll be able to declare victory—or at least, celebrate early wins.

Be Bold

You've probably heard of the BHAG—a big hairy audacious goal—or of the phrase *go big or go home*. To build a billion-dollar business, your purpose needs to be big, audacious, ambitious, and ideally almost impossible. It needs the visionary quality that enables a Disruptive Innovation to emerge. It needs to envisage transformation. Tesla's purpose to recreate the global economy fits the bill; Fisker's goal to lead the auto industry is predictable and pedestrian by comparison. Fisker's goal could be achieved with one vehicle, and then what? (Musk is good at being bold. His other company, SpaceX, set out to revolutionize space technology with the goal of enabling people to live on other planets—presumably in case the solar electric economy thing doesn't work out so well.)

Musk also seems to believe that failure simply isn't an option. "We have to have sustainable means of power generation anyway," he told TED founder Chris Anderson in 2013, going on to say, "I'm confident that solar will beat everything, hands down, including natural gas . . . . It must, actually. If it doesn't, we're in deep trouble." (This reminds me of Paul Polman accepting the need for change as fact in Chapter 1.)

Take the Long View

A purpose statement isn't a quick fix, something to get you through the next quarter. It's a North Star to guide your business through fads and fluctuations, to build an enduringly great company.

Musk shows he was aware of this from the start—remember, he talked about "the *long term* plan . . . to build a wide range of models, including affordably priced family cars." Taking this long-term, holistic view has directly driven success at Tesla because, given the barriers to EV adoption, the car alone was never going to be enough. You couldn't achieve breakout success by parachuting a new product into the old system because the issues of battery cost, charging infrastructure, manufacturing capacity, and cost of power would have undermined the vehicle, no matter how good. To win, you'd need to change the system. Musk knew this and from the start created a company to build the system, not just the car. Tesla's recent undertaking to build a gigafactory—a factory to produce lithium-ion batteries—makes it clear that the company is more than a car company. Fisker focused on the car alone and went the way of other EV wannabes.

Unilever's purpose of making sustainable living commonplace has a similarly expansive quality. Paul Polman is overt in his criticism of short-termism. "The 'short-termism' of so much modern business—'quarterly capitalism'—lies at the heart of many of today's problems,"[18] he has said, on one of the many occasions he has expressed his view that business needs to refocus on long-term value creation. But it's also good business. Because Unilever's purpose is a job that might never be complete, it opens up endless opportunities for new product development, new market penetration, and new business models.

Toyota, too, emphasizes the importance of the long term. Principle 1 of *The Toyota Way*, a 2004 book in which Dr. Jeffrey Liker, a

University of Michigan professor of industrial engineering, codified the 14 principles that underlie Toyota's management philosophy, says: "Base your management decisions on a long-term philosophy, even at the expense of short-term financial goals. Have a philosophical sense of purpose that supersedes any short-term decision-making. Work, grow, and align the whole organization toward a common purpose that is bigger than making money." In Japan, this notion of a long-term purpose that guides the organization is widespread. According to Lynn Stout of Cornell University Law School, there are more than 20,000 Japanese companies that are more than 100 years old, with a handful that are more than 1,000 years old. There is even a specific word for long-lived companies in Japanese: shinise. Stout says Professor Makoto Kanda, who has studied shinise for decades, has found that Japanese companies can survive for so long in part because they focus on a central belief or credo that is not tied solely to making a profit. A billion-dollar business can't be built overnight. It needs a long-term vision and strategy. Fisker didn't have it, and its shelf life was as short-lived as its purpose.

WHY PURPOSE DRIVES PROFITS

With the philosophical piece out of the way, let's turn to the practical side of purpose: *why* it drives profits. There are three key reasons why a social purpose drives profitability:

1. Purpose = plan

2. Motivated people

3. Loyal customers

1. Purpose = Plan

The problem with a North Star of "build profit" is that it doesn't tell you how you're going to do it. It's like me saying my purpose in life is to get really rich. Fine. But how am I going to get there?

Students of Jim Collins's *Good to Great* are familiar with the Hedgehog Concept. Collins writes that *Good to Great* companies have "a simple, crystalline concept that guides all their effort," and he identifies having a clear concept as one of the key factors that drives business greatness. The "Hedgehog" terminology is derived from an essay by Isaiah Berlin who compared the hedgehog to the fox. "Foxes pursue many ends at the same time . . . never integrating their thinking into one overall concept or unifying vision. Hedgehogs, on the other hand, simplify a complex world into a single organizing idea, a basic principle or concept that unifies and guides everything," Collins explains.

The purpose statements of Green Giants function as their Hedgehog Concepts. They provide the clarity of the single organizing idea, and this clarity of concept guides clarity of action.

Tesla has a lofty purpose, but Musk made the purpose practical by translating it into a deceptively simple plan, which he summed up in the "*Secret Tesla Motors Master Plan*" blog post in 2006 as follows:

1. Build sports car

2. Use that money to build an affordable car

3. Use that money to build an even more affordable car

4. While doing above, also provide zero emission electric power generation options

So far, Tesla has stuck to the plan with uncanny discipline. Remember, this entry was posted in 2006, before this book was written. In 2015, Tesla is somewhere between steps 1 and 2. The Roadster, with a price of $100,000, was followed in 2012 by the Model S, starting at $62,400—certainly a more "affordable car." The Model 3, priced between $35,000 and $40,000—the "even more affordable car"—is expected to begin deliveries in 2017. Tesla has broken ground on the gigafactory, designed to bring down the cost of batteries, a key input to make possible step 3. Charging stations have been established across the country, allowing a Tesla owner named John Glenney to become the first person, in January 2014, known to drive coast-to-coast in a Tesla Model S, using only the company's network of free Supercharger stations for fuel.[19]

Meanwhile at one of Musk's other business concerns, SolarCity, the plan to make solar the cheapest energy source in the United States is well under way (and while most solar companies have been struggling to survive, SolarCity has seen its shares go up sixfold since its IPO in 2013[20]). Shares of Tesla have beaten the market by 101 percent per year since 2011. Sales growth has been 158 percent per year over the same period.[21]

As mentioned elsewhere, Tesla now has half the market capitalization of General Motors, despite selling 300 times fewer cars. It seems the plan is paying off.

IKEA is similar. *The Testament of a Furniture Dealer* captures IKEA's purpose and outlines the strategy that flows from it. It's all in there: the importance of low cost, the primacy of efficient design, the benefit that size brings to purchasing relationships, and the avoidance of waste—all packed into 14 pages, written almost 40 years ago. Even though IKEA has grown to a company with €28.5 billion ($31.91 billion) in revenues since the *Testament* was written, the document remains, quite recognizably, the operating system of the business. IKEA

has stayed the course with its purpose and remained absolutely faith-
ful to the master plan.

A plan alone is, of course, not enough. You have to stick to it with
the kind of focused discipline Tesla and IKEA have displayed.

"There is nothing mushy about [purpose]—it is pure strategy,"
Harvard Business School Professor Hirotaka Takeuchi has said. "Purpose is very idealistic, but at the same time very practical."[22]

Your purpose gives you clarity on the question we asked earlier:
Why does my business exist? It works for *Good to Great*, and it works
for Green Giants.

2. Motivated People

At a recent advertising awards dinner, actor Jerry Seinfeld gave a
speech. "Spending your life trying to dupe innocent people out of
hard-won earnings to buy useless, low-quality, misrepresented items
and services is an excellent use of your energy," he told the assembled
representatives of the marketing industry, with only a hint of irony.

The quote got a ton of buzz among my Facebook friends, many
of whom are in the advertising industry, in part because it cut a little
too close to the bone. It's the reason I asked the CEO of Ogilvy to let
me cofound a sustainability practice. As I often say, I couldn't go on
selling people stuff they didn't need for a living. I needed to find my
purpose and pursue it through my work.

Today, many employers, including the Green Giants, are unlocking the rewards purpose provides. A passionate purpose attracts—and
retains—passionate people. Employees of Green Giants I've interviewed are more like disciples than staff members. Nike's culture, for
example, is famously cult-like; staffers I've met are all competitive run-
ners and wear sneakers all the time, even to top-tier business meetings.

Gary Sheffer, GE's VP of communications and public affairs, told me that the process of introducing Ecomagination had reminded GE of the power of purpose. "We remembered that we'd always been a purpose-driven company. We were founded by Thomas Edison," said Sheffer. "This was so powerful for our people that we decided to introduce purpose statements for all our lines of business, and we're seeing people feeling more energized and engaged as a result."[23]

A mounting body of data backs this notion up. Employees who derive meaning and significance from their work were found to be more than three times as likely to stay with their organizations. Employees who say they can make an impact while on the job report higher levels of job satisfaction than those who can't by a 2:1 ratio. And it's even more pronounced among the generation who are officially the majority of the workforce as of 2015,[24] Millennials. A recent study found that 83 percent of graduate school students would take a 15 percent pay cut to have a job that seeks to make a social or environmental difference in the world[25]; 97 percent want to work for a green company. As the influence of Millennials grows, demands on employers to match their need for meaning will too.

When employees believe in your purpose, their motivation is intrinsic, not something you have to bribe them to have. I've watched employees at companies all over the world "get religion" about their work once a purpose has been defined. They get that fire in the belly for which there's no substitute. They embrace your purpose because it's their purpose too and they want to succeed—together.

3. Loyal Customers

In August 2014, a Long Island couple, describing themselves as "two VERY highly satisfied Tesla customers," took out a full-page ad in two Palo Alto, California, newspapers to publish an open letter to Elon

Musk, whom they called an "Automotive Visionary." "Thank you for building the great American car," they said, going on to offer suggestions to make the car even better, including moving the cup holder, addressing the car's blind spots, and running a marketing campaign to create "many additional enthusiastic Tesla owners." Musk responded to them on Twitter within the day, promising to address their requests.

Tesla's blog features posts from many more passionate owners. On August 7, 2009, for example, a former U.S. Naval officer, John McEwan, posted an ode to his new Model S and its purpose, entitled "Promoting National Security Has Never Been So Much Fun." In it, McEwan expresses his joy at being "liberate[d] from foreign oil and wild price fluctuations at the pump." He compares his Model S to "the first horseless carriage or the first radio or first television or the advent of the personal computer, fax machine, cell phone, or even the Internet itself . . . . It represents the fundamental paradigm shift that will define the 21st century." He loves the car's performance but (to steal from Indra Nooyi) he loves that the performance comes with purpose even more. By comparison, when I looked for stories on Fisker's erstwhile customers, all I could find was an article from an owner who sorely wanted to love the car but had to return it owing to a glut of technical issues.

A passionate purpose and the products it produces attract passionate consumers. I have a client who moved to Edinburgh, Scotland, from New York. He's a vegetarian, can't eat gluten, and is a hard-core sustainability advocate. When he visits New York, he heads straight to Chipotle for a veggie burrito bowl (they don't have Chipotle in Edinburgh). The team knows we'll be eating Chipotle every day for a week when he's in town, but I don't get too many complaints. My client loves Chipotle because it's delicious and has vegetarian and gluten-free options, and even more because its purpose aligns with his values.

He's not alone. There is a growing body of evidence that what people are looking for from brands has radically changed. We no longer want simply to buy products; we want to buy into a purpose. In fact, 90 percent of consumers around the world want the brands they do business with to share their core values.[26] In addition, 87 percent want a more meaningful relationship with brands, and 87 percent believe that business needs to place at least equal weight on society's interests as on business interests.[27]

Indeed, public relations firm Edelman's recent brandshare research identified what it called "a new need state": societal need. This is defined by business behaviors like "uses its resources to drive change in the world," "takes a stand on issues I care about most," and "lets people know the company's mission and vision for the future." The research found that meeting a societal need doesn't just contribute to making people feel warm and fuzzy; it actually drives hard business outcomes, delivering an 8 percent increase in intent to purchase, a 10 percent increase in likelihood to defend the brand to detractors, a 12 percent increase in likelihood to recommend, and a 12 percent increase in sharing branded content. Again, this is a trend that is more pronounced among Millennials.

Edelman's research team also found that the prominence of purpose as a purchase trigger has risen globally by 26 percent since 2008. In certain regions, that growth is even more pronounced: Since 2010, it has increased by 100 percent in Japan, by 79 percent in China, by 43 percent in the Netherlands, by 43 percent in India, and by 36 percent in Germany. And by the way, consumers have no problem with you making money out of purpose; 76 percent of global consumers believe it is acceptable for brands to support good causes and make money at the same time, a 33 percent increase globally from 2008. In fact, when quality and price are equal, the most important factor influencing brand choice is purpose, outpacing design and innovation and brand loyalty.[28]

Many other studies have yielded consistent findings. The bias is especially pronounced among a social group that one firm names the Aspirationals. Representing a third of the global population, Aspirationals are defined by their love of shopping (93 percent), their desire for responsible consumption (95 percent), and their trust in brands to act in the best interest of society (50 percent). "Aspirationals represent a powerful shift in sustainable consumption from obligation to desire," says Raphael Bemporad, cofounder and chief strategy officer at brand innovation consultant BBMG, one of the report's authors. In other words, people want to buy from purpose-driven companies. These people can also be powerful advocates; nine in 10 Aspirational consumers say they encourage others to buy from socially and environmentally responsible companies.

Customers of Green Giants are believers, allies, and advocates—not just consumers. A purpose confers crucial competitive advantage in an otherwise prevalent culture of brand ennui. In a world of marketing where one study found that people around the world would not care if 73 percent of brands disappeared tomorrow (the figure is 92 percent in the United States), and think only one in five brands make a meaningful difference in people's lives,[29] purpose can mean the difference between commercial success and complete irrelevance.

FIND YOUR PURPOSE

Now for the fun part. What is your purpose? In other words, why does your business exist?

You should be able to answer that question in one clear, simple sentence. According to author Daniel Pink, Clare Booth Luce—who served in Congress and as a U.S. ambassador—famously told John F. Kennedy, "A great man is a sentence," as in "Abraham Lincoln preserved the Union and freed the slaves." A great business is a sentence too. Your task is to figure out what your business sentence is. *To make sustainable living commonplace. To transition to a solar electric economy. To improve the everyday life of the many people.*

Finding your purpose may not be easy. Remember the data I mentioned earlier showing that 90 percent of consumers want brands to share their core values? They also said only 10 percent of brands get it right.

But there are tools, techniques, and talent you can draw on for help. The ideas that follow are based on work I've done with clients including Unilever, Coca-Cola, Tetra Pak, Delhaize Group, Siemens, and Kraft. They can help to set you on the right path.

Corporate Archaeology

Let me describe an idea for a business. The basic premise is to make available, at a price almost anyone can afford, a product that has life-saving health properties but has until now been accessible only to a rich elite. The product is relatively inexpensive to mass-produce, so margins can be commanded at a low price point. Since everyone should use it every day, the market is potentially vast. And this product has revolutionary potential. As people start buying and using it, they'll become healthier. They'll grow more productive and begin to emerge from poverty. This benefits them, and it benefits the business; more affluent people become more valuable customers.

Rather than pay its workers minimum wage and see them living in slums, the business builds them homes and provides schools, libraries, and swimming pools. It gives to philanthropic causes. While the business funds all this out of its profits, the enterprise views it as an investment rather than a cost because it will pay back in employee productivity, brand image, and customer loyalty.

The business states its purpose as "to make cleanliness and hygiene commonplace."

Do you buy into the idea? Does it sound cutting edge?

The product I'm describing is soap, and the business is Lever Brothers (now Unilever), shortly after its founding in the 1880s by British industrialist William Hasketh Lever.

I learned this story on a trip in 2011 to Port Sunlight, the model village built by Lever to house his workers outside the British city of Liverpool. The trip was organized by Marc Mathieu, then newly minted as head of the Unilever corporate brand. An enigmatic Frenchman with a history of big creative ideas and an advocate of purpose in business, Mathieu took us back to where it all began in search of Unilever's corporate brand purpose.

He led us through the original factory, past neat rows of red brick Arts and Crafts houses with manicured front lawns, to the Port Sunlight museum. As we explored the museum, there it was in black and white, in Lever's own vintage copperplate: the purpose "to make cleanliness commonplace."

It was scintillating to be part of this piece of corporate archaeology, to sift through the artifacts and find brand gold dust: guts and soul, a legacy that oozed authenticity and still felt enlightened more than a century later. I'd worked with Unilever on and off for nearly a decade before this trip and had had no idea the story existed—a fact

I had in common with almost 100 percent of Unilever's staff. It took this history tour and a committed team under the leadership of an Iconoclastic Leader to disinter it.

Over the weeks that followed, the Unilever team evolved the historic purpose into its contemporary expression: "to make sustainable living commonplace." It then set about restoring that purpose to the heart of the business and the culture. This rediscovered purpose has completely revitalized the company, creating a continuous narrative arc from the past to the present, and it now guides every action the company takes.

More corporations than you might expect had social purpose in their DNA when they were founded. Indeed, many of the great industrialists of the past—Milton Hershey of Hershey Chocolate, George Eastman of Kodak, John D. Rockefeller, Arthur Guinness of the Guinness Brewery, and many more—embraced social purpose as integral to or even the focus of their enterprises. Each of them believed—and proved—that profit and purpose need not be competing agendas but can be and should be united as one.

So to answer the question "Why does my company exist?" you might start by uncovering the intention of the person who founded it. Dig into company legacy. Make friends with your company archivist (if, like Coca-Cola, American Express, Kodak, and Unilever, you have one). Google your founder's history and visit his or her home if it's open to the public. Find out as much as you can about where your company came from. The goal is not to recreate the past but rather to find the nugget of inspiration that brings everything into focus, answers the question of why you exist, and provides the raw material for an authentic purpose that can propel you into the future. Don't take the past as gospel, but do use it as a springboard to what you can become.

Internal Investigation

Sometimes the raw ingredients of a purpose may already exist some-where inside your organization. Start by finding out what people al-ready know. After conducting a thorough literature review and landscape analysis, speak to the experts inside your business. What information has Jane in R&D or Ron in supply chain been gathering? What killer data do they have? What secret projects are people al-ready working on? Who has a brilliant idea no one knows about? In-clude a broad cross-section of individuals, not just the marketing or sustainability teams. Treat this as a formal process, involving an ob-jective third-party moderator and guaranteeing anonymity. Listen for big ideas, new stories, and people's passions. Find the themes and con-nect the dots.

Once, when I was working for a company that made a humble and rather passé "powdered beverage" (think Kool-Aid or Crystal Light), this process uncovered that an employee had conducted a car-bon footprint assessment of the lifecycle of a powdered beverage ver-sus a bottled beverage—which no one else knew about. The employee found that because with powdered beverages you take the plastic bot-tles and the need to transport large quantities of heavy water around the country on trucks out of the equation, you remove 97 percent of the carbon footprint. You read that right: Powdered beverages have a 97 percent lower carbon footprint than their bottled equivalents. By simply switching from bottled, ready-to-drink beverages to powered beverages prepared in the home with tap or home-carbonated water, we could eliminate 97 percent of the carbon footprint of an $84 billion global industry overnight—or so this employee's data suggested.

Our purpose for this client became: "To reduce the carbon foot-print of the entire beverage industry by encouraging people to shift to 'smart hydration.'" Every 1 percent share our client stole from bottled beverage competitors would reduce the category's carbon footprint, so purpose and profit were beautifully aligned.

Similarly, Ecomagination began with a range of products GE already made—from energy-efficient locomotives to Energy Star–certified refrigerators—that had bubbled up spontaneously across the organization. It took Jeff Immelt and Beth Comstock to connect the dots and commit the purpose to paper. Finding your purpose this way can mean it's aligned with what your employees already care about and feels more like evolution than revolution. Ensure it stands up to scrutiny and that third-party experts endorse it, and build from there.

Hack Your Brand

Sometimes, by default or by design, you are starting with a blank canvas. This is thrilling and terrifying in equal measure. Do not try to figure this out alone. Bring in the reinforcements: external experts.

Contrary to popular belief, sustainability experts are not rabid anticorporate activists. Seek out the pragmatists who respect the role business can play and will be invested in helping you succeed. Don't just ask allies who'll tell you what you want to hear. Find people with a range of perspectives relevant to your business. Think laterally about whom to look for. Consider people at NGOs, academics, entrepreneurs, authors, artisans, practitioners, artists, and totally unusual suspects. Empower them to tell you the truth. Then listen.

Conduct a series of interviews to learn the following: What do they think social or sustainable business leadership looks like in your category? What are your competitors doing that's caught their eye? What are their expectations of a company like yours? How do you measure up? What will it take to get there? Also include customers in the mix. What are their needs? All this will start to uncover areas of focus.

Then bring four or so of the external experts into a room with a small group of internal experts drawn from diverse aspects of your business for a one-day workshop to "hack" your brand. Find out what happens when you create your equivalent of this experience. The Hellmann's mayonnaise team wanted advice on how to weave sustainability into their brand. The team had been working to overcome a consumer belief that the mayo was artificial. In fact, it is made of just a handful of real ingredients—eggs, oil, and vinegar, hence a positioning of "Real Food." So we put the team from Hellmann's (a Unilever brand) into a room with David Barber, the CEO of the incredibly popular New York restaurant Blue Hill; Rick Field, founder of the indie Brooklyn-based pickle brand Rick's Picks; Callum Grieve, an expert in business and climate change; and Tamara Giltsoff, of a sustainable business incubator. They spent the morning in the business version of speed dating, with client teams rotating through experts, interrogating each other with questions, and sharing points of view. We took the afternoon to confer, connect the dots, narrow down, and ultimately land on ideas with the greatest potential.

Through the day it became apparent that in American culture, the bar had been raised on "real," and that to be considered real today, it wasn't enough just to be not artificial; you had to be sustainable too. We realized there was an opportunity to evolve the real positioning to what we called "Real 2.0" by expanding the definition of real to incorporate sustainability. We worked together to develop a purpose statement, "To make real, sustainable food a reality in America," by transforming the supply chain to source the eggs, oils, and vinegar sustainably. The first step: a goal of 100 percent cage-free eggs (which they'll achieve in 2016). Oils are next with a mission to reach 100 percent sustainable soy by 2015. Of course, the workshop was just the beginning, but it catalyzed Hellmann's pivot from a classic condiment to a brand on a mission, one the brand is still on today, eight years later.

When you invite outside experts in to "hack" your brand, they can help you test your boundaries, raise your sights, find your purpose, and set you on a path to leadership. And remember, don't jettison them once the purpose is on paper. Retain them as advisers, advocates, and partners because the path forward won't always be easy or obvious, but if they collaborated in the creation of your purpose, they'll be invested in seeing it succeed.

CRITERIA FOR SELECTING A PURPOSE

There are some additional criteria that should be applied throughout your process of selecting a purpose.

- *Is it material?* The issue you really want to tackle is the material one, meaning the area that drives the greatest negative impact of your business and that you have the greatest ability to fix. So, if you are a food brand like Chipotle, your material issues are likely to include the footprint of your agricultural raw ingredients—hence, Food with Integrity. If you're an apparel brand like Nike, it's probably the materials you use to make your products and the human rights and waste implications of where and how you make them. A purpose that plays around the edges of issues or ignores your company's major impacts will tend to feel opportunistic or smack of inauthenticity, AKA greenwashing.

- *Does it fit the business and brand?* The purpose can be an opportunity to build an existing brand relationship, so if you're a company that already exists, it should enhance who you already are rather than completely change your face. For Hellmann's mayonnaise, as previously discussed, that meant taking the opportunity to deepen its existing commitment to "Real Food" by shifting to better eggs and better oils. For GE, using its engineering ability and legendary "Imagination" to find opportunities to drive energy efficiency and revenue for clients was an organic evolution of the company's core business. You don't want to emerge from this process unrecognizable to your stakeholders; rather, the process should help you become an even better "you."

- *Is it original?* Differentiation is one of the most fundamental tenets of business strategy, and it's one of the reasons many business leaders are eager to incorporate an element of social good into their brands. They see an opportunity to stand out from the crowd. And yet, in the execution, many end up doing the exact opposite. They default to ideas that have been tried before or a clichéd language of tree frogs or polar bears. These are worthy tropes but they neatly slot a company into an undifferentiated sea of businesses that call themselves green or promote social causes. Michael Porter, the seminal thinker on the role of differentiation in business strategy, said, "The worst error in strategy is to compete with rivals on the same dimensions." Don't compete to be the best. Instead, as Porter says, "Compete to be unique." Ensure that your purpose doesn't make you sound like that of every other purpose-driven company out there. Limited differentiation produces a limited ability to drive profit. The purpose statement of Method, the natural home products company—to inspire a happy and healthy home revolution—is completely distinct from other cleaning product statements, conventional and eco-friendly alike, and it's given rise to a highly differentiated company and product range that has driven business success.

IN CONCLUSION

In summary, the Green Giants prove that a social purpose is anything but antibusiness. They prove that, done right, social purpose can be a driver of profitability for brands, not a barrier to it. It can be a spur to innovation of both new product lines and new business models. It can build trust and foster authenticity in an age when people have lost faith in a business world they see as out to screw them. It can give brands in commodity categories new stories to tell while unlocking new target markets. Consumers feel the vibe and respond by granting brands greater emotional resonance.

In today's world, purpose = profits.

The Purpose Paradox proves there is nothing sacred about the Friedman ideology, a doctrine that holds profit and social good as competing objectives. Friedman's thesis is just that—an ideology—and business dogma changes all the time. It is changing now.

Consider this: In 1981, legendary former GE CEO Jack Welch gave a speech at New York's Pierre Hotel entitled "Growing Fast in a Slow-Growth Economy." Welch did not use the specific term "creating shareholder value" in the speech, but it was unabashedly profit-first, and it is viewed (along with the Friedman essay) as the other defining moment in the formation of the shareholder value movement. Shortly thereafter, Welch set GE's mission: to be the world's most valuable company.

He was wildly successful at it. During his tenure, GE's value rose 4,000 percent. One of his primary leadership directives was that GE had to be Number 1 or Number 2 in the industries it participated in. He fired the bottom-performing 10 percent of managers every year. GE had 411,000 workers at the end of 1980, just before he took charge, and 299,000 at the end of 1985. His policies earned Welch the moniker "Neutron Jack," but *Fortune* magazine named him "manager of the century" in 1999.[30] Welch maximized stock value, then retired, no doubt taking his retirement pay in stock. Not long after he retired, the stock lost 88 percent of its value, and even now it has rebounded to only 40 percent of what it was when it peaked.

Then, in 2009, about eight years after he resigned from GE, Welch did what appeared to be an about-face, telling the *Financial Times* he never meant to suggest that boosting a company's share price should be the main goal of executives. "Shareholder value is the dumbest idea in the world," he said. "Shareholder value is a result, not a strategy."[31]

Welch did not go so far as to embrace purpose, and it's not entirely clear what precipitated his pivot. But when the guy credited with inventing shareholder value renounces it, it's probably time to look for a new business philosophy.

We are in the midst of a battle for the soul of business. And while it's too soon to declare a winner, one day soon, we may wake up to discover that a new generation of billion dollar brands, the Green Giants, has taken over and that Milton Friedman's idea of business has gone the way of the dinosaurs.

CHAPTER

Built In,
Not Bolted On

"We're just really good at operationalizing things"
—**Deb Frodl**, Global Executive Director, Ecomagination at GE

Recently, I had an interesting call from a new business prospect inviting us to bid on building a new Signature Citizenship Program for her multinational technology company. We asked what her objectives were for the program. Would she be looking for business results?

"Oh no," she said, sounding faintly horrified. "This isn't about business. It's about delivering social good." The subtext of her answer was clear: Keep the citizenship (another term for CSR) and the selling separate.

I'm almost certain there's a person somewhere else in the organization whose job is selling the products that generate the company's revenue. This person is probably equally convinced that his or her job has little or nothing to do with social responsibility or sustainability. This person probably views those functions, such as volunteer programs and charitable gift matching, as cost centers, not revenue drivers.

This version of the separation of church and state is still the norm at the vast majority of businesses. It's the physical manifestation of the Friedman philosophy explored in Chapter 3. But it is out of date.

At Green Giants, things are different. As we saw in Chapter 3, Green Giants see business and social and environmental responsibility as one agenda. And that has crucial implications for the way in which they are structured. Rather than bolting sustainability or social responsibility on via a separate department and structure, they build it into the heart of their business.

Building it in, not bolting it on, is the fourth shared trait of Green Giants. The $2.8 billion Brazilian beauty company Natura provides an excellent illustration of this trait in action. In 2002, Natura became one of the world's first companies to adopt integrated reporting, a pioneering practice in which a business integrates social and environmental performance metrics into its annual report alongside financial ones. Managers at Natura have their performance ratings and bonuses tied to environmental and social goals as well as financial results, so their decisions are guided by all of them. Natura won't make a decision that creates financial benefit to the detriment of its environmental and social goals. For example, Natura declined to enter China, a huge potential growth market, because the company has an ethical commitment against animal testing and China insists upon using it. And yet Natura has a leading market share of 23.2 percent in Brazil (greater than Unilever's or Avon's). From 2002 to 2011, the company's revenues grew 463 percent, and it had an average gross margin of 68 percent, compared with the industry average of 40 percent.[1]

Sustainability and social responsibility are not the work of Natura's CSR department, nor its eco sub-brand, although it has both. They are integral to—and are integrated into—Natura's corporate strategy and the core structures of its business.

Natura stands in contrast to much of the business establishment, which is still aligned with the mindset of the potential client I mentioned at the beginning of the chapter in regarding sustainability and/or social responsibility as an expense to be shouldered, an initiative to be undertaken, or a department to be built—in other words, a sideshow to the main event of making money.

For Green Giants, sustainability and social responsibility are not merely a way to burnish their reputation or atone for sins elsewhere in their operations, nor are they philanthropic or citizenship endeavors, as deeply important as those things are. As we discussed in the last chapter, sustainability and social responsibility are integrated into the purpose of the business. It's not just where they *spend* their money; it's how they *earn* it.

This chapter is about the profound implications that philosophical orientation has for how a company is structured. It's not enough to *believe* that sustainability and/or social responsibility can be integral to how you earn your money. You need to get to the sheer hard work of "operationalizing" the philosophy—integrating it into the structures that form the guts and sinews of your organization.

THE SIX STRUCTURES

The structures upon which most businesses are built today were not created to enable a Green Giant–style business to emerge. Getting there is among the thorniest challenges companies face. Nothing short of business transformation is called for.

It's a challenge Green Giants are taking on, working to build sustainability into six core structures of their businesses:

1. Corporate strategy

2. Organizational structure

3. Governance structure

4. Cost structure

5. Incentive structure

6. Reporting structure

Not every Green Giant is doing all of these, but several of them are doing more than one. Here's how.

1. Corporate Strategy

The corporate strategy is the operating system of the business. It is the filter through which your purpose passes to be translated from a big idea into a business road map—the more formal, in-depth version of the "Secret Tesla Motors Master Plan" explored in Chapter 3. It's the plan for how the company will make money, and if something isn't in there, it's clearly not a priority and probably won't get done.

Let's examine two corporate strategies. First, let's visit the tab on Procter & Gamble's website entitled "Company Strategy." There is lots of information here. The first paragraph of text explains: "We are focused on strategies that we believe are right for the long-term health of the Company with the objective of delivering total shareholder return in the top one-third of our peer group." It then goes into more detail: "We are focusing our resources on our leading, most profitable categories and markets." Details of these, along with activity streams relating to operating efficiency, productivity, and innovation, are also described.

The only place the word "sustainability" appears on this page is in a tab in the top navigation bar.[2] Click on the tab, go to the Overview, and you find a headline that reads "Sustainability is part of everything we do." Interesting, then, that it appears nowhere in the Company Strategy.

Over on the website of key competitor Unilever, things look a little different. Unilever's corporate strategy, which it calls The Compass, is to "double the size of our business, while reducing our environmental footprint and increasing our positive social impact . . . ."[3]

This is captured and expanded upon in the Unilever Sustainable Living Plan (USLP). The USLP outlines three pillars: (1) improving health and well-being, (2) reducing environmental impact, and (3) enhancing livelihoods. Beneath the pillars sit nine focus areas (e.g., Greenhouse Gases, Sustainable Sourcing). The focus areas are subdivided into 50 specific targets (e.g., "We will purchase all palm oil from sustainable sources by 2015" falls under Sustainable Sourcing, while "By 2015 we aim to reach 200 million consumers with products and tools that will help them to reduce their greenhouse gas emissions while washing and showering. Our plan is to reach 400 million people by 2020" falls under Greenhouse Gases). The USLP strategy is not Unilever's sustainability strategy; it is its *business* strategy—the only one the company has.

You can see, at a glance, how different the corporate strategies of Unilever and P&G are. Sustainability is fully integrated into one and rather segregated in the other. This is a key difference between Green Giants and their competitors. Sustainability and social purpose are as integrated into the corporate strategy of Green Giants as they are into their purpose. And this is partly what makes Green Giant business strategies successful. Sustainability and social responsibility are an integral part of the plan to drive value creation—not a completely separate workstream.

In a video created to celebrate the second anniversary of the USLP, Paul Polman is adamant that sustainability and business can, and indeed should, coexist in corporate strategy, asserting, "There is no contradiction between sustainability and profitable growth."

Market results bear him out. Prior to Polman's taking the helm at Unilever, the company had been through a 10-year no-growth period. Since he took over, sales and returns have grown consistently, outpacing P&G as well as other rivals Kimberly Clark and Colgate Palmolive.[4] In its 2013 USLP update, Unilever revealed that, for the second year in a row, the brands growing faster than the rest of the portfolio were those that were ahead on their journey to embrace sustainability or a social mission. Examples include the Lifebuoy soap brand, on a mission to save lives in the developing world through hand washing, and Domestos, also trying to save lives but by focusing on access to toilets and good sanitation (more on this later in the chapter).

Similarly, from the start, GE's Ecomagination was a business strategy, not a separate sustainability one. "Ecomagination is both a business strategy to drive growth at GE and a promise to contribute positively to the environment," Jeff Immelt told a rapt audience at the 2005 Ecomagination launch at the George Washington School of Business. He punctuated his speech with the now famous statement, "Green is green."

So successful was this strategy that in 2010, Immelt upgraded the ambition, setting a goal of growing revenues from Ecomagination offerings at twice the rate of total company revenue in five years. In 2012, Ecomagination met this objective with revenue totaling $25 billion. Today, the cumulative revenue generated since 2005 is $180 billion. For reference, that can be compared with the $300 million that GE's ESG (environmental, social, and governance) team (the team tasked with the sort of work most sustainability departments are focused on) saved from operational efficiencies during the same period. It is true that $300 million is a large number, but the outcome achieved from a business strategy into which sustainability was built was 600 times greater.

It may seem self-evident, but had GE approached this as merely a CSR or sustainability play, it would never have achieved these business results. GE achieved them because it was looking to earn money by embedding sustainability into its business strategy.

Notably, NGOs and other watchdogs did not have a problem with GE's profit motive—in fact, they endorsed it. According to Gary Sheffer, during the course of a year-long listening tour instigated to inform the nascent Ecomagination strategy, NGO partners told GE, "Be true to who you are. Don't try to paint the company green just for green's sake. You are a profit-making infrastructure company, and you're doing this for profit because your customers want to buy these products. Just say it; otherwise, your credibility is shot."

NGOs would rather see a profit motive because that's what makes the strategy stick. It's too easy for initiatives that are being undertaken as reputational or philanthropic endeavors to be "sunset" (a nice way of saying "cut") when times get tough. Indeed, fully 80 percent of executives said they expected to cut their spending on sustainability and CSR as a result of the financial crisis; a third of companies shelled out 40 percent less on these things in 2009 than a year earlier. (By contrast, IKEA increased its investment in sustainability over the same period, for example announcing a plan in 2009 to increase the amount of wood in its products that comes from responsibly managed forests between 2010 and 2012.[5] Today IKEA's target is for 50 percent of its wood to come from more sustainable sources by 2017 and 100 percent by 2020.

So, as long as there are clear criteria and a measurement system in place to ensure the social or environmental outcomes, it's okay to make money.

And at dedicated Green Giant brands like Chipotle and Tesla, there is no other strategy. These businesses were created because their inventors believed that updating existing models by embedding sustainability or social responsibility into corporate strategy would make for a better business. And they were right. The third quarter of 2014 was the third consecutive quarter of double-digit same-store sales growth for Chipotle, with sales up 31.1 percent from the same quarter the previous year,[6] while in 2014, Chipotle outperformed comparison companies like McDonald's and Yum! Brands by 30 percent.[7]

Sustainability and social responsibility have to be built into the operating system of the business—the corporate strategy—before a billion-dollar, Green Giant business can emerge. "It is nothing less than a new business model," says Paul Polman. "One that focuses on the long term; one that sees business as part of society, not separate from it; one where the needs of citizens and communities carry the same weight as the demands of shareholders. This is why we have put the Unilever Sustainable Living Plan at the heart of our strategy."

2. Organizational Structure

When you believe that sustainability/social responsibility and business are separate agendas, you locate them in your organization accordingly. That's why in many businesses today, the CSR and sustainability teams sit either within the corporate communications function or in their own silo. The primary focus of many sustainability departments is to set and help achieve goals for the business to reduce carbon emissions, reduce water usage, and increase energy efficiency. The CSR department is usually tasked with identifying and building philanthropic programs or partnerships, with the primary goal of improving corporate reputation.

Without wishing to diminish the excellent, necessary work done by these often first-rate teams, their agenda is rarely transformation, and their functions are usually not sufficiently well integrated into the business or corporate strategy to enact it. I've worked with many sustainability or citizenship clients who'd love to be working on business transformation but who do not have the license, the budget, or the influence to effect that kind of change.

This is what I mean when I say that CSR and sustainability are bolted on, not built in, to the majority of organizations. But a billion-dollar, Green Giant business cannot be built from the margins.

Green Giants are at different stages on the journey to integrate these concepts and skill sets into the core functions of the organization, but they are all clear that this is their task. Nike is a fascinating study in organizational integration—so fascinating, in fact, that in 2014, Harvard Business School (HBS) taught the case as part of its required course on Leadership and Corporate Accountability. Eric Sprunk, NIKE's chief operating officer, and Hannah Jones, its vice president, innovation accelerator, and chief sustainability officer, attended class to hear students' analysis of the case study, entitled "Governance and Sustainability at Nike," which was discussed by all 900 first-year MBA students.[8]

The students learned that the journey to build corporate responsibility and sustainability more fully into the organization was turbocharged by Jones upon her appointment as head of CR in 2004. She had inherited a team whose responsibility was primarily to police and enforce the right decisions in terms of worker rights in the Nike supply chain. Jones quickly saw the potential to transform the team's role and its contribution to the business.

As the HBS case that was developed for the class tells it,[9] a cross-functional team overseen by Jones and other members of Nike's top management team spearheaded a project, code-named Rewire, to make sure, in Sprunk's words, "we weren't having kind of a compliance arm versus a business arm; we [would] just have a business arm doing the best thing for our profits, for our shareholders, for our consumers, for the world."[10] The project got a shot in the arm in 2009 when Nike decided to completely restructure its business in response to the financial crisis.

What resulted was a complex web of reporting lines and other systems of accountability designed to break down the walls between the business and the CR department, and to create a kind of two-way street in which CR and sustainability considerations and expertise were built into the decision-making processes of the finance, strategy, design, innovation, and operations teams. Finance, design, and operations expertise were added into the CR and sustainability team, newly dubbed Sustainable Business and Innovation (SB&I).

The key players in the new structure were the CSO, Hannah Jones; the CFO, Don Blair; the COO, Eric Sprunk (at the time, Jones held the title of head of SB&I, while Sprunk was VP of merchandising and product); and the teams that reported to them. All reported ultimately to CEO Mark Parker and the corporate responsibility committee of the board of directors.

Some of the relationships between the teams included the following:

- As the case describes it, there were dual reporting lines between SB&I and the business functions as well as between SB&I and operating activities such as product development and the supply chain. For example, the SB&I team under Jones included finance personnel, while the finance function under Blair included personnel with "dotted-line" reporting into SB&I.

- The head of Considered Design within SB&I reported both to Jones and to the vice president for innovation.

- Jones, as head of SB&I, was brought into the executive leadership team, and Sprunk, as head of Nike's "product

engine," began attending meetings of the board of directors' CR committee.

- The sustainability audits of the contract factories were
  moved to auditing, freeing SB&I up to work more on innovation and forward-looking strategy, and the head of
  sustainability audits now reported to the CFO, so that
  audit expertise could be brought to bear on these specialized audits and sustainability issues could be worked into
  business strategy and investment models. "This may seem
  like a small point, but it's important. Moving the sustainability audit into the general financial audit function and
  trying to bring auditing expertise to bear shows Nike is
  taking the sustainability audit much more seriously," one
  of the HBS case's authors, Lynn S. Paine, told me.[11]

- An SB&I Lab was created to focus on innovation. The
  lab was part of SB&I, but it was also "sponsored" by Blair,
  with a dotted-line reporting relationship to the VP of
  strategy. A senior management group—including the
  heads of innovation, logistics, IT, and other functional
  areas—helped define the lab's strategy, but approval of
  strategic investments was by Nike's sustainable investment management committee, made up of Blair, Jones,
  and the heads of corporate strategy and development,
  with ultimate oversight by Parker.

In the company's sports parlance, this two-way street enabled
Nike to shift from playing defense to "this 'offensive' element of sustainability and corporate responsibility that we see as a growth driver
. . . . We're not just managing risk. We're putting down investments
around long-term growth and innovation," according to Blair.[12] This
new organizational structure enabled sustainability and social respon-

sibility to be integrated into decision making about how, and the functions by which, Nike makes its products and its money—and gave the people responsible for making the money insight into sustainability and CR concerns.

Nike wouldn't claim to have it all worked out; indeed, this complex structure creates plenty of opportunity for healthy tension. But it is a structure that has enabled the Flyknit shoe to emerge and come to scale. Could that have happened without the leadership team's commitment to building sustainability and social responsibility into the heart of the organization and vice versa? I doubt it.

Embedding sustainability into the organization emerges as key at other Green Giants as well. GE, for example, has "Ecomagination Champions" embedded in leadership roles across the organization who wear two hats—their day job hat and their Ecomagination hat. Natura invests in continual training for its managers to make sure they are aligned with its values. The training program is called the Cosmos Program. It teaches management, organization, and sustainability, and its four levels have been completed by 600 managers at the company.

Appointing a chief sustainability, citizenship, or corporate responsibility officer is important, but by itself is not enough. The goal is to get these topics out of their silos and into the heads and hands of the people making decisions about the business so that expertise in sustainability and social responsibility can flow into the line functions, while business thinking flows the other way.

3. Governance Structure

At the People's Climate March in September 2014, 400,000 people poured down New York's Central Park West to show their support for global action on climate change. Among them, in blue T-shirts emblazoned with their corporate logo, were 120 Unilever employees, including North American CEO Kees Kruythoff.

This was a bold move since many of the march participants were vehemently anticorporate. Standing guard over Kruythoff and his crew, in a bright orange "peacekeeper" T-shirt, was Hunter Lovins. Lovins is one of a small cadre of individuals who is embraced by both the activist community and the business establishment, and her presence sent a signal to any anticorporate folk who might get the wrong idea: These are the good guys. Don't mess with us.

Lovins is one of six members of the Unilever U.S. Sustainable Living Advisory Council, an entity formed in 2013 to advise the Unilever leadership on how to operationalize the USLP in the U.S. business. Unilever is one of only a relative handful of businesses that has such a board. In 2014, the *Harvard Business Review* ran an article by Lynn S. Paine (the HBS faculty member who prepared the Nike case cited earlier in this chapter) in which she makes the case for sustainability as a board-level issue, a notion that is not yet fully embraced by mainstream business. Paine estimates that no more than 10 percent of U.S. public company boards have a committee dedicated solely to corporate responsibility. She adds that sustainability and corporate responsibility issues are consistently ranked at the bottom of more than 20 possible board priorities.[13]

Green Giants Nike and Natura are among the companies that do have such committees. Both have created board-level entities dedicated to CR and sustainability (respectively) that literally embed the topics into their corporate governance structures. In addition, Unilever and GE have sustainability advisory boards to advise their senior executives. While these are not formal governance entities, they serve similar functions and also offer their counsel to the C-suite.

Besides vouching for the companies to the activist community (in Lovins style), the committees at Green Giants serve multiple roles, including:

- *Ensuring that sustainability and financial concerns are both represented in corporate decision making.* For example, Natura had to choose whether or not to continue to use synthetic alcohol as a key raw material in its manufacturing process or to switch to a more environmentally friendly organic alcohol. The committee was drafted to evaluate the decision. "Based solely on traditional economic criteria, analyses showed that organic alcohol was 30 percent more expensive. However, once environmental and social externalities were included, the cost of synthetic product was in fact higher," according to Luciana Hashiba, manager for partnerships and technological innovation at Natura.[14] The organic version won the day, owing in part to the role of the committee in ensuring that sustainability concerns were embedded in the decision-making process.

- *Advising on enterprise vision and goal setting.* In May 2014, Unilever North America announced a commitment to source 100 percent clean energy for all energy use at Unilever's U.S. sites by 2020. Andrew Winston, who is on the Unilever U.S. Sustainable Living Advisory Council, told me that he and his fellow members became convinced that committing to 100 percent renewable energy across the company's operations was a crucial next leadership step for Unilever. The company was already buying renewable energy certificates (RECs), but agreed it was time to be bolder by adding "on-site and off-site renewable generation" to the mix. Producers of renewable energy can sell certificates equivalent to the megawatt hours of energy they generate and upload to the grid; purchasers can claim to be using renewable energy although they are not literally consuming the renewable electricity generated.

Winston and the others on the council believed the move would help Unilever reach its goal of halving its carbon footprint but also represent a better financial solution over the long term than buying certificates. "Investing in renewables creates more direct value for a business—it's a hedge against energy prices, possible resilience against grid outages (if you have your own power and storage), and enhancement of customer and employee value and loyalty," Winston told me. "RECs are also facing questions about whether they really reduce carbon, so there's an effectiveness question. Investing in renewables directly is more legitimate."[15] (Since the most recent analysis suggests that leading global companies get an average internal rate of return of 27 percent on their low carbon investments, which include investments in renewables,[16] Winston may well be proven right.) Winston recounts the board recommending that Unilever partner with NRG Energy to achieve the ambitious goal, and things moved quickly from there. The decision was not easy, but it was incredibly rewarding, according to Winston. "That's when you feel you made a difference," he says.

"We had spoken at length [with the council] on climate change policy in the U.S. and the need for Unilever U.S. to have a stronger POV," Jessica Sobel, sustainability manager at Unilever North America, confirmed. "With the council's help, we decided that leading the way in our own operations is a critical and iconic step. They helped us reach the decision and provided critical insight and support as well as connecting us to the right partner."[17]

- *Guiding companies through complex and even contentious decisions.* Deb Frodl, the global executive director of Ecomagination at GE, says the Ecomagination Board helps GE navigate its tougher challenges. "As we embrace some of the tougher industries like oil and gas and mining," she says, GE looks to the board to "give us some feedback, help us, [tell us] where should we be careful, where should we partner, is [shale gas] fracturing something we should lead and be on a platform talking about?"[18] Not a topic with easy answers, but having the right counselors can help.

- *Providing deep expertise on topics that are not widely understood in the mainstream business community.* At OgilvyEarth, we collaborated with our sustainability advisory board (on which Andrew Winston served) on a guide to avoiding greenwashing in communications. The board members flagged their concerns to us that greenwashing had become something of an epidemic in advertising and marketing, probably driven more by a lack of knowledge than by malign intent. The guide was grounded in the board's deep understanding of the issues but packaged so as to be accessible to the lay reader. We applied the principles to all our campaigns moving forward—indeed, we ran all strategic and creative work by the board prior to launch to make sure we'd eliminated all risk of greenwash and therefore preempted backlash before it arose.

These types of committees are typically made up of between four and 10 senior counselors, each representing a different perspective on sustainability or CR issues material to the business. For example, Nike's committee includes Jill Ker Conway, a former president of Smith College and a historian of women's participation in the paid workforce. Conway, who also serves on Nike's main board, has played a major role in helping Nike work through labor issues in its supply chain. She famously insisted that then-CEO Phil Knight attend every meeting of the committee[19], presumably to ensure that it was not marginalized or subjugated to the financial issues that can trump sustainability or CR issues in other, less well integrated businesses.

GE's Ecomagination board has included a range of prominent thought leaders representing expertise in issues including sustainability and governance, closed loop (also known as circular economy, a school of thought aiming to redesign the product value chain so as to entirely eliminate waste) or cradle to cradle design, sustainable investment strategies, and business solutions to climate change. In 2013, Deb Frodl added a perspective from the fossil fuel industry to help GE think through the role it should play in fracking and the shale gas boom. The mix of perspectives is a crucial part of any board or committee, so as to ensure that issues are examined with sufficient rigor and vigor.

These boards or committees typically meet on a quarterly basis, but I know I have my own advisers on speed dial, and I suspect executives at Unilever and the other organizations do as well.

Integrating sustainability or responsibility into the governance structure of the business—whether through a dedicated committee, expert board member, or advisory board—creates oversight and, crucially, accountability to consider sustainability concerns alongside financial ones. It also provides a vital sounding board and support system as executives feel their way through the uncharted territory of building a Green Giant.

Much as a formal governance structure can influence positive decision making around sustainability, if a board member is vocally *un-*convinced of the business case for sustainability or the mandate for business to evolve, he or she can block progress on these issues, as some CEOs I've worked with have found to their chagrin. Hunter Lovins recalls a time when legendary sustainable business leader Ray Anderson of Interface Inc., a leading carpet maker, whom she advised, faced mounting pressure from vocal board members. Anderson had gone extremely far out on a limb (he was the unquestioned sustainable business leader of his day). Lovins recalls:

> In the run-up to Y2K, no one was buying carpet. The bottom fell out of the carpet market. Interface stock went from something like 61 to 13. Various members of the board fought him, demanding that he abandon all this "sustainability crap." But he refused to change course, and ultimately was vindicated. Several of his competitors went out of business. Interface kept its customers through the downturn and stayed alive. I was not in the boardroom, so I don't know exactly how he did it, but Ray always blended inspiration with a velvet fist. He was irrepressibly good humored. But indomitable.

Best to know where your board sits before setting forth. And know you'll have to channel your inner 4 Cs to see things through.

4. Cost Structure

One of the biggest sticking points for many companies seeking to drive sustainability or responsibility deep into the heart of their business is cost. Some sustainable or socially responsible practices (like energy efficiency and waste reduction) save businesses huge amounts of money. But it remains the case (for now, at least) that many other more sustainable or socially responsible business inputs—from ingredients and raw materials to labor and energy—cost more.

Trying to retrofit an existing business model to accommodate those costs can be challenging, especially when an entire business category may be predicated on access to cheap labor, cheap raw ingredients, or abundant, cheap energy, as many of today's businesses are. This is especially true when the decision is "unilateral"—that is, your competitors aren't doing it. You have to make the decision as to whether you can pass the additional cost on to the end customer or consumer, and thus risk being priced at a higher price point than your competitors, or whether you need to absorb the cost and take a hit on margin. That's why many business leaders increasingly favor the introduction of clear policy signals in certain business areas, such as a formal price on carbon, which could be implemented through either a carbon tax or an emissions trading system; it levels the playing field. And it's why many feel they can't make the business case add up for building a Green Giant–style brand.

Sustainable business advocates believe that over the long term, business leaders who opt to make their value chains more sustainable and responsible will reap the benefits of having built a more resilient, future-proof business. This is a theme that is explored elsewhere in this book with examples like the Prius, the success of which is partly due to its ability to insulate the consumer against volatile gas prices. And many of the Green Giants have been willing to invest on the understanding that the payback period may be longer.

But most business leaders want to know if they can make the costs work now. Often, the answer is no. However, the Green Giants suggest it may not always be necessary to wait. They are delivering their stellar results now, not 10 years hence. How have they done it?

Chipotle is a business that's gotten cost right. The most obvious way in which Chipotle's cost structure differs from that of its conventional competitors, especially its fast food rivals, is in the higher costs of the humanely reared meats and organic or local produce upon which it insists. Despite these higher costs, Chipotle commands margins that are significantly higher than its fast food competitors. How? Chipotle has quite deliberately built its business to account for these higher costs by taking a holistic look at its cost structure and working the higher costs of the raw ingredients in, not treating them in isolation or just tacking them on.

To explain this in more detail, there are three main costs in the restaurant business: food, labor, and occupancy. Figure 4-1 shows that Chipotle's ingredient costs are indeed high for the industry, but its total restaurant costs are low—and its profit margins are consequently healthy.

The efficiencies come through labor and real estate. But labor efficiencies are not achieved the usual way, by underpaying people. (In fact, the compensation for a general manager at Chipotle—which the company calls a restaurateur—is $63,000, compared a McDonald's general manager salary of $45,495[20]. A restaurateur can earn up to $129,000 in total compensation, and more than 95 percent of Chipotle managers are promoted from within.) Rather, Chipotle prides itself on what it calls its "people culture," training staff to work exceptionally efficiently to increase the speed of service and therefore same-store sales.

As for real estate, Chipotle opts for high visibility, often leased, locations with high traffic, but with much less square footage than the usually owned, often less central locations of traditional fast food players. It's a strategy that has made Chipotle the most profitable of publicly traded restaurants, at $840.69 per square foot. Compare that

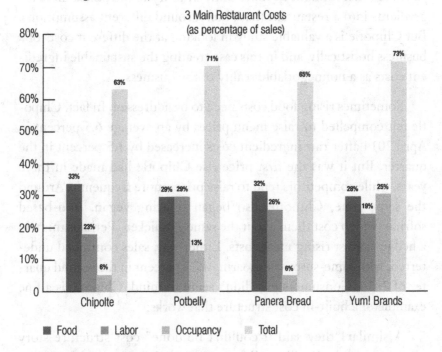

Figure 4-1 Chipotle's costs relative to some of its competitors.[22]

3 Main Restaurant Costs
(as percentage of sales)

to Panera Bread at $548 per square foot, Wendy's at $504.67 per square foot, and Burger King at just $392.27 per square foot.[21] In its earnings report for the second quarter of 2014, Chipotle's CFO Jack Hartung announced plans to go smaller, creating "really, really small, scrappy" stores, focused on serving takeout—which now represents two-thirds of Chipotle transactions, up from 50 percent in 2000.[23] If successful, the strategy will further enhance margins, making more space in the budget for better ingredients.

Chipotle's communications director, Chris Arnold, reflects on this point. "I guess it's because the business has been built up around these higher ingredient costs so we've built our business to allow us to invest more in food and still run really profitably," he told me.[24] He conceded that it might be more difficult to try to introduce these ingredients into a restaurant that's built around different assumptions. But Chipotle is a valuable study in looking at the different costs of a business holistically, and in this case treating the sustainable ingredient costs as a nonnegotiable reality of the business.

Sometimes rising food costs need to be addressed. In fact, Chipotle felt compelled to raise menu prices by an average 6.5 percent in April 2014 after raw ingredient costs increased by 1.5 percent in the quarter. But it was the first price rise Chipotle had made in three years, while competitors tend to raise prices more frequently. Around the same time, Chipotle also began offering vegan, tofu-based sofritas, which cost them about the same as chicken. Perhaps this was a hedge against rising meat costs. Either way, sales continued undeterred, with same-store sales soaring 17.3 percent in the second quarter of 2014. Consumers just didn't seem to mind. Chipotle is a fine example of a built-in cost structure that works.

A similar "they said it couldn't be done" cost structure story emerges at Tesla. You'll recall from Chapter 2 that part of the reason General Motors killed its electric vehicle, the EV1, was because it said there was no way to make the business case add up. GM said that creating a vehicle that was competitive with gasoline-fueled cars in terms of performance and practicality, at an affordable price, just couldn't be done. There was one particular cost structure culprit: When it comes to EVs, the cost structure is all about the battery.

The key variables in an EV battery are capacity, measured in kilowatt hours (kWh), and range, the distance you can drive on a single charge. Range is determined almost exclusively by capacity, so people naturally want more capacity to overcome "range anxiety"—the fear of running out of juice. But here's the rub: Manufacturers' costs are tied directly to capacity. They pay for capacity by the kWh. So, as capacity and range go up, so does cost—by an estimated $400 to $500 per kWh[25]. For reference, a 2014 Nissan Leaf has a capacity of 24 kWh, giving it a range of between 75 and 100 miles,[26] and presumably costing Nissan somewhere between $9,600 and $12,000 for the battery alone—roughly half the retail value of the vehicle.

Tesla's ambition was to introduce an EV with the kind of range and performance no previous EV had been able to match. This could be done only by dramatically increasing capacity. Tesla had to find a way to do it that wasn't completely cost prohibitive. The engineers' breakthrough came in bypassing a proprietary battery in favor of using commercially available 18650 lithium ion cells—the same cells used in laptops. Tesla batteries contain thousands of these cells, but each costs only about $4, and the decision brought Tesla's costs per kWh down to $350[27], a crucial $50 per kWh advantage over competitors. The car was then built around the battery.

This made the cost of a luxury vehicle viable. The 2014 Model S delivers capacity of 85 kWh—more than three times that of the Leaf—and a range of 250 miles per charge at a price point of $70,890 to $94,390. While steep, the capacity/range/cost formula works commercially: The Model S is selling like hotcakes.

But battery cost is an ever-present concern for Elon Musk, who's next ambition is to deliver a more mass market Tesla, at a price point closer to $35,000. It's impossible within the existing cost structure, so (as previously described) he's building a gigafactory, a huge plant capable of producing 35 gigawatt-hours' worth of lithium ion cells a year—more than the world's entire 2014 production of lithium ion cells—to get battery costs down to less than $250 per kWh. At that price point, he can get closer to his dream of mainstreaming the EV. The gigafactory required a massive capital investment (estimated at $5 billion), but Musk is convinced the payback will justify the outlay.

If it were anyone else, one might doubt him, but remember, this is the guy who's other company, SpaceX, is the only private company ever to return a spacecraft from low-earth orbit, or to have a space-craft attach to the International Space Station, exchange cargo pay-loads, and return safely to earth—a feat previously accomplished only by governments.[28] An affordable lithium ion battery seems positively simple by comparison.

Space stations aside, whatever the size of your business, getting the cost structure right need not be a moon shot. Build your business model around the salient costs, rather than trying to shoehorn a new cost into an old model. Build the costs of sustainability in; don't bolt them on.

5. Incentive Structure

Of all the points in this chapter, this is perhaps the simplest concept to grasp. If you want to send a clear signal that sustainability or CR goals are valued as highly in your organization as financial ones, there are few better ways to do it than by building them into the perform-ance targets and compensation and incentive structures of your staff—not just of the sustainability or CR teams, but of everyone, from the CEO on down.

Expecting success when these targets are voluntary while financial ones are mandatory is not a way to encourage ownership or behavior change among employees. In many of the companies I've consulted with, the absence of incentives around sustainability or corporate re-sponsibility has been a major barrier to change, especially in cases where the cost structure needs to go through a period of transition to kick-start the transformation.

As a case in point, I worked with Unilever teams in the pre–Sustainable Living Plan days that wanted to make their products more sustainable. However, they found it hard to sell their ideas to middle management because the ideas required an upfront investment that would pay back, but over a medium- to long-term horizon. The middle managers were incentivized on purely financial goals—as most middle managers are—and were working in the context of a two-year rotation in a given position. In other words, they were being evaluated on their ability to meet certain financial targets within a two-year time horizon as a prerequisite to promotion. There was zero incentive for them to approve the recommended changes. Quite the opposite, in fact, and so the changes were not approved.

This situation was one we encountered numerous times. In fact, this experience and others like it led us to dub the issue "the concrete middle"—a place where bottom-up sustainability ideas go to die. For when executives are committed to a bold vision, junior staff may be galvanized, but unless middle managers in particular are incentivized to deliver, the system blocks change. It's not that the middle managers are bad people. It's simply that the system they are functioning in does not incentivize them to value the sustainable outcomes the teams are trying to deliver as highly as short-term financial ones.

Things are very different at Unilever now. Delivery of the Unilever Sustainable Living Plan forms part of the personal work objectives of CEO Paul Polman and CFO Jean Marc Huët, as well as those of every individual brand team. Indeed, Polman reportedly received a $722,230 addition (or 37.5 percent) to his 2013 bonus payment for his work in driving progress on the USLP, according to Unilever's annual report.

Similarly, Natura's business is built around the concept of the triple bottom line, where economic, social, and environmental considerations carry equal weight. This is reflected in the way executives are evaluated and compensated. The criteria are:

- *Economic:* Consolidated EBITDA (earnings before inter-est, taxes, depreciation, and amortization), covering Brazil and international operations

- *Social:* Organizational climate survey for employees in the Brazilian and international operations and loyalty rate for Brazilian consultants

- *Environmental:* Carbon emissions in Brazil and in the in-ternational operations

Executives are expected to fulfill all three.

Building sustainability targets into incentive structures like this doesn't just help clarify expectations and attach value to the right things; the process of defining appropriate goals for each division and function also helps translate the Green Giant strategy from a lofty ideal into a tangible, actionable plan with ground troops lined up to execute. At Unilever, employees have targets linked to specific areas of the USLP, worked out via collaboration between the sustainability team and individual functions or brand teams. Those in the supply chain may be incentivized according to their performance against the goal to source 100 percent of the agricultural products sustainably, while marketers working on the Dove brand may be evaluated in part against how many girls they have reached with self-esteem messages. It all adds up to a strategy to achieve the overall plan.

Sustainable business NGO Ceres estimates that 24 percent of America's 613 largest companies now link executive compensation to sustainability performance, up from 15 percent in 2012.[29] So while Green Giants are progressive in this regard, they are not exceptional. Building sustainability and social responsibility into employee and ex-ecutive compensation structures encourages and empowers teams to operationalize and execute on Green Giant goals, rather than leaving it to chance.

Reporting Structure

Let me share a quote with you:

> Life is a chain of relationships. Nothing in the universe exists alone.
> Everything is interdependent . . . . Commitment to the truth is the
> route to perfecting the quality of relationships . . . . The search for
> beauty, which is the genuine aspiration of every human being, must
> be free of preconceived ideas and manipulation.

Sounds like a new age yoga brochure, doesn't it? In fact, it's pulled
from the front page of Natura's annual report.

For those more accustomed to finding PE ratios and EBITDA in
the pages of an annual report, this softer language might come as a
surprise. But this is no ordinary annual report. It is an integrated report, an example of the vanguard practice of reporting on financial,
environmental, social, and governance issues via one process and in
one document.

It's an old adage that what gets measured gets managed, and certainly business is increasingly embracing the need to report on sustainability and corporate responsibility, with 95 percent of the largest
250 companies in the world now producing a sustainability report.[30]
(Beyond that group, though, the news is less good. First-generation
sustainability reporting—the process of reporting on employee
turnover, energy, greenhouse gases, lost-time injury rate, payroll,
waste, and water is still limited to just 3 percent of the world's largest
3,972 listed companies and 0.04 percent of the world's small listed
companies.[31])

But while a CR or sustainability report may detail a business's
strategy and actions in these areas, most businesses report on them
via a separate process rather than in the context of the company's financial reporting. They typically don't do so in a way that demon-

strates the business value of CR and sustainability, which means the businesses struggle to evaluate how this work contributes to value creation. It's therefore hard to make sound business decisions around them and to justify them to skeptical stakeholders, especially shareholders (as demonstrated by the story of activist shareholders in Chapter 3). It's another way the balkanization of sustainability and CR continues.

Not at Green Giants, though. Several of them are experimenting with integrated reporting. Integrated reporting is a vanguard practice of integrating sustainability, social responsibility, and business together, in one process and one document. Hunter Lovins dates its origins back to a meeting she and several peers—including Dr. Robert Massie—attended with Ray Anderson of Interface in the early 2000s. "As he went about implementing his passion for more sustainable practices, Anderson noticed that everything he was doing was enhancing shareholder value," Lovins said. "We discussed what constitutes shareholder value. Cutting costs will show up on the bottom line, but the fact that his corporate commitment to behave more responsibly makes it easier to recruit and retain the best talent will be buried. Its contribution to reducing risk, making it easier to access capital, to building brand loyalty (a feature that may have kept Interface in business during the downturn in sales during Y2K), to driving innovation, and all of the now 13 different aspects of what he and I then called the Integrated Bottom Line get lost in current accounting systems."

Since then, leading companies have experimented with ways to measure and communicate this value. One of the first was the Global Reporting Initiative (GRI), first released in 1999. Conceived by Robert Massie—the founder of Ceres (the Coalition for Environmentally Responsible Economies)—it was constructed by teams of accountants, NGO representatives, the Tellus Institute, and the UN Environment Programme. Headquartered in Amsterdam, it is a voluntary standard that has gained widespread adherence in Europe, although less so in the United States. Next came the International Integrated Reporting Council (IIRC), then the Sustainability Accounting Standards Bureau (SASB). Clearly, the field predates the Green Giants, but they are among the leaders helping drive it into the mainstream of business practice.

This is where the chief financial officer enters the scene. Unilever CFO Jean Marc Huët appeared on the cover of *Financial Management* magazine in 2013 to declare "The call for integrated reporting is rising" and to talk about why Unilever had become part of a pilot program of the IRRC to "test the principles, content, and practical application of Integrated Reporting" and develop"[32] an international framework for it. Unilever was one of 75 businesses and 25 investors from around the globe participating. For Unilever, the results first showed up in the 2013 report, which Huët described as a first step toward a fully integrated report for the company.

To see what this theory looks like in practice, visit the front page of Unilever's 2013 annual report. Here, you're confronted with the company's purpose in large type, "to make sustainable living commonplace," and by the strategy to double the size of the business while reducing its environmental footprint and increasing positive social impact. This is a marked change from the standard annual report that typically opens with a letter from the CEO or chair with nary a mention of sustainability.

In Polman's letter, which comes next, he says, "This Annual Report seeks to highlight the integral link between our long-term business purpose of making sustainable living commonplace and Unilever's overall results."

It does so by, for example, showing that the brands farthest along in pursuing a social purpose are growing faster than others, that reducing waste reduces environmental impact and financial costs, and that managing risk must include managing the availability of more responsible ingredients and the risk that sustainable solutions may not be delivered. These are not things typically acknowledged as material business risks. The report also talks about the benefits to all stakeholders, not just shareholders (although as the analysis conducted for this book by Jason Denner of POINT380 showed, that benefit absolutely exists, with Unilever stock outperforming rival P&G's by 3.5 percent over the last 5 years[33]). And among its governance committee reports, it includes material from the corporate responsibility committee, which is rarely included in an annual report.[34]

Natura was an even earlier pioneer of the integrated reporting process. Like Interface before it, Natura embarked on the journey because its leaders were convinced the company's leadership in sustainability and social responsibility were adding value to the business but didn't have a way to prove it, particularly to the investment community. Natura also needed better valuation models to support management in making integrated decisions.

For example, a Harvard Business School case[35] details how Natura tried to assign financial, social, and brand value to a policy to have 30 percent of new hires at a new distribution center be workers with physical disabilities. The financial cost was fairly straightforward to assess, but what of "the value to society, the value from increased employee morale and long-term productivity, and the positive impact on Natura's reputation and brand"? How do you place a value on those? The company's CFO, Roberto Pedote, admitted the journey had been challenging. He described the process of trying to understand the true costs and benefits of performing integrated analysis as "far more complex" than traditional reporting, and the methods for measuring them as "still embryonic."[36]

Integrated reporting is still far from mainstream. But there are signs this is changing, driven by policy, exchanges, and investors. While integrated reporting is voluntary in most parts of the world, it is now a requirement for companies wishing to be listed on the South African stock exchange. In addition, Brazil ranks companies listed on its exchange, BM&FBOVESPA, in terms of sustainability and social responsibility, and it encourages them to disclose sustainability data. Other exchanges are taking action, with developing market exchanges foremost among them.

There are also signs that investors are placing increasing emphasis on environmental, social, and governance data. For example, 722 investors with $87 trillion in assets, representing about a third of the world's invested capital, had become signatories to CDP (formerly the Carbon Disclosure Project) in 2013, which means they requested that companies disclose their carbon emissions data via a standardized process investors can use to determine if a company is managing its carbon emissions. As stated earlier, companies that are leading in this have 18 percent higher ROI than companies that are lagging, and 67 percent higher than companies that refuse to report. CDP data is now available on Bloomberg terminals, where it is downloaded an average of 1 million times every six weeks. While this is not specifically a demand for integrated reporting, it is a major step in the right direction.

The next evolution in the journey to integrate sustainability and social responsibility into corporate reporting may be brought about through the work of the Sustainability Accounting Standards Bureau. SASB is working to integrate sustainability standards into the Form 10-K, which all public U.S. companies must file with the Securities and Exchange Commission. It therefore works within the current system of financial reporting, so that investors can compare financial and sustainability fundamentals side by side. This will enable it to prove what sustainability issues are material to financial performance in a given sector, information that is currently unknown. "SASB will totally transform accounting as well as management," Hunter Lovins told me.

Corporate strategy and integrated reporting are of course intimately linked. It's a bit of a chicken and egg situation; did the strategy give rise to the need for a new kind of report, or did the process of trying to compile the report yield the strategy? Perhaps it is a bit of both. Paul Polman has said that when the Sustainable Living Plan was launched, it was "as much an act of faith as careful thinking about all the angles."[37] An integrated report helps you get beyond the act of faith to a measurement framework with clear goals and metrics, and the ability to understand whether the new business model is actually working.

Polman's CFO, Huët, compares integrated reporting today to the advent of management accounting in the Victorian era, which, he says was led in part by Unilever's founder.[38] It's a new system of accounting for a new era of business.

STRATEGIC PHILANTHROPY

All of the above may give you the impression that in this new era, corporate philanthropy has been displaced by more strategically integral aspects of sustainability. In fact, the opposite is true.

I have a client who is responsible for corporate fund-raising at a medium-size nonprofit based in Washington, D.C. She'd engaged us to help her revamp her approach to building relationships with prospective corporate sponsors because she was having increasing trouble getting traction. About a month into our engagement, she called in a panic. A new head of marketing had taken over at the largest corporate sponsor of their flagship program and had announced, very unexpectedly, that she would be winding down their multiyear, multimillion dollar relationship within the quarter. The problem? The new CMO simply couldn't see the strategic alignment between her company's mission and the nonprofit's cause.

Our client was devastated, but we were not surprised. The days of corporate giving built on the back of the CEO's friendships or personal passions are on the wane, being replaced by a new, more strategic form of philanthropy where the corporation's giving is designed to deliver its purpose, build its brand, and complement its business, as well as deliver measurable social impact (for which the brand can claim credit).

This is the other side of the coin, for just as Green Giants are integrating purpose into business, they are also integrating more business thinking into their philanthropy and corporate giving. In this instance, we counseled our client to treat her prospects as we at an agency would treat ours: Seek to wow them with how deeply we understand their business and show them how working with us will help them achieve their goals—both business and social.

Again, Unilever presents an interesting example of this philosophy in action. This is how Unilever describes the relationship between the corporation and its foundation: "The Unilever Foundation is a key action we are taking to help meet our ambitious goal of helping more than 1 billion people improve their health and well-being and, in turn, create a sustainable future—a core commitment of the Unilever Sustainable Living Plan."[39]

While the Unilever Foundation has its own mission—to improve quality of life through the provision of hygiene, sanitation, access to safe drinking water, and basic nutrition and by enhancing self-esteem— it sits within the context of the corporate strategy and is a tool for delivering on corporate strategy goals. The foundation and the brands often combine forces to up their impact. For example, Domestos, a Unilever brand of toilet cleaner sold in the UK and several other markets globally, has a purpose to provide a safe and germ-free toilet for all. To achieve it, the Domestos brand team has brokered a partnership with the Unilever Foundation and UNICEF to reach communities in the developing world where a lack of good sanitation and hygiene facilities and practices causes diseases that kill a child every two minutes.

The topic is a delicate one. I have had the dubious honor of being in meetings with the foundation team where "open defecation" is discussed freely. This topic is among society's last great taboos, so to non-profits laboring to make improvements on it, a private sector entity willing to embrace and fund the work is a welcome turn of events. The goal just happens to align beautifully with the Domestos business and brand because as more people get toilets, stay healthy, and need their new toilets kept clean, Domestos opens new markets and drives demand for its products.

The partnership includes a Domestos cause marketing program targeting consumers in developed markets. Five percent of sales of special bottles go to fund work in developing communities. These funds are bolstered by a multiyear, multimillion dollar commitment from the foundation. Together, they support such programs as UNICEF's drive to get education and facilities to communities that need them and World Toilet Day, an effort to raise awareness for, support of, and behavior change around the issue globally. The first-year goal of reaching 400,000 people was beaten by 50 percent, and in 2014, Unilever committed to help 25 million people gain improved access to a toilet by 2020. During year one, Domestos sales increased by 9 percent, making it one of Unilever's fastest growing brands.

Jean-Laurent Ingles, Unilever's global SVP of household care, says, "This is more than corporate social responsibility. It is about establishing a clear link between tackling development issues and our business ambitions."[40]

You can see how different this all is from the request the prospective client made regarding her citizenship program at the beginning of the chapter. When you integrate purpose and business, the lines between business and philanthropy can start to blur. It's the new face of philanthropy, and it seems to be better for everyone.

IN CONCLUSION

What these stories share in common is the attempt to break sustainability and corporate responsibility out of their silos and embed them into the organization—to reframe them from vertical functions to business horizontals. In the process of building these ideas into the core structures of the business, Green Giants are reshaping those structures, forging a new kind of enterprise.

It might be easier in the short term just to bolt sustainability or responsibility on, rather than painstakingly working through the process of building them into the structures of business as the Green Giants are doing. But know that as long as their location is peripheral, their impact will be too.

To build a Green Giant, you need to embrace sustainability as a business reality, a business opportunity, and a business driver, and then you need to build it into the core structures that drive your business. For as this chapter shows, far from being wide-eyed idealists, Green Giants mean business—and they structure their companies to deliver.

CHAPTER **5**

Mainstream
Appeal

"Our 17-year-old consumers tell us they want a better world. They don't call it sustainability."

—**Hannah Jones,** Chief Sustainability Officer, Nike

In 2007, I was sitting behind a two-way mirror in Paramus, New Jersey, listening to everyday moms react to scripts for potential mayonnaise ads. The focus group moderator read the following in a soothing tone: "Picture chickens pecking in an attractive farmyard as the announcer says, 'Hellmann's mayonnaise is made with just three real, natural ingredients: free-range eggs, natural oils, and vinegar.' "

"Ewwww!" interrupted a blonde woman with nail wraps, a pristine white T-shirt, and a disgusted look on her face. "That's so gross! I do *not* want to be reminded that eggs come from chickens!!" Several other women furiously nodded their assent. For these women, chickens, apparently, were off the table.

This was one of my early lessons in ensuring that your sustainability positioning has mainstream appeal. While to me, chickens in farmyards equal natural and healthy, to these moms, it was a short mental leap from there to chicken poop and salmonella in their refrigerator. These ladies wanted their free-range eggs sanitized.

This corroborated what Graceann Bennett, a leading brand strategist, and I found in 2011 when researching our report *Mainstream Green: Moving Sustainability from Niche to Normal*. Through our research with people from all over America—and from all over the map, sustainability-wise—we came to realize that traditional green or ethical brands had a fundamental flaw. They prioritized the greenness or sustainability over everything else. In the process, they did a great job of appealing to the Super Greens, the already converted choir who make up about 16 percent of the U.S. and UK populations and are heavily motivated by sustainability. But in the process they inadvertently alienated the 66 percent who make up the mainstream. To the mainstream, "green" products seem to be aimed at crunchy granola hippies or rich elitist snobs—not at them. Instead of enticing them into better ways of living, green marketing was counterproductive, driving a greater wedge between them and the product, brand, or behavior it was designed to promote.

Green Giants are different from these traditional green brands. They understand that for most people, sustainability is increasingly desirable, but it still comes in as a runner-up in the relevance stakes to whatever primary functional or emotional benefit they seek, be it flavor, usefulness, cachet, health, or value. Green Giants build their marketing around human wants, needs, and desires first, showing that sustainability delivers the benefits people want, rather than flagging sustainability itself. And this enables them to cast a much wider net for customers than focusing on sustainability alone.

Mainstream appeal is the fifth shared trait of the Green Giants. It may seem self-evident that if you want to build a Billion Dollar Brand, it will need to have the potential to appeal to a whole lot of people who will buy enough of it to get you there. But it has proven tough to do this with sustainability and social good. This chapter explains how to position your sustainable product or service for mainstream appeal and how to avoid common pitfalls associated with building brands with sustainability and social good at their core. While the research was done with consumers and this chapter focuses mainly on consumer brands, my work with target audience groups (including business decision makers, investors, policy makers, and key opinion formers) suggests the principles have broader application.

MAINSTREAM GREEN: A RECAP

"The mainstream has completely confounded us when it comes to green." That's what Graceann Bennett and I wrote in 2011. At the time, we both worked at OgilvyEarth, the sustainability communications practice I cofounded. We were trying to figure out how to help our clients unlock what we felt sure was a huge market opportunity in incorporating sustainability or social good into their brands, but we were being thwarted by what we called the Green Gap. In research studies, mainstream consumers had expressed a strong desire to live a more sustainable life, but in real life, few converted their intentions into action. This is a major problem for the planet, but our concern was also with its impact on the business case. We saw corporations eager to experiment with more sustainable products and services losing confidence and interest when the promised sales failed to materialize. The culprit? Often the Green Gap. Consumers simply weren't putting their money where their mouths were.

We set out to understand why. What was holding the masses back from adopting a more sustainable lifestyle? What separated the doers from the mere believers and the skeptics? And what secrets could we uncover to close the gap so that brands and marketers could drive behavior change and business growth?

We conducted a series of interviews with behavior change and sustainability experts, then spent time in the homes and neighborhoods of Americans across three markets: San Francisco, Chicago, and the New York metropolitan area. And we fielded two surveys with

1,800 demographically representative Americans in order to triangulate the truth.

The first thing we did was to plot the U.S. population on a continuum of green (as shown in Figure 5-1). We found that most of America is smack dab in the middle ground—not hard-core green, but not completely unaware or unappreciative of issues surrounding sustainability either. In fact, about two-thirds of Americans characterized themselves as "somewhere in the middle" when it comes to living a green or sustainable lifestyle. And while 82 percent say they have good green intentions, only 16 percent follow through and convert the intention to action. The 16 percent who do are the Super Greens. The 66 percent who do not are the Middle Greens. The Middle Green area is where the Green Gap lives, and if you are anything more than a niche brand, this is most likely where your consumer lives too.

If you have an ambition to build a billion dollar brand around sustainability or social good, as the Green Giants have done, the Middle Green is the group you need to crack. Forget about the Green

Figure 5-1 The U.S. population plotted on a continuum of green

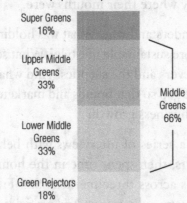

Super Greens
16%

Upper Middle
Greens
33%

Middle
Greens
66%

Lower Middle
Greens
33%

Green Rejectors
18%

Rejecters. They are unlikely ever to be motivated by these issues. The Super Greens absolutely are, but they are a small group and they may have anticonsumerist tendencies, making them a less promising pool of customers. The Middle Green mainstream is where the potential lies, but to tap it you need to figure out how to close the Green Gap.

One note on the spectrum: One of the curious things about sustainability is that the proportions of the groups have not changed significantly over time. Most social trends follow a fairly standard adoption curve. Think about a new piece of technology, such as the iPad. It was embraced first by the innovators, and then in order by the early adopters, the early majority, the late majority, and finally perhaps by the laggards, until it was ubiquitous. This is how most trends cycle. But it never really happened for sustainability. When I began looking at green segmentations in 2006, the Super Green group was around the 16 to 18 percent mark. It is still about the same today. And the Middle Green group has still not embraced Super Green behaviors. Sustainability seems to play by different rules, which is one of the reasons building a business around it has proved to be so challenging.

But the Green Giants prove it can be done, and the rewards for success are significant. To show how it's done, consider the case of Chipotle versus Otarian. (And if you've never heard of Otarian, you're about to find out why.)

HOW (NOT) TO DRIVE MAINSTREAM APPEAL

Imagine this scenario. You're pottering around New York City's West Village, a veritable foodie haven, when you start to feel hungry. As you turn onto Bleecker Street, you notice a bright, clean, new restaurant with a slightly odd name: Otarian. "Thank goodness you're here!

Your planet needs you!" says a sign on the door. You decide to give it a try and head inside.

The server greets you with a chirpy "How do you want to save carbon today?!" Not allowing this slightly unexpected greeting to distract you, you select the tandoori and mushroom paneer wrap from the meat-free, mostly local and fair-trade menu. The server hands over your meal in a box emblazoned with the slogan "LOW CARBON cuisine that loves health and the planet."

"Thank you for saving the planet, one Otarian meal at a time!" she says.

You seat yourself at a table made from recycled buttons on a recycled plastic and aluminum chair and unwrap your sandwich. "Enjoy our low carbon wrap that is made with sustainable and local ingredients that are never air-freighted and has a carbon footprint 0.91 kilograms smaller than that of chili burrito with beef," says the packaging. As you take a bite, your eye is drawn to a huge, flat-screen TV on the wall where a cartoon is playing on a loop featuring sad-looking cows headed to a slaughterhouse and the world's poor looking pale and hungry.

Are you enjoying your meal yet?

Otarian, which opened in New York and London in 2010, billing itself as "the world's first low-carbon restaurant chain," ought to have been a slam dunk. The concept was thoughtful, and a great deal of work went into calculating the carbon footprint of every dish; Otarian partnered with the World Resources Institute on the metrics.[1] Reviews were slightly mixed, but most declared the food "fresh and well-seasoned." (The *New York Times* was an exception: "With sleight of hand, Otarian serves airplane-quality food without the environmental guilt of flying."[2]) Trends pointed to the potential of the concept: Vegetarianism is on the rise in the United States and the UK, with 12 percent of Brits now following vegetarian or vegan diets,[3] and U.S. meat consumption was down 12 percent between 2007 and 2012.[4] Consumers were saying they wanted to live a more sustainable lifestyle. Food is one category in which they seem willing to put their money where their mouths are (pardon the pun). Otarian's launch party at the West Village location was buzzing and star-studded.

And yet a year later, in 2011, Otarian had shuttered its UK operations and a lone New York location (down from an original three) was all that remained.[5] What happened?

On the face of it, the concepts behind Otarian and Chipotle share a lot in common. Both seek to offer food that is healthier and has a lighter environmental footprint. Both have lobbied for a better way of making food, especially as it pertains to meat. And both feature nontraditional information regarding the food on their menus, Otarian about the carbon footprint and Chipotle about the calories. Yet today, Chipotle is inching closer to 2,000 locations globally, with 200 slated to open in 2015 alone,[6] while Otarian is down to just one.

We didn't ask our research subjects to compare Otarian and Chipotle specifically. But Otarian fell into many of the textbook green marketing traps we highlighted in *Mainstream Green*, while Chipotle deftly avoids them. Together, they demonstrate the delicate art of achieving mainstream appeal and the difference it makes to business results. Here are some of the principles from the report in action.

Make It Personal

The first clue to Otarian's problems is in the greeting the server used and the concept that was plastered all over your lunch. You didn't go to a restaurant to save carbon. You went there to get some yummy food. If it was more sustainable, even better, but carbon does not trump taste. A lot of early green marketing fell into this trap. It led with the benefit to the planet, assuming it's a primary motivator for people. For most of us, the mainstream especially, it isn't. Imagine concentric circles around the individual with me at the center, my family next, my community next, and the world on the outside. The closer you get to the center of the bull's-eye, the more motivating your message becomes. The planet is on the outside. It's super-motivating for Super Greens, but a distant second, third, or fourth for the majority. That's why, for the mainstream, eco messages about polar bears will never beat ones about personal health, status, prosperity, or happiness. Make it about people first, not the planet.

Chipotle gets this right. Chipotle's Food with Integrity philosophy has always been presented as in service to taste. As its communications director, Chris Arnold, told me: "Chipotle is a chef-founded and chef-run company, so food is what drives us. For us, this is about better food. It just so happens that these ingredients are better in many ways—better for you, better tasting, and better for the environment, better for family farms . . . but everything we do is about making the food better."[7]

This concept—that sustainability can be good for me as well as for the planet and society—is sometimes called co-benefits.[8] Getting the hierarchy of the co-benefits right is key. So, Chipotle is a burrito restaurant with ethics, not an ethical restaurant with burritos. Not so Otarian. Otarian's marketing positions the food as second fiddle to the sustainability. If you're a restaurant, the food just has to come first. At least, it does if you want the mainstream to buy in.

Behavior First, Attitudes Second

Psychologists now understand that attitudes often follow behaviors, rather than the other way around. A lot of communication in the sustainability space has focused squarely on changing people's beliefs and attitudes, and it has done so with a wealth of rational arguments behind it; think of *An Inconvenient Truth* or the overwhelming evidence that has now been shared by the Intergovernmental Panel on Climate Change about the realities of global warming. And yet behavior has not significantly shifted. Our research confirmed what neuroscientists and behavioral economists have shown: that attitudes and beliefs are shaped by behaviors, and behaviors drive belief systems more than the other way around.

We compared closing the Green Gap with eliminating cigarette smoking. Despite decades of clear public service messages about the dangers of smoking, attitudes toward cigarettes did not significantly change until corporations and governments worked together to make smoking no longer the norm. Once smokers had to stand shivering outside or cluster in depressing lounges, looking like outcasts, people started to act on the idea that smoking is unusual and dangerous.

Otarian's overly didactic marketing is textbook Green Marketing 1.0. It is attitude-focused, trying to argue customers into agreeing with it. "If Americans gave up eating meat, we could feed a billion Africans on the grain saved," read the napkins. I'm a Super Green so this stuff is wildly persuasive to me. To the mainstream, though, it's a turnoff.

Chipotle has worked this out. Its marketing is designed to lure people in with food and fun before unleashing its principles on them when they least suspect it. One example of this is at the brand's extremely successful Cultivate Festivals, where food, music, and culture are the main dish, served with a stealthy side of sustainability education. Chris Arnold told me:

The whole idea with our Cultivate Festivals is to draw people in through bands and big name chefs, so people come and listen to the music and enjoy great artisanal food. While they're there, we have five or six attractions that explain the difference between processed and whole foods or the difference between small, pasture-based agriculture and industrial animal agriculture. The first year we had a gestation crate [a tiny crate sows are kept in while pregnant, without room to move, which has become a touchstone in the debate over industrial agriculture], and we had a line dozens deep of people all day wanting to take their picture in this sow stall. To motivate people to learn, we give them a passport, and if you get stamps from five out of six attractions, we give you a free burrito. We bring them in under the auspices of entertainment and give them an incentive to learn something new. Significant majorities leave the event knowing things about us or about food they didn't know before.

This jujitsu move has the added benefit of making people feel better about something they were already doing and enjoy, therefore having the potential to increase their loyalty, rather than scaring them off at "hello." But more important, it turns customers into believers—almost without them realizing what happened. "That's our goal: Draw people in, then make them more curious about food and where it comes from," says Arnold.

But the strategy of "lure them in, then whack them over the head with your message," like all good marketing, has to be well executed. Here's how not to do it: Otarian founder Radhika Oswal reportedly invited guests to a party at her Australian mansion, then gave an impromptu 40-minute lecture on vegetarianism. "Meat eaters are literally covering the world in s*&%!" she lectured.[9] Several guests got up and left. In sustainability, as in all things, a little subtlety can go a long way. Chipotle 1, Otarian 0.

Guilt Doesn't Sell

A lot of early green marketing tried leveraging guilt to persuade people to change their behavior. We've all seen the videos of sad polar bears, children standing in parched deserts, and the like. That is indeed the reality we face, but our research found that reminding people of it in a bid to motivate behavior change is counterproductive. Guilt doesn't work. It overwhelms and sends people into a tailspin of denial, dead-ending in inertia. We compared it to Eve and the apple; once people start to learn about green, they are inflicted with the curse of consciousness and everything they do is suddenly another reason to feel guilty, from the coffee they drink to the car they drive. People go a long way to avoid feeling guilty, and so guilt shuts them down. But they want the relief that absolution from guilt provides.

Here's where Otarian got it wrong: There's nothing like the image of a bunch of cows going to a slaughterhouse to kill your appetite completely, even if you're not eating beef. Chipotle has used messaging that's not so different from the videos in Otarian's restaurants, but it didn't play them in people's faces at the point of purchase.

In 2011, Chipotle created a two-minute video called "Back to the Start." In this sweet animation, a farmer starts off with cute pigs roaming in an open field, but over time, he succumbs to the lure of industrial agriculture. His fields become factories, and trucks and chemicals arrive. The farmer looks increasingly sad, and as the gentle soundtrack (a cover version of a Coldplay track sung by Willie Nelson) reaches its chorus, "I'm going back to the start!" he leaps into action, converting his fields back to the rural idyll he began with. His family and animals look content, and a signpost reading Food With Integrity appears alongside a discreet Chipotle logo.

The video was invented, Chris Arnold explained, to be shared digitally with Chipotle's most loyal fans, but as an experiment, the company decided to run it in 5,000 movie theaters. It was so successful that Chipotle upped that to 10,000 theaters and then ran it during the Grammy Awards to an audience of 40 million. After that, the video lived on online, where it's had more than 8 million views on YouTube. Meanwhile, proceeds from downloads of the song on iTunes went to support sustainable agriculture. The video followed the lessons given in the previous section: It was so gentle and charming that you almost didn't notice there was an educational message hidden beneath the entertainment. But you sure felt good about the happy free pigs. Still, neither the video nor its imagery ever went anywhere near the stores.

This was deliberate, and it was a strategy Chipotle figured out through trial and error, Arnold told me:

> What we've learned over the years is that if we went too far down the path of communicating what we're doing [to make the food more sustainable], people checked out. They felt like Chipotle, which had always been this fun and irreverent brand, is now preaching at them over food issues and they didn't like that. So we dialed it back and made the information available on our website and in our PR so it was there if people wanted to find it, but it was never the driver of our marketing.[10]

Arnold did note that as culture has changed and the conversation around sustainable food has become more mainstream, the brand has felt able to "push the envelope more." But Chipotle sticks to its strategy of keeping its ethics mostly out of its restaurants, focusing the dining experience on the food and allowing the campaigning to take place in more conducive environments, like online. So when you enter the restaurant, you get the benefits of absolution without guilt being flung in your face. Less guilt + more pleasure = more purchases.

Make It Easy

"I can't tell you exactly what the term 'carbon footprint' means. I understand the detrimental effects of leaving a carbon footprint, and I understand the ways that we need to prevent doing so. But scientifically, I don't know what that means," Daniel in Connecticut told us in our 2011 research. He's not alone; 82 percent of Americans from our survey said they don't have a clue how to calculate their carbon footprint. People explained how they struggled with the crazy carbon calculus. They specifically called out an Otarian-esque scenario: How do you calculate the impact of eliminating meat consumption while factoring in long drives in your SUV to reach out-of-the-way vegetarian restaurants? (In a similar vein, critics of Otarian called attention to the fact that its billionaire founder owns multiple homes, one with a garage containing 17 cars. Her personal carbon calculus, they suggested, could use some recalibration.)

People need this information simplified and interpreted into a form they can process, ideally in a split second at the point of purchase. The idea that eating at Otarian has a lower carbon footprint than eating at other restaurants is not so hard to grasp. But people have no frame of reference for how meaningful it is in the grand scheme of things to eat a vegetarian wrap with a carbon footprint that is 0.91 kilograms smaller than that of a beef burrito. How much is 0.91 kilograms, anyway?

Having done all that excellent homework, Otarian missed an opportunity to translate the impact into something people could wrap their brains around and feel good about. Chipotle may have over-simplified slightly in its charming animation of happy, free-roaming pigs, but people easily got the point (and the associated virtuous feelings). Simple is good. Otarian inadvertently ensnared its customers in the complexity of the carbon conundrum. Thanks, but no thanks, Otarian.

Make It Normal

The most powerful barrier of all to people trying to live a more sustainable lifestyle surprised us: the power of social norms. Our research confirmed what neuroscientists and behavioral economists had already shown: We are social creatures and look to others around us to help us make decisions on how we live our lives. As we discussed in the "Contrarian" section of Chapter 1, it's lonely being the only vegan at the barbecue. Unless we live in certain communities on the East or West Coasts of the United States or a few other progressive enclaves where riding bikes, recycling, using solar panels, and eating local organic food is the social norm, most of us, in America at least, receive cues from those around us that living a more sustainable life is still the exception, not the rule.

One of our subjects, a young mom, lived in Chicago. "I ride my bike when I'm going to meet my 'earth mom' friends, but when I'm meeting my soccer mom friends, I'll drive my car because otherwise they look at me weird," she told us. Another woman from a New Jersey suburb demonstrated that stereotypes associated with legacy images of greener living are persistent. "My neighbor recycles, and I often feel like she's looking down her nose at me, judging me," she said. "But she doesn't dye her hair and [whispering] *I don't think she even shaves her legs.*" Indeed, we found that more than 50 percent of people in the United States and nearly 80 percent of people in the UK think green products are for crunchy granola hippies or rich elitist snobs—neither of which they want to be. The mainstream just wants to be normal.

You can see where marketers got this wrong. Take the example of eco-friendly cleaning products. In the early days, marketers' instincts were to package them in bottles covered in yellow flowers and green leaves, give them a distinctive eco-sounding name, and put them in a different part of the aisle. Choosing them therefore had to be a conscious and visible choice for the consumer. Marketers didn't realize that in the subtleties of the unspoken social code, in order to pick that product off the shelf and walk around the store with it in their basket, consumers felt they were being asked to make a personal statement they didn't necessarily want to make. And so they preferred to stick with a known quantity, an un-green product that said to their peers, "Nothing to see over here. I am totally normal."

Even motivated consumers fear attracting the negative judgment of their peers if they go out on a limb and purchase green products; instead, they embrace the comfort of conformity. With its militantly vegetarian stance, tribelike name, and in-your-face philosophy, Otarian challenged consumers to commit to an identity in order to eat its food. As we saw in Chapter 3, brands today do need a point of view, and people want to buy into your purpose. But Otarian just came on too strong. Chipotle doesn't demand the same level of commitment. You can embrace its ethics, or not. If all you want is a great burrito, sure! Come on in! That pragmatism makes it much easier for the mainstream to swallow than a paneer wrapped in polemic.

Lose the Labels

Language in the green space has been particularly hard to nail. Terms like "green" and "sustainable" are plagued with legacy issues and do little for the mainstream consumer beyond raising suspicion and confusion. "They've co-opted the language. Everything's green and everything's sustainable. I just don't know what it means anymore," Erin from San Francisco told us in 2011.

In 2014, a team from Edelman Berland, the insights and analytics arm of Edelman PR—Mike Berland, Samantha Tritsch, and Jeremy Guterl—as well as independent consultant Peter Hempel conducted new research for this book. We engaged 100 Americans representing a range of genders and age groups. They confirmed that little has changed. " 'Green' doesn't really mean anything to me because it's such a misguided word used by many companies to boost sales," one respondent told us. " 'Green' or 'sustainable' has been expanded to mean just about everything, so it loses impact," said another.

Green Giants have found a way around this: They talk about more specific benefits of their products without stepping on the landmines of the "G" or "S" words themselves. They lose the labels—and with them, the associated stigma. Consider Chipotle. For this book, Edelman Berland also conducted an analysis of press releases, blog posts, and other long-form communications of each of the Green Giants. The organization analyzed an average of 7,384 words of marketing language for each company and brand. It found that top-used words in Chipotle's marketing lexicon include foodie favorites *better, fresh, grow, local,* and *quality.* Among its top 20 marketing terms, only two are traditionally "green" (*sustainable* and *organic*).

You can see this in action across the Green Giant brands. Rather than using eco terms, their vocabulary is redolent with optimistic, aspirational ideas like innovation, health, modernity, and technology. Tesla's top-used words are *forward-looking, long-distance, cost, energy, fast,* and *performance.* It never uses *green* and only rarely *sustainable.* Nike's words are *design, innovation, performance, movement/motion,* and *technology; sustainability* is in the top 10, but *green* is second from the bottom. Unilever is a heavy user of *sustainable*—after all, it's in the name of its plan—but the rest of its language includes *children*, *life*, *future*, *open*, and *world*. Whole Foods leads with *responsible* and then uses *fresh*, *health*, *new*, *pesticides*, *protect*, and *transparent*. And in its Eco-magination communication, *power*, *technology*, and *solutions* dominate GE's vocabulary.

These are all benefits people want. Most of them live close to the center of that bull's-eye you imagined earlier in the chapter. They speak to things people expect from products in their respective categories—*fast* for a car, *fresh* for food, *solutions* for B2B products. They are relevant, personal, easy to grasp, and, well, normal. Indeed, of the Green Giants, only Toyota uses the word *green* very much at all to describe the Prius; *environment* is the Prius's most frequently used word, and *green* its fourth.

In Otarian's glossary, *low-carbon* and *planet* dominate. While Chipotle and the Green Giants are talking everyone's language, Otarian is speaking Super Green. One attracts the mainstream while the other, unfortunately, repels.

Losing the labels is what Hannah Jones is talking about in the quote that opens this chapter: "Our 17-year-old consumers tell us they want a better world. They don't call it sustainability." Lose the labels, normalize the language, and you normalize the concept.

Make It Modern

One outcome of losing the labels and following the other principles outlined in this chapter is that consumers don't really think of the Green Giants as green at all—or at least, not green-first. Edelman Berland asked our research respondents to talk about what the Green Giant brands had in common. The most popular words people used

Figure 5-2 Attributes most commonly chosen to describe Green Giants versus control companies

Green Giants	Control Companies
Forward-thinking	Established
Innovative	Traditional
New	Mainstream
Modern	Tried-and-true
"Green"	Affordable
Environment	Conservative
Community	Old
Eco-friendly	Business-as-usual
Higher-priced	Stuck in their ways

were *forward-thinking, innovative, new,* and *modern. Green* and *environment* came fifth and sixth on their lists, as you can see in Figure 5-2.

Moreover, Green Giants make their conventional counterparts look old-school. A control list of direct competitors, chosen for our survey because they have not taken strides to place sustainability and responsibility at the core of their businesses, were described as *established, traditional, mainstream,* and *tried-and-true,* as well as *conservative, stuck in their ways,* and *old,* when placed next to the Green Giants.

This is striking. In our 2011 report, we urged companies, "Don't stop innovating, make better stuff," because we'd learned that consumers think of sustainable products as primitive and as coming with an associated trade-off in performance or quality. "We don't like going backwards. High performing sustainable choices are key for mass adoption," we wrote then. The Green Giants prove it now. Each of them is founded on a Disruptive Innovation, not a technological step backward. As we said in Chapter 2, they have used sustainability as a spur to invent the products and services of the 21st century. That's what the language they use conveys too.

Consumers sense it, and they respond. In Chapter 3, I asserted that Green Giants will increasingly be seen as the brands of the future, while conventional businesses will seem out-of-date. This research shows that the Green Giants are already on their way. They have succeeded in communicating sustainability and social responsibility as integral parts of a modern brand—not just greener, but better. And in the process, they've achieved mainstream appeal.

* * *

Hopefully, it is now apparent why Chipotle was able to generate mainstream appeal while Otarian was not. You can't motivate mainstream behavior with what are essentially niche marketing techniques. Otarian positioned its brand around environmental benefits, not human benefits. That reduced its potential audience from "all humans" to the subset "humans who care about carbon"—which is to say at best 16 percent of us. People will buy Otarian's food first for the reasons they buy any other food—Is it tasty? Is it affordable? Is it convenient? Is it healthy?—and if it checks those boxes, the fact that it's low carbon is a great added benefit. But it's still the rare consumer who would put carbon at the front of that list.

Just because sustainability is the desired outcome doesn't mean it has to be your marketing strategy. But if you can make eating low carbon food feel normal, as Chipotle has made ethical meat and dairy, you'll drive more business and hopefully do more good in the process. Indeed, you may become the de facto "new mainstream," a title to which Chipotle could legitimately lay claim, having overtaken Burger King in the United States with same-store sales increasing by an astonishing 19.8 percent in the third quarter of 2014 (16.8 percent for all of 2014.) At the same time, sales at McDonald's slumped 3.3 percent, its fourth consecutive quarter of declining sales.

Chipotle's explosive growth is coming not just from the same people eating its food more often but from drawing new customers in, including male teens.[11] That's the very definition of mainstreaming. Chipotle has succeeded in moving sustainability from niche to normal, and it shows no signs of stopping.

FROM ECO-FRIENDLY
TO MALE EGO-FRIENDLY

There's an angle of mainstream appeal that is less relevant to Chipotle and Otarian but has been crucial to Tesla's breaking the billion-dollar ceiling. As we were spending time with our research subjects in 2011, we began to notice that men got kind of squirrelly around the topic of green. The reusable shopping bag was an especially divisive item. Emmanuel from Oakland, California, wanted to be more eco-friendly, but he just couldn't bring himself to use one. "It's kind of embarrassing. It looks like a man-purse," he said.

On the other side of the country, Michael in New Jersey felt the same way: "That is one of my downfalls. I don't really like carrying around canvas bags. It's easier for girls to use them because they have their purse already, so they can just throw them in there," he said. We caught him in his office stuffing a canvas tote in the drawer beneath his desk so his coworkers wouldn't see it.

But it went way deeper than canvas bags. Eco-friendly cars and reusable water bottles were problematic too—anything, it seemed, that was visible. Even more than women, men did not want to be seen being green.

We wondered what was going on. So we just outright asked our research subjects: Do you feel the green movement is more masculine or feminine?

A staggering 82 percent said feminine.

We'd already seen that the greener you were on our spectrum, the more likely you were to be female. But we hadn't put two and two together until then. Here, then, was another barrier to mainstream adoption. Green is just too girly for guys. Carry a tote, give up your 4WD truck and your steak, eat quinoa, compost . . . . It's true that the everyday domestic choices we need to make in favor of sustainability offered little to make the NASCAR fan's heart race.

Then along came Tesla. I remember the first time I actually saw a Tesla. Cars had been a bone of contention in my marriage since my eco awakening. I wanted a Prius. He wanted a Porsche, or until we could afford one, something Porsche-esque. Then one day, a black Tesla rolled past us on New York's Sixth Avenue. Everything went into slow motion. My husband watched it, his jaw on the ground. "What was *that*?" he gasped as it glided away. "Oh, that?" I said lightly. "That's a Tesla." We had reached consensus.

Tesla is the first car company to roundly crack the code on selling an eco-friendly vehicle to men. The company knew exactly what it was doing. The first-ever post on Tesla's blog, written by Tesla co-founder Martin Eberhard, was called "Attitude." The title referred to what the post described as Tesla's "pro-driver attitude":

> My observation is that most electric cars were designed by and for people who fundamentally don't think we should drive. Ideally, we should walk or take public transportation; EVs are a necessary evil

for when these don't work. This mentality has led to dozens of unappealing electric "punishment cars" . . . . We at Tesla Motors love cars. We love to drive; we appreciate beautiful and fun cars. And Tesla cars are built for people who love to drive. So our optimization is not for ultimate low cost, but rather for performance, aesthetics, and sex appeal.

That is Tesla's pro-driver attitude. The company understands why people—not only men, but definitely men—like cars. So instead of making a less bad car, they made the best one ever.

Compare the early days of eco car marketing to Tesla. There were many things the eco marketing got wrong. In fact, as we were wrapping up the *Mainstream Green* report in the spring of 2011, a poster for the Nissan Leaf—Nissan's compact plug-in electric vehicle that goes 70 to 80 miles on a single charge—appeared on a billboard outside our office window. The poster had a picture of planet earth divided into four quadrants, one of which was a kelp forest while another was a baby seal. From the vantage point of our research, everything about that poster and the car—from the plaintive look on the seal's face, to the planet, to the curvy, girly little car, to the eco-obvious name (Leaf)—gave the mainstream consumer reason to believe this was another of Eberhard's "punishment cars." It screamed "hello crunchy granola hippy, good-bye mainstream." Good-bye mainstream men, especially.

Tesla is the polar opposite of that poster. It is tailor-made to quicken the pulse of any self-respecting man (and plenty of women, too). With its sleek curves and ability to accelerate from 0 to 60 faster than any other car in automotive history, its available torque, its multi-transmission gears, and its status symbol price point, Tesla checks all the boxes. There's a good reason why, for decades, sports cars have been sold to men in commercials showing vehicles driving much too fast around hairpin bends on courses in Switzerland, ideally with a chick in red lipstick somewhere in the mix. That is what gets men to buy cars. They want their car to tell the world how manly and successful they are. Baby seals? Not so much.

It's a philosophy Tesla extends to other consumer touchpoints. Often held at Tesla's showrooms, events to launch new vehicles feature loud music, dry ice, and leggy models. There is not a whisper of hemp or greenery in sight. Tesla's showrooms too are temples to technology and speed. Tesla is another great example of not confusing your desired outcome with your marketing strategy. Elon Musk may be trying to transition the world away from fossil fuels, but he knows the best way to do that is to make the car as desirable as humanly possible—and that means keeping the planet out of it.

Driving a Tesla is more like drinking champagne than eating your broccoli. It conforms to all the luxury car social norms, so it gives mainstream men air cover if they take the leap. And as with Chipotle's burrito, the hierarchy of benefits is great core benefit first, sustainability an added bonus. There's the guilt-absolution too since it has the promise of being a guilt-free luxury vehicle. Genius.

Like Chipotle, Tesla displays an understanding of human nature. It makes eco-friendly into something that is male ego–friendly. Marlboro famously cracked this same code when it replaced the concept "Mild as May" in its ads with the now iconic Marlboro Man. This strong, silent type turned smoking filtered cigarettes from girly to guy-thing almost overnight.

In our report, we said sustainability could use its Marlboro Man moment. With its danger, speed, and status, Tesla gets us there. This is eco-friendly driving for the *Top Gear* set.

LOSE THE CRUNCH

Let's return to the Leaf for a moment. After that initial ad, which Nissan said was always intended to target the early adopter, the Super Green, Nissan did something brilliant. During the 2010 Apple Worldwide Developer Conference, the one at which Steve Jobs used to give his signature annual keynote, Jobs debuted the new iPhone and the world's first iAd—for the Nissan Leaf. The stunt earned Nissan several minutes of marketing gold dust as Jobs played the ad, positioning the Leaf as the car of the future, and walked through the Leaf app, preordering a vehicle for himself. The ad, app, and Jobs endorsement positioned the Leaf not as a car for tree huggers but as the latest Silicon Valley must-have boy toy. This pivot from Super Green to mainstream was perfectly judged, and from there, the Leaf has gone from strength to strength. In 2014, it broke its own record for the most U.S. electric vehicle sales in a single calendar year, with a total nearing 22,700. That puts it halfway to the billion-dollar benchmark that qualifies a Green Giant, and definitely qualifies it as a Next Billion.

This story illustrates another of our keys to mainstream appeal: Lose the crunch. In our 2011 report, we asked why a product has to be packaged in burlap just because it's green. Everywhere we looked, there were hemp bags, hemp-effect packaging, or their metaphorical equivalents. This sends a signal to the mainstream consumer that the product is not for them and, worse, is of inferior quality. (Not to mention that everyone's hemp packaging looked the same. In an attempt to differentiate through sustainability, they actually did the opposite.) The Leaf's early ads were the poster equivalent of hemp packaging. But while the Leaf might have started its marketing journey with overtures to the crunchy eco set, it then lost the crunch and morphed into a modern brand—to which sustainability was integral, but not everything. The Leaf's sales success is the result in part of its having cracked the code on mainstream appeal when it lost the crunch.

KILL THE SUSTAINABILITY TAX

Price and perceptions of premium pricing have bedeviled sustainable and green products from the get-go. For consumers, the cost/benefit analysis has not always added up. "Pay more for a product that doesn't work!" is essentially what they read into the green cues of many consumer goods as a result of a decade of experience. In fact, in our 2011 research, price was the Number 1 barrier holding Americans back from buying more green products and services, and it came through loud and clear again in 2014. "I can't afford the green products. They are too expensive," one respondent succinctly put it.

The expense was not imagined. An informal study at the time we wrote *Mainstream Green* found the price premium on more sustainable products could be significant, including 16 percent for an eco-friendly car, 48 percent for organic milk, 60 percent for organic eggs, and as high as 100 percent for eco-friendly cleaning products. We called this premium the Sustainability Tax since that's de facto what it is.

The Sustainability Tax is a profoundly literal barrier for many. In a universe where the average Walmart shopper has $65 a week to spend on groceries for her family,[12] she simply can't factor a price premium like that into her budget, no matter how much she might want to. But the tax creates psychological barriers too. It fuels the perception that green products are for a rich elite and not for "people like me." An abnormal price suggests an abnormal product.

The tax also creates mixed messages. We usually tax behaviors we want people to do less of. In the green products market, we've got the opposite going on. We're taxing virtuous behavior. (The same is true in some parts of the B2B world, for example, where carbon-intensive fossil fuels receive more generous subsidies than renewables like solar.) It just doesn't make sense. Losing the Sustainability Tax should therefore be a Green Gap killer app, eliminating multiple barriers to behavior change in one fell swoop. Job done.

Except that an exploration of the Green Giants suggests the cost/benefit equation is more nuanced than that. For this is not just a question of price. It's a question of value.

To demonstrate the complex relationship between sustainability, price, and value, let's consider a brief history of Whole Foods. When Whole Foods launched in Austin, Texas, in 1980, it was, by co-CEO and founder John Mackey's estimation, "a bunch of hippies selling food to other hippies." Then the store moved to a new location, began selling alcohol and "gourmet" items, and lost the crunch. "I lived in Austin at the time and recall this as the moment Whole Foods shifted to more of a 'hipster organic' vibe," our 2014 research collaborator Peter Hempel told me.

Whole Foods prices were always a little higher. The chain stuck to this higher price strategy as it brought the organic, natural products that had once been niche to locations in affluent, urban neighborhoods across the country. Whole Foods didn't really have a viable competitor and continued its rise to become the nation's largest organic supermarket. Along the way, it earned the nickname "Whole Paycheck," but that didn't stop its meteoric rise: By the end of 2013, it had 380 stores and revenue of $12.9 billion. Its market cap has at times topped that of Krogers, which as the nation's largest grocer has many times more stores than Whole Foods.

The strategy seemed to run out of runway rather abruptly in the second quarter of 2014, when the Whole Paycheck reputation finally came home to roost. Whole Foods saw same-store sales growth, its primary indicator of business health, slump from 8 percent in 2012 to just 5 percent in 2013, the lowest levels since 2008. Analysts cited two primary drivers. First, Whole Foods faced lower-priced competition. Walmart announced it would be launching a range of 100 mostly organic products in partnership with Whole Foods competitor Wild Oats. The range will be priced 25 percent below national brands—for which read Whole Foods. Second, Whole Foods has saturated its traditional locations, and to continue to grow, it has begun moving into smaller cities and some less affluent neighborhoods—most notably Detroit, where Whole Foods opened its first store in 2014. These communities are more likely to be price-sensitive, and that was impacting sales growth, analysts said. Both limits to growth came down to price. While Whole Foods had been heavily promoting its private label, 365 Everyday Value, and had launched The Whole Deal, a section of its website devoted to coupons and tips for getting more for your money, John Mackey admitted, "We haven't been investing in price as aggressively as we probably needed to."[13]

This news of Whole Foods' slowdown kicked off a media firestorm. Bloomberg did a basket-to-basket comparison of Whole Foods versus key Manhattan competitors, concluding that Whole Foods was actually cheaper than city favorites Fresh Direct, Gristedes, Food Emporium, and D'Agostino.[14] Beyond New York (which is not exactly a fair comparison), the bargain hunter website Cheapism.com and consumer finance site Kiplinger.com both found that many items were cheaper than average at Whole Foods, including organic milk and such staples as pasta and Greek yogurt.[15] But on the other side, some questioned whether Whole Foods' Detroit store was really the success story management painted. They challenged whether the store was merely serving the local affluent and student populations, while its organic, natural foods remained out of reach for the underserved populations Whole Foods claimed it had gone there to help. Whole Foods states that two in five of its customers in the Detroit store use food stamps, much higher than at its stores elsewhere in the country, and an indicator of appeal beyond the affluent. Plans to open a second Detroit location are underway.

Whole Foods committed to significantly step up its focus on price going forward, but the company also pointed out that eliminating the Sustainability Tax altogether was never its endgame. "We're never going to be in a race to the bottom; chase [customers] only on value, only on price. That's not who we are," Walter Robb, Whole Foods' co-CEO, told analysts. As if to prove it, Whole Foods launched its first major national advertising campaign in October 2014. Called "Values Matter," the signature piece of the ad campaign was a film in which images of a hazy hipster version of Americana were accompanied by a voiceover that read:

> We want people and animals and the places our food comes from to be treated fairly. The time is right to champion the way food is grown and raised and caught. So it's good for us, and for the greater good, too. This is where it all comes to fruition. This is where values matter. Whole Foods Market, America's healthiest grocery store.

"We're hungrier for change than we've ever been," the text of another ad read. "Whole Foods, where value is inseparable from values."[16]

In October 2014, Whole Foods shares were up more than 7 percent on fourth-quarter profit that beat analysts' targets and sales growth that was in line with expectations. For the year, Whole Foods reported total sales of $14.2 billion and a 10 percent growth in square footage with 38 new stores.[17] It seems reports of Whole Foods' demise may have been overstated. What the analysts perhaps failed to realize, and that Whole Foods ads aimed to communicate, is that there is more to value than price alone.

The other Green Giants point to this too. Indeed, few of them have achieved mainstream appeal by being price-competitive with their conventional counterparts. Some do offer an obvious financial advantage. Ecomagination offers the customer the promise of superior business performance (usually in the form of fuel savings) coupled with sustainability performance, as enshrined in the Ecomagination Product Review process. IKEA's Products for a More Sustainable Life at Home help you save money as you lower your footprint. Unilever has made it a point not to pass price increases along to the consumer—for example, while cage-free eggs cost the business more, the consumer has not been asked to bear the extra cost on the sticker price of a jar of Hellmann's.

But Chipotle foods, Tesla autos, the Prius, and the Flyknit shoe are all priced at a premium. While competitive with other fast casual chains (like Panera Bread or Qdoba), they are higher than those of the traditional fast food players. Chipotle's prices are among the highest in the fast food industry. Consumers spent an average $11.60 per visit there in 2013 compared to $3.88 at McDonald's.[18] Chipotle's customer spend is growing every year while that at McDonald's is flat, and when Chipotle raised prices by 6.4 percent in 2014, the increase did not hurt sales a bit.

Tesla autos are luxury vehicles at luxury prices, although the company is working hard to make even current models more affordable. (Tesla announced new leasing terms in October 2014 that, once tax incentives and other specifics are accounted for, can bring the monthly lease for a Model S down to $500.[19]) Both Tesla autos and the Prius may cost more up front, but they insulate the customer against gas price volatility, and the upfront investment is amortized over the lifetime of the vehicle.

Flyknit shoes are expensive when compared to generic sneakers, but perhaps no pricier than other iconic Nike shoes. Natura has products at a range of price points.

The common link is not obvious. There is no one Green Giant formula when it comes to price. But what they do share is an understanding of where the value resides—in the "me" benefits the sustainability delivers, not the sustainability itself. Where Green 1.0 manufacturers went wrong was in assuming that being green or offering sustainability were a value add to the consumer in and of themselves that enabled the companies to command a price premium. The flaw in this logic, as we've seen in this chapter, is that for the mainstream consumer, green alone is not a value add; indeed, it may be seen as undermining value if it leads to inferior performance or quality. But the "me" benefits—many of them intangible—are extremely valuable to consumers and can command a price commensurate with that value.

There's another concept at play too, one that is beginning to gain traction: lifetime value. These products often carry a higher sticker price, but over a lifetime of use, they can pay for themselves many times over in savings on energy, water, fuel, and even grocery bills. The same is true of more healthful products that ultimately increase life expectancy and lower healthcare costs. In our instant-gratification society, where "value" has become synonymous with "cheap," lifetime value can be a tough story to tell, less motivating than the immediate callout of the sticker price. But Green Giants provoke us to ask questions like:

- Are inexpensive appliances and vehicles really a good value if they guzzle gas and drive up our utility bills?

- Are conventional cleaning products really a good value if they make our homes unhealthy, not to mention pollute our lungs, our communities, and our planet?

- Is inexpensive fast food really a value if it makes you fat and sick?

Plus, now that Green Giants have proven there need be no trade-off between sustainability and quality, why shouldn't we expect to have it all?

In short, the Green Giants challenge the notion that we need to kill the Sustainability Tax after all. But if we intend to charge a premium, we better make sure we're delivering a benefit that justifies the cost. We need to make sure we're delivering true value, which is to say a product people really want, produced in a way they feel good about. Once you offer both, you have the kind of brand formula that makes decision making more emotional than rational, and commanding a higher price then becomes a whole lot easier.

OVERCOMING CYNICISM

One final insight that emerged from our 2014 research was surprising. Our 2011 research had found that eco-suspicion and eco-confusion abounded. People just had a really hard time believing companies' intentions were benign when it comes to sustainability and social good. Perhaps this isn't surprising when by one estimate, as many as 98 percent of all green marketing claims are guilty of greenwash.[20] This has resulted in an environment in which 64 percent of Americans no longer trust sustainability-related marketing claims.

So we were extremely surprised to learn that when we asked respondents what drives decision making at Green Giants and the companies we selected as controls, they thought decisions at Green Giants were significantly more likely to be guided by a desire to make the world a better place, while at control companies decisions were significantly more likely to be guided by self-interest. All Green Giants scored 40 percent or higher on making the world a better place (altruism), while control companies without exception scored 40 percent or lower.

The most extreme comparisons were Whole Foods at 53 percent altruistic versus Walmart at 19 percent, Chipotle at 46 percent altruistic versus Burger King at 17 percent, and the Toyota Prius and Tesla both at 48 percent altruistic versus General Motors at 20 percent.

These results suggest consumer cynicism is significantly lower for Green Giants than for control companies. The Green Giants' position on social purpose is coming through, and people seem to believe them. And more important, the perceived altruism affects consumer favorability. Green Giants and control companies tend to score similarly on overall favorability when "somewhat" and "very favorable" responses are combined. When only "very favorable" responses are counted, however, it becomes clear that companies with a social purpose—the Green Giants—are more successful at inspiring dedicated fan bases who view them highly.

But let's not sugarcoat this. People don't think the Green Giants are saints. Even the top companies are barely above the 50–50 split; the strongest score for "make the world a better place" is Unilever at 53 percent (though to be fair this is a relatively new endeavor and trust takes time to build).

Clearly, there is much work still to be done. What that work looks like is the subject of Chapter 6, which examines the New Behavioral Contract that Green Giants are forging with their stakeholders—because in today's world, while communication matters more than ever, actions ultimately speak louder than advertising.

CHAPTER **6**

A New Behavioral Contract

Mensch, n. *a person of integrity and honor.*

In June 1996, the pages of *Life* magazine carried a shocking image of a 12-year-old Pakistani boy, Tariq, sitting on a dirt floor, carefully sewing, while surrounded by incriminating evidence: soccer balls emblazoned with the iconic Nike swoosh. It was an image that shook the company and the world. Nike was a respected, beloved business, assumed by its millions of global customers to be one of the good guys. Yet here was evidence, in living color, that its soccer balls were being made by children. The article that accompanied the image was damning, alleging that children like Tariq were working 60 hours a week while earning as little as 60 cents a day.

Over the previous decade, Nike had experienced a period of rapid growth and had shifted its manufacturing to whichever market could deliver product at the lowest cost. No company back then was thinking about labor rights. No company realized it needed to. But the brand had begun to draw increasing criticism from publications as varied as *The Economist* and *Rolling Stone*. Nike had mostly shrugged it off. "Our initial attitude was, 'Hey, we don't own the factories. We don't control what goes on there,'" Nike's former head of compliance, Todd McKean, would admit in 2001.[1]

As the issue burgeoned in 1996, President Bill Clinton formed the Apparel Industry Partnership, a coalition of companies and labor and human rights groups assembled to draft an industry-wide code of conduct. Nike was the first corporation to sign up. But media investigations continued to uncover issues involving Nike, adding Vietnam and Cambodia to the hot spots where labor rights were apparently being violated. As the coverage escalated through 1997, outraged customers staged anti-Nike rallies in 50 U.S. cities and 11 countries.[2] Student groups encouraged their universities to boycott the brand. The comic strip "Doonesbury" ran a series of Nike-focused pieces, comparing the outsize budgets the company spent on marketing and star athletes to the meager wages paid to factory workers—a favorite theme in critiques. Things hit an all-time low when "gotcha" documentary filmmaker Michael Moore captured Nike CEO Phil Knight on camera, apparently unconcerned that child laborers were making his products. The footage was released in 1998 as part of the documentary *The Big One*.

Nike wasn't the only brand implicated, but it became the lightning rod for the issue. As the evidence became overwhelming, Knight finally admitted, in a 1998 speech at the National Press Club in Washington, D.C., that "The Nike product has become synonymous with slave wages, forced overtime, and arbitrary abuse."[3]

Knight went on to outline a new vision for the company's supply chain. He committed Nike to taking responsibility for the conditions of the million-plus contract factory workers (by far the largest group of workers in the Nike supply chain), eliminating child labor, and allowing independent monitoring of conditions, among other things. "We believe that these are practices which the conscientious, good companies will follow in the 21st century," he said. Prescient words.

Thus began a change of course that would set Nike on a path to the leadership position on sustainability and corporate responsibility, including labor issues in the supply chain, that it holds today. It began with hundreds of factory audits. Board member Jill Ker Conway, an expert on women's role in the workforce, personally went to multiple factories in such countries as Indonesia and Vietnam. She visited the dormitories where the predominantly young, female workers lived, ate with them in the cafeteria, and observed them at work. Conway decided to engage a third party to conduct face-to-face interviews off-campus and learn more. Some 67,000 workers were interviewed, giving Nike a wealth of information about how to improve conditions. Overtime and supervisors emerged as key issues; in Indonesia, for example, the supervisors were often Taiwanese or Korean men who didn't speak the same language as the workers. Supervisor training and managing surges in demand were key fixes.[4]

In 2001, at Conway's suggestion, Nike established a board-level committee for corporate responsibility and became one of the first companies to publish a CR report. Then, in 2005, Nike took the dramatic step of publicly disclosing the names and addresses of contract factories producing Nike products—the first company in its industry to do so.[5] More recently, it made this information available on an Interactive Global Manufacturing Map; there, you can click on a factory to view its name, number of workers, percentage of female and migrant workers, and what's made there, among other things.

The work continues. In 2011, Nike released its Manufacturing Index, part of a plan to put sustainability and workers' rights on an equal footing with quality, cost, and on-time delivery as selection criteria for supplier factories. The index took 30 Nike employees a year to develop.[6] Nike plans to source only from contract factories achieving a bronze rating or above on the index by 2020. The company says it has already seen workplace violations fall since release of the index.

In fact, in almost a complete 180-degree turn from where it began, Nike is now telling its suppliers "If you're going to be on the journey with us . . . we're going to need you to really think about investing in your workers."[7] As the Nike website says, "Our greatest responsibility as a global company is to play a role in bringing about positive, systemic change for workers within our supply chain and the industry." A far cry from "not our problem."

The journey continues at Nike; struggles remain over overtime and wages. But the transformation from laggard to leader is undeniable. While the sweatshop story persists for other companies, Nike has remained above the fray in recent scandals (including the 2013 factory collapse in Dhaka, Bangladesh, that killed more than 1,100 workers, as described in Chapter 1).

BUSINESSES BEHAVING BADLY

This story illustrates what this chapter is all about: a New Behavioral Contract for business. From avoiding taking responsibility for anything beyond what was necessary to comply with the law, Nike embraced what I call Pre-sponsibility across its supply chain. From turning a blind eye to the conditions of workers in its factories and perhaps hoping others would do the same, Nike opened up the proverbial kimono in several acts of what I call Truthsparency. Yes, it began under duress, but the company then went on to exceed stakeholders' demands, and anything that had been done before, to set new standards for supply chain responsibility and transparency.

Pre-sponsibility and Truthsparency, along with Experimental Collaboration, are the three pillars of the New Behavioral Contract. This chapter explains what these pillars are. Previously thought of as antithetical to the corporate world, these new ways of behaving are increasingly seen as the hallmarks of leadership. And embracing this New Behavioral Contract is the sixth shared trait of Green Giants.

Why is a New Behavioral Contract necessary? Certainly the litany of businesses behaving badly over the past 10+ years is a factor. The misdemeanors of Enron, Lehman Brothers, BP, and Bear Stearns, and of course the financial meltdown of 2008, left consumers reeling and trust in business at an all-time low. A 2014 study found, for example, that only 17 percent of Americans believe that big business can be trusted to do what is right always or most of the time.[8] Another study found that trust in business among the general public in 2014 was at its lowest levels since the 2008 financial crisis. And while trust in government is even lower, people still crave greater government regulation of business. Indeed, more than half of the general public globally sees the role of government as protecting consumers from businesses—specifically irresponsible ones.[9]

Chris Pinney of the High Meadows Institute argues that the new contract is also necessary because business has gotten so big. At a time when 58 of the world's 150 largest economies are companies,[10] business has more influence over our lives than ever before. License to operate is no longer granted by government alone but must be negotiated with a much more complex web of stakeholders, often represented by increasingly sophisticated civil society organizations. As an example of scale, consider that 2 billion people around the world buy Unilever products—that's more than a quarter of the people on planet earth.

"We have 2 billion consumers so we have to be clear about what our role in society is," says Unilever's chief finance officer, Jean Marc Huët. "With public trust in business undermined by scandal after scandal, we would do well to listen and act quickly."[11]

As the power and impact of business grows, so do our expectations of how it should behave. For example, one study found that people around the world expect business to protect the environment, treat employees fairly, and ensure a responsible supply chain more than they expect it to provide quality products at the lowest price.[12]

The Nike example bears this out. Nike perhaps assumed that consumers wanted cool, affordable sneakers and didn't really care what it took to make them. As it turned out, and as the protests revealed, they did care—quite a lot.

And with the rise of social media, a company's ability to control its image is gone. Transparency is the new normal, and everything is discoverable.

Trust today is built through actions, not advertising. Your behavior is your brand. And your license to operate depends on behaving well.

While none of them is perfect, the nine companies discussed in this book are experimenting with a New Behavioral Contract that replaces some of the bad behaviors of the past with better ones. It is one of the shared factors driving their success.

THE THREE PILLARS OF THE NEW BEHAVIORAL CONTRACT

Pre-Sponsibility

Recently, I was part of a meeting at a large agricultural company. The executives were bemoaning the fate of their industry, under siege by groups they call "the People Against Everything." (Big Ag is not the environmentalists' favorite sector.) "They're attacking [Competitor X] because the farmers are using more than the recommended dose of their fertilizer, and it's causing algal blooms [a rapid expansion of the population of algae] in the ocean. But [Competitor X] can't be held responsible for how farmers use their products!" exclaimed the CEO.

Unilever would beg to differ. In 2010, Unilever discovered that about 95 percent of the carbon footprint of its soaps, shampoos, and shower products came from the consumer use phase of each product's lifecycle. This means that the impact of producing the raw materials to make the product, manufacture it, ship it, and dispose of it is dwarfed by the impact generated by the consumer as we use the product in our showers. The culprit is the energy required to heat the water. This burns through energy, cranking out carbon emissions. (It's the equivalent of the farmers and the fertilizer in the quote above.)

Upon learning something like this, under the old behavioral contract—the one espoused by my agriculture client—most corporations would have shrugged and said "not our problem." But Unilever, being a Green Giant, instead took responsibility for it without being asked to. Unilever decided to build the consumer use phase into its emissions reductions goals, and it set out to persuade people to take shorter showers. This is an example of Pre-sponsibility, the act of proactively taking responsibility for your entire footprint, *before* someone else puts pressure on you to do so.

Unilever estimated that cutting shower times by one minute a day for 200 million households in the United States alone would save 26 billion gallons of water and 1.3 million tons of carbon. That's roughly equivalent to taking 271,000 cars off the road.

The plan to achieve it started with research. In 2011, Unilever installed shower sensors in the bathrooms of 2,500 UK consumers. Study participants were asked to keep diaries so the company could understand whether what people thought they were doing lined up with what they were actually doing. It turned out people were spending much longer in the shower than they thought—eight minutes as opposed to the five people claimed. At an average water flow rate, that's equal to about 16 gallons, or 62 liters, of hot water. And at that rate, showers are really no worse for the environment than baths, as we had long believed.

Unilever experimented with all kinds of things to bring the time down. It tried three-minute shower playlists, affordable low-flow shower heads, and shower "pebbles," which are small devices that turn amber and then red as your three-minute goal approaches. To engage the adolescent guys who buy its products, provocative personal care brand Axe ran an ad campaign suggesting customers "showerpool" with friends. Unilever ran a campaign in partnership with the Guardian Sustainable Business to crowdsource people's ideas on how to cut shower times, receiving hundreds of submissions. Innovations like dry shampoo and quick-rinse body wash have been conceived, designed to shave all-important seconds off shower times.

But getting people to shorten their showers has turned out to be significantly more challenging than anticipated. In the 2013 Unilever Sustainable Living Plan update, it was one area in which the company admitted making only limited progress.

I'm not surprised. When I went through my initial green awakening, I created my own personal shower challenge. It wasn't fun. On the days when I don't have to wash my hair, it's no big deal. I can be in and out in a minute or so. But on days involving hair washing, leg shaving, and exfoliation, it's impossible. Turning off the taps while you lather, as Unilever suggests, is miserable. You stand there, dripping and shivering. When the water comes back on, it's cold, and by the time you've got it back to the right temperature, you might as well not have turned it off. Getting the shampoo out of my hair takes forever. I tried washing my hair less frequently, but it resists all efforts to be tamed by dry shampoo. And I'm someone who's trying. Five minutes of shower time is the best I can manage.

But Unilever is not giving up. On the Open Innovation section of its website (a great example of Experimental Collaboration, and which will be discussed at length later), Unilever is hosting a Sustainable Shower Sensations challenge to solicit new ideas from scientists, engineers, and designers. The site asks for ideas on "chemicals, formulations, ingredients or solvents which enhance or accelerate the cleaning process; improved foaming agents; modified shower designs; [or] combinations of new products with new shower devices." I'm eagerly awaiting the results.

Unilever's efforts to tackle the carbon footprint of its customers' showers are an example of Pre-sponsibility in action. Pre-sponsibility is different from corporate social responsibility, the more familiar form of business responsibility. It is about taking ownership of the impact of the full lifecycle of your business and proactively seeking out opportunities to improve, not waiting for stakeholders to shock or shame you into it. It's a behavior Green Giants are increasingly displaying.

An even closer counterpoint to the Big Ag fertilizer dilemma described previously can be found at Method Home, the home products purveyor and Next Billion. Method learned that 53 percent of Americans were wasting laundry detergent (and money) by overdosing—that is, using more detergent than needed in every wash. The dirty secret of the laundry industry is that often detergent companies often ignore or actively encourage overdosing by making large caps with vague directions, because overdosing benefits their business. Method decided to take responsibility for the issue and invented 8X ultra-concentrated laundry detergent packaged in bottles with a special nozzle to ensure precision dosing. On the shelf, the product is so small that it looks more like a bottle of body lotion than laundry detergent. It's easy and clean to use, light to carry around, and ends up saving you money too.

You may be wondering if Pre-sponsibility contributes anything at all to business growth. The answer seems to be yes. Unilever's biggest effort to convince consumers to take shorter showers to date is a national promotion it developed in partnership with the Nature Conservancy, Walmart (its largest retail customer), and Suave (its leading U.S. shampoo brand). The Suave Turn off the Tap promotion ran in American Walmart stores in 2011 with promotional packs of Suave touting the cost and carbon savings offered by shorter showers. (The packs claimed that the average American family could save up to $100 and 3,200 gallons of water per year by turning off the water when shampooing and conditioning hair, and could also save up to $150 and 4,600 gallons of water per year by shortening the shower time by two minutes.) The packs completely sold out in just three weeks,[13] totally busting projections, a success that encouraged Unilever and Walmart to repeat the effort. Likewise, Method's 8X ultra-concentrated detergent is one of the company's most successful product launches to date. These are direct top-line impacts. Less tangible but just as real are positive impacts like reductions in supply chain vulnerability, securing your license to operate, eliminating vulnerabilities to and enhancing corporate reputation, and strengthening stakeholder relations across the value chain.

Let's imagine how Unilever or Method would handle the Big Ag fertilizer dosage dilemma. Maybe they would work with the farmers to address the dosing. Maybe they'd find a way to capture and recycle the phosphate in the runoff or create an Open Innovation challenge to invite ideas for ingredients to replace phosphate that don't cause algal bloom. I'm not a fertilizer expert, so I don't know. But what they probably wouldn't do is take the "we can't be held responsible" approach.

Many of today's business leaders define responsibility too narrowly. For example, I worked with an asset management firm that defined responsibility as making sure that its pension funds and mutual funds were able to offer people the returns they expected. To achieve this, the firm has become America's largest investor in coal and oil. But its primary responsibility doesn't absolve it of the consequences of all that dirty energy. That's a pre–Green Giant definition of responsibility. (The recent movement for funds to divest from fossil fuels is an example of Pre-sponsibility.)

How to Do It

Persuading folks like my Big Ag client to take Pre-sponsibility is delicate and difficult. To persuade these people, help them find and then face facts. Enlist credible outsiders to measure impacts and present them objectively. If possible, catalyze a personal epiphany by suggesting they witness the impacts of their business at first hand. (Many executives have never seen the vast barns where their chickens are raised, the clear-cut rain forest from which their palm oil is sourced, or the Great Pacific Garbage Patch a gyre of plastic the size of Texas in the Pacific Ocean—where their waste plastic packaging ends up.) Above all, present it as a shift from compliance to leadership—which it is. Pre-sponsibility begins with understanding the full impacts of your business and taking action to minimize, mitigate, and enhance wherever you can. Nothing should be off the table. If you are making a product, you're at least partly responsible for it, from sourcing all the way through to end-of-life. Don't wait for regulation or consumer demand to act. Pre-sponsibility can make your business more liked, trusted, and respected. It can inspire employee and customer loyalty. It can open up opportunities to innovate and improve quality. That, in turn, makes your business more successful.

Truthsparency

On the morning of April 21, 2008, Unilever employees arrived at the organization's London headquarters to find Greenpeace activists dressed in orangutan suits swarming the building's front steps and scaling its facade. Up at the company's Merseyside factories, more costumed protestors chained themselves to factory equipment, shutting down production lines.

This made-for-media stunt was designed to draw attention to what Greenpeace alleged was a supply chain including palm oil from producers, causing the destruction of the orangutans' Indonesian rain forest habitat. Palm oil is a substance that shows up in everything from ice cream and margarine to soap and shampoo. It is an efficient crop, producing 10 times the oil for the land used as alternatives. But the establishment of palm oil plantations, especially in Indonesia, has been associated with destruction of the rain forest on an epic scale. And along with driving the great apes to the edge of extinction, deforestation causes 15 percent of all global carbon emissions—more than all the cars and trucks on the road today—thus contributing significantly to global climate change. So the unsustainable harvesting of palm oil is a big deal.

The weird thing was that no one thought Unilever still had a palm oil problem—or at least, it was far from the worst actor. The company is the world's largest purchaser of palm oil, but it had been working to address the issue for some time, becoming a founding member of the Roundtable on Sustainable Palm Oil (RSPO) in 2004, conducting third-party audits of its suppliers, and taking steps to aggressively clean up its palm oil supply chain.

But in exhaustive, graphic, and detailed documents, Greenpeace presented proof that Sinar Mas—the largest palm oil producer in Indonesia, the second largest in the world, a member of RSPO, and a supplier to Unilever—was engaged in widespread clearing of high conservation value forests and draining of peatlands without proper permits. The fake orangutans were Greenpeace's way of bringing this to the attention of Unilever as well as the global media.

Unilever wasn't the only target. Greenpeace also posted a fake commercial on YouTube showing people biting into Nestlé's KitKat chocolate bars (Nestlé produces KitKat outside the United States), only to find they were biting orangutan fingers—with bloody results. The video received 1.5 million views and more than 200,000 customer requests for action. HSBC was also targeted with fake ads pointing out that it was a major investor in Sinar Mas.

In the old days of opaque business, if something like this happened, a company might have responded fairly predictably: It would try to hush things up as fast as possible. In today's world of radical transparency, it's more complicated. The social media and social good movements have converged to create the perfect conditions for transparent business to thrive and for opaque, insular business to come apart at the seams.

So, upon reviewing the revelations in the Greenpeace report, rather than stonewall or spin, Unilever digested the evidence and then announced that it would suspend a contract with a Sinar Mas affiliate until the affiliate was proved innocent. "The Greenpeace claims are of a nature that we can't ignore. Unilever is committed to sustainable sourcing. Therefore, we have notified PT SMART [a subsidiary of

Sinar Mas] that we have no choice but to suspend our future purchasing of palm oil," Marc Engel, Unilever's chief procurement officer, said at the time.[14] Nestlé and HSBC soon followed suit.

What's interesting about this case is that the issue arose not because Unilever, Nestlé, and HSBC were trying to hide something but because they didn't have enough visibility into what was going on in their own supply chains. Their businesses weren't sufficiently transparent, even to themselves. The Greenpeace documents offered more information about what was really going on than the companies themselves had.

But in today's world, turning a blind eye is no longer acceptable; ignorance is no longer a defense. That's what Truthsparency is about. For Green Giants, transparency is not a passive concept. It's about aggressively driving for visibility into the far reaches of your business, getting a handle on what's really going on, and sharing what you learn as you try to fix it.

Since this incident highlighted just how murky and fraught the palm oil supply chain is, Unilever has pivoted to Truthsparency. Instead of relying on GreenPalm certificates (which are like carbon offsets for palm oil) to achieve its sustainability goals, Unilever announced that it would drive for full traceability for every drop of oil it uses by 2020, introducing a Traceability Reporting and Verification Program and reducing to just a few suppliers to achieve it. Complete transparency is the goal. It won't be easy; as of 2014, 10 years after RSPO was formed, only 16 percent of palm oil worldwide is certified sustainable.[15] In any given batch, supplies from different origins are mixed together, making it hard to know where your specific oil originated. But being a Green Giant, Unilever believes it has to try. It knows its reputation depends on it. (As of this writing, Unilever had reached 58 percent traceable.)

Truthsparency isn't just for the benefit of activists. In 2014, Edelman's brandshare research found that 68 percent of consumers globally want a brand to communicate openly and transparently about how its products are made and sourced, but only 15 percent say brands are doing it well. That's a 53-point gap,[16] and it's up 14 points from a year earlier. In a world where it's possible to discover you've inadvertently been feeding your children pink slime, BPA, and horse meat, consumers are increasingly anxious about where the products they buy have come from, especially those that go in or on their bodies.

Whole Foods' early grasp of this insight and consequent drive to bring Truthsparency to bear across its stores has long been one of that company's crucial competitive advantages. There's now not much on Whole Foods shelves that doesn't give you a glimpse into where it's from, how it was produced, or how good it is for you, and that information is mostly presented so that it is quick and easy to grasp as you dash through the aisles.

Take the fish counter. Recognizing the challenges facing global fish stocks as a result of overfishing, Whole Foods was instrumental in forming the Marine Stewardship Council in 1997, and it became the first retailer to sell sustainably sourced seafood. Then it developed a three-tiered system for seafood: "best" (green), "good" (yellow), and "avoid" (red), banning red-designated products in 2012. Each type of fish in Whole Foods' extensive displays is clearly color-coded, making it easy to navigate. (Even the chopsticks I used for my Whole Foods sushi lunch today carried the slogan "No endangered fish.")

In the meat section, you encounter another navigation system, this time a five-step animal welfare standard on every package of meat. You can choose from the lowest designation, which requires producers to simply ban crates and cages to confine livestock, on up to Step 5+, where animals spend their entire life on a farm where their well-being is the prime focus. Prices go up as the standards do, but at least you understand exactly what you're paying for.

And in the home cleaning aisle, you find that each product is rated on the Eco-Scale rating system. Orange, yellow, and green ratings let you know how products stack up against third-party standards, toxicity of ingredients, environmental impact, animal testing, and so forth. Whole Foods doesn't even sell products with red ratings.

As for personal care products, the Whole Foods website assures you they are subject to standards and are simply not carried if they contain any of 50 ingredients common in personal care products but ruled out by Whole Foods. These include phthalates (used to hold colors and scents but known to be hormone disruptors), triclosan (found in antibacterial soaps and alleged to be a hormone disruptor and to lead to antibiotic resistance), and microbeads (tiny beads found in exfoliating products, often made from plastic and alleged to be toxic to marine life).

As of 2014, there was a new, Responsibly Grown labeling system for produce and fresh flowers. The system includes an extremely comprehensive range of measures, including soil health, impact on pollinators, water conservation, use of renewable energy sources in production, and inclusion of genetically modified organisms. The system is rigorous; one farmer remarked that the scorecard asked him to count the number of earthworms in his soil, which he joked might take him some time to complete.[17] But for the shopper, it's all boiled down to a simple orange, yellow, or green system—peace of mind, at a glance.

The proliferation of eco- and related labels in general is a response to the desire for transparency; there are at least 458 eco-labels in 197 countries and 25 industry sectors today[18], each aiming to give us greater transparency into what we are actually buying. Ironically, consumers tell us this sea of labels actually makes things more opaque, not less so. Whole Foods' simple rating system cuts through the clutter to make choosing well easy and obvious.

Whole Foods' Truthsparency is infecting the industry. The seafood system has been embraced by the majority of major supermarkets and restaurants in America, including Walmart. And after developing the meat standards, Whole Foods set up a nonprofit called GAP (Global Animal Partnership) along with Niman Ranch (which supplies Chipotle's pork) and the Humane Society, among others, to grow it, donating the intellectual property behind the system and continuing to sponsor it. The system has since been embraced by many farmers and by other producers, notably Tyson, one of America's largest poultry producers.

There's one more manifestation of Whole Foods' culture of Truthsparency: payroll. At Whole Foods, everyone can see what everyone else earns by simply looking it up. It's been this way since 1986. CEO John Mackey says he believes this level of transparency is important to drive trust and insists he's never lost an executive he wanted to retain over pay transparency.

I'm not sure about this one. Salary transparency may be too much transparency for many palates. But this example doesn't undermine the legitimacy of the trend. In today's world of social media, transparency is just a given. The lack of it makes companies look increasingly out of date. Consider that, today, anyone can track deforestation with an accuracy of 250m square meters, updated every 16 days, from their smartphone using the World Resources Institute's Global Forest Watch. Soon there will be nowhere left to hide. Businesses wishing to emulate the success of the Green Giants need to reject the corporate bias toward secrecy and embrace openness. You can no longer expect to stay, Oz-like, behind the curtain. People expect to peek back there, and they better like what they see.

How to Do It

You don't have to have it all figured out to get started with Truths-parency; people won't accept a cover-up but they will forgive you for not being perfect, as long as you're honest and humble about it. Consider Patagonia's Footprint Chronicles, an online portal where consumers can trace the impact of some of their Patagonia gear. With source material hailing from all over the world, Patagonia knew that not every product it profiled would have a sterling supply chain, though some would. But it trusted that its consumers would value the no-holds-barred info. So Patagonia divulged the bad along with the good and let consumers explore. This full-disclosure dialogue was the first of a series of examples of proactive transparency that have propelled Patagonia from outdoor outfitter to cultural icon.

It starts with measurement and reporting, and creating a plan to act on what you learn. The major business movement toward sustainability disclosure and reporting is a response to the new mandate for transparency. As previously stated fully 95 percent of the world's 200 largest companies now produce a sustainability report,[19] and 73 percent of the Fortune 500 disclose their carbon footprint to CDP.[20] Third-party professionals specialize in different areas of business transparency; they probably already have a point of view on your business, and if they don't, they'll soon formulate one. The groups behind certification and labeling systems have a wealth of experience, data, and energy that they're eager to share. Follow their advice and they may even go to bat for you; I regularly hear those "people against everything" praising Unilever in public, for example.

Then figure out an engaging way to share. Natura and Unilever are among the Green Giants that issue annual updates on their progress toward their goals with refreshing transparency. When they've failed to achieve a goal, they admit it, and they offer an honest appraisal as to why, along with how they plan to course-correct next year. There's no effort to sugarcoat things: In Natura's updates, the areas where it missed the mark are labeled in all caps with NOT ACHIEVED.[21] (The research agency Trendwatching presented this as an example of its cheekily named "Full Frontal" trend in its 2013 report.) Unilever favors a color-coding system where each of its 50 goals are assigned blue for "achieved by target date," green for "on-plan for target date," and yellow for "off-plan for target date." In the 2013 update,[22] it was easy to see at a glance that while the vast majority of targets were on track, "Reduce GHG [greenhouse gases] from skin cleansing and hair washing"—those shorter showers again—was one of six workstreams where Unilever was off-track.

In the past, sharing negatives was antithetical to business, which sought to maintain tight control of its image at all times. Yet times have changed, and today consumers trust you more, not less, if you share the bad and the ugly along with the good. One study found that 68 percent of consumers trust reviews more when they see both good and bad scores, while 30 percent suspect censorship or faked reviews when they don't see anything negative at all.[23] None of us are perfect. Today's consumers know that and will thank you for dropping the facade.

Think about how else you can demonstrate that you have nothing to hide. Method Home's synthetic competitors package their products in opaque white plastic with harsh, artificial colors on their labels. Next to them on the shelf, Method's clear bottles and clear formulas offer literal, not just metaphorical, transparency. Chipotle's open kitchens let you see exactly what's going into your burrito bowl. Tesla committed tech heresy when it released its patents for anyone to use, citing the need to accelerate the adoption of EV technology.

Mind you, transparency has limits. Hell might freeze over before we get a peek into Nike's fabled Innovation Kitchen to see what new ideas are in the pipeline. In general, innovation is typically off-limits. But supply chain, impact, ingredients, progress . . . this is information for which your stakeholders are hungry, and revealing it is likely much less risky than you think, as long as it is delivered with acknowledgment of the journey, appropriate humility and a ban on hubris, and evidence that a robust process (ideally third-party verified) is in place.

As Green Giants and their ilk raise the bar on Truthsparency, it will become harder for everyone else to remain opaque. Best to out your skeletons and your plans on dealing with them before somebody (most likely Greenpeace) does it for you.

Experimental Collaboration

If I asked you to name the most infamous corporate rivalries in American business history, chances are you'd put Coke versus Pepsi close to the top of the list. The cola wars have been waging for close to a century, with the brands' closely guarded secret formulas at the center. (Coke's is apparently kept under lock and key in Atlanta, and only a tiny inner circle of employees have access to it.) I've worked for agencies where one or the other was a client, and I can tell you that if Coke is your client, you'd better make damn sure there are no Pepsi beverages served during meetings, for sale in your staff cafeteria, or otherwise visible on your premises. The same is true in reverse. Both brands insist on category exclusivity if they're sponsoring a major event, like the World Cup or the Olympics, and seek exclusive deals with major restaurant chain partners like McDonald's, Burger King, Chipotle (all Coke), and KFC (all Pepsi).

So when Indra Nooyi, CEO of PepsiCo, took to the stage alongside Rob Gehring of the Coca-Cola Company at the inaugural Walmart Sustainable Product Expo in April 2014 in Bentonville, Arkansas, it gave the audience pause. What could be so important that it had persuaded these longtime rivals to set their differences aside and come together?

The answer: Recycling.

Nooyi and Gehring were among a group of top executives on stage to sign a pledge to commit between $5 million and $10 million apiece to the Closed Loop Fund, which aimed to make recycling available to all Americans. The other players were Walmart, which convened the event and cofounded the fund; A. G. Lafley, chair and CEO, Procter & Gamble; Roberto Marques, company group chair for Johnson & Johnson; Monique Oxender, senior director of sustainability for Keurig Green Mountain; John S. Weinberg, vice chair of Goldman Sachs; and of course the North American CEO of the Green Giant Unilever, Kees Kruythoff.

The idea for the fund came out of a Walmart-convened supply chain summit in which 30 recycling, consumer product, and supply chain experts (including the fund's cofounder, Ron Gonen, who previously served as deputy commissioner for recycling and sustainability for former New York City Mayor Michael Bloomberg) got together to discuss why recycling rates for common packaging materials like plastic, paper, and glass had stalled in America over the past decade. The issue is more than environmental; it leaves manufacturers seeking to add more recycled content to their packaging supply chain with a shortfall in access to materials, and equates to $11 billion in wasted packaging every year. Increasing recycling rates reduces greenhouse gases, saves companies money (recycled materials are typically cheaper; landfill fees are expensive), and has the potential to increase jobs in local communities. Much of the issue is pretty fundamental: A staggering 40 percent of U.S. homes don't have curbside recycling.

The group unanimously agreed on the cause of the problem: a lack of access to capital for municipalities to invest in the large-scale infrastructure projects needed to increase curbside recycling and materials processing. The individual companies had been investing their own funds into piecemeal efforts to upgrade the infrastructure, but these independent efforts weren't the right way to move the needle.

That's when Walmart and Gonen conceived the idea of inviting businesses with a financial interest in solving the problem to collaborate on a solution. The businesses would be invited to co-invest in a social impact fund that would be used to generate zero-interest loans to municipalities to invest in the kind of large-scale recycling infrastructure projects needed. The total could be deployed more strategically by a group with a holistic overview, thereby exponentially increasing the value of the money and the pace of change. Because of the savings in the system once the infrastructure is in place, investors would be guaranteed their money back. They would also stand to reap the financial benefits of access to the recycled materials they needed back into their supply chains. The fund would also create economic value for cities by reducing landfill disposal fees and increasing revenue from the sale of recyclable commodities and creating local jobs. In fact, by 2025, the fund expects the initial $100 million to lead to:

- A reduction of more than 75 million tons of greenhouse gas emissions

- The diversion of 27 million cumulative tons of waste from landfills

- The creation of 27,000 new local jobs

- A saving of more than $1.9 billion in waste disposal costs for municipalities

- Provision of much greater access to recycled material for packaged-good companies[24]

The argument was so persuasive that it compelled Coke and Pepsi—as well as the other businesses, including Unilever—to put their differences aside and come together.

Kruythoff explained why Unilever agreed to sign up: "While we are making progress, the environmental, social, and economic issues we face as a society are far too complex for any individual, company, or government to tackle alone. The Closed Loop Fund is a great example of how we can drive transformational change through partnership."[25] That's as ringing an endorsement of collaboration as I've read.

As I write this, the fund had completed its first round of fundraising, having attracted an additional group of corporate partners including 3M and Colgate Palmolive, and it was accepting applications from municipalities. Awards were expected to be made early in 2015.

This kind of precompetitive collaboration is a new way of operating in the age of the New Behavioral Contract. Conventional business doesn't like to collaborate. Collaboration runs counter to a culture built on the back of secret formulas locked away in safes, an arms race for patents, and the nondisclosure or confidentiality agreement. To suggest that you need to collaborate may also be to admit that you don't have all the answers—something few businesses are willing to do. And it may run the risk losing that all-important competitive advantage.

But when it comes to sustainability, collaboration can enhance outcomes for everyone. There are issues, like recycling, that are too large or complex for individual companies to solve alone. In addition, with such issues, while acting alone can be a drag on the business, acting together to enact a systems change can create efficiencies, avoid duplication of efforts, level the playing field, and even lift all boats. When the changes to be made are precompetitive, and the advantages of collaboration outweigh potential costs, increasingly Green Giants and their ilk are choosing to fight the instinct to compete and are collaborating instead.

By way of comparison, here's a side note involving an anecdote about Coca-Cola. When my colleague Graceann Bennett and I presented the *Mainstream Green* report at breakfast at a Sustainable Brands event in 2011, a former client of mine from Coca-Cola joined our panel to share her reactions to the report findings. Over the previous year, her team at Coca-Cola had invested heavily in a nationwide recycling campaign featuring Coke-branded recycling bins and TV commercials. "The research has made me question whether we were really trying to change behavior or we were just looking for the reputational benefits of being seen to be promoting recycling," she said. I admired her candor. She was admitting that her intent was not really to drive change but to be seen as doing so. The difference with the Closed Loop Fund is that Coke's dollars are now being used to genuinely drive change, in a less flashy and more impactful way. That's part of the New Behavioral Contract: doing rather than telling, and putting outcomes ahead of image. Of course, if the fund is successful, the reputational benefits will also come, and with them, business results.

Hannah Jones at Nike sums it up this way: "The art is knowing when to compete, and when to collaborate. Let's collaborate in adapting public and private infrastructure worldwide to a low carbon economy. Let's compete on innovation."[26]

Making Frenemies

The Closed Loop Fund is an example of making frenemies, which is one of the two forms of Experimental Collaboration that Green Giants embrace. (The other form is Open Innovation, discussed in the next section.) Another example of making frenemies is the Sustainable Apparel Coalition (SAC). The SAC began life in a not dissimilar way to the Closed Loop Fund: with a letter issued by Walmart and a more socially oriented company, Patagonia, calling on fellow business leaders to put their differences aside and collaborate to address a common challenge. In this case, that challenge was the lack of a common standard for measuring sustainability in the apparel industry. On top of its complex social challenges, the apparel industry also has a surprisingly large environmental impact, touching issues that include greenhouse gas emissions, land and water use, environmental toxins, and waste. It uses dyes, solvents, and huge amounts of water and petroleum. Decisions made across the value chain—fabric choices, pattern making, packaging, shipping, and disposal—therefore have major consequences. Choosing conventionally grown cotton, for example, locks you in to a material that is hugely water-intensive and uses more insecticides than any other single crop (25 percent of the insecticides applied worldwide). Yet there was no common way to measure and manage that impact.

Patagonia agreed to the collaboration, warily at first, because it was guided by its purpose: to use business to inspire and implement solutions to the environmental crisis.[27] Working with Walmart was a way for Patagonia to achieve much more than it could alone. The two hatched the plan of convening industry counterparts to work on industry-wide metrics together. They deliberately did not choose an existing industry group, preferring the independence of something new.

They needed to attract members of the industry to engage them. Because of its cultural status and its Considered Index (a tool for predicting the environmental impact of different choices made at the design stage), Nike was at the top of their partnership wish list. Launched in 2010, the Considered Index had reportedly taken seven years and $6 million to develop. (It served as an input to the development of the Flyknit technology.) The SAC had neither the appetite, budget, nor time to reinvent the wheel. But surely Nike wouldn't share its precious IP (intellectual property), would it?

Actually, it did, agreeing to share its database with the coalition, as well as releasing it to the public. It was not the first time Nike had experimented with sharing its sustainability-oriented IP. Along with other partners including Yahoo, Best Buy, and salesforce.com, Nike had formed GreenXChange in 2009, a web-based platform where patent owners could share portions of their IP portfolio. But the SAC collaboration is much larger.

The SAC group collaborated on the creation of what became the Higg Index, released on June 26, 2012 and refreshed in a 2.0 version in December 2013. This is a tool that enables apparel companies to assess impacts at the facility, product, and brand levels, rolling choices up to an overall score out of 70. An investigation of the tool reveals its value; not all outcomes are intuitive. For example, while recycled polyester scores higher than virgin fiber, as you'd expect, bamboo, which is often marketed as a greener alternative, scores worse than leather, cotton, or wool because turning bamboo into fabric is such an energy- and chemical-intensive process.[28] This can help guide designers' choices in radically different ways. Brands can also get points for asking consumers to wash items in cold rather than hot water, as Levi's does, or for using recycled components like Nike's polyester, made from used water bottles.

Today, the SAC includes 100 apparel brands, plus retailers (including IKEA), suppliers, NGOs, academic experts, and the Environmental Protection Agency. The 2.0 version of the Higg Index now covers 45 materials, begins to incorporate social and labor issues, and—in the spirit of transparency—has a sharable aspect that allows companies to see where they are relative to competitors.[29] Its ultimate goal is to be consumer-facing, with a simple hangtag that gives you the kind of easy-to-interpret information the Whole Foods ratings do for food, cleaning, and personal products. But the SAC says they need to pressure-test the index some more before they go there.

Giving away IP that resulted from so much work and investment money may seem on the surface like a bad business decision for Nike. But the company didn't look at it that way. By the time it made that move, the Flyknit technology was already well advanced, and Nike had already reaped the rewards of first-mover advantage. The information contained in the Higg Index avoids divulging Nike's most crucial secrets. (Remember the legal battle with Adidas that ensued when that company sought to copy Flyknit?) And it's actually better for Nike if the whole industry moves together. SAC members suggested that part of the reason they were willing to collaborate is because they'd experienced the challenges of developing and implementing proprietary approaches to solving the worker rights issues discussed above, resulting in unnecessary complexity and cost for them and their suppliers.

Nike believes that collaboration helps level the playing field. Other proponents of making frenemies agree. It takes the risk out of going it alone. It provides businesses cover as you get up to speed. It offers resources and information on areas that may be unfamiliar. It enables you to share the burdens, the risks, and the costs of problem solving and gives you a sense of how you're doing on the journey. For

Green Giants that are ahead of the curve, leading the formation of a coalition confers eternal leadership. For businesses that might rather be somewhere just behind the bleeding edge, industry collaboration provides safety in numbers and the opportunity to lead without being a lone wolf. Finally, the combined buying power can help overcome issues on the supply side (like availability of humanely raised or fair trade ingredients) and force suppliers to catch up. And once there are common standards and common goals, future bets on sustainable materials and processes become less risky, enabling investment.

The sustainable business community has become fond of the African proverb "If you want to go fast, go alone. If you want to go far, go together." That's what making frenemies is about.

Open Innovation

"There's a new hallmark of leadership," sustainable business expert Hunter Lovins told me over drinks in New York in December 2014. "Setting bold goals, then saying, 'we have no idea how we will get there.' And then figuring out whom you need to work with to get it done."

I can guess whom she was talking about. When Unilever CEO (and Iconoclastic Leader) Paul Polman launched the Unilever Sustainable Living Plan in 2010, he was up-front about the fact that he didn't know how his company would meet some of the 50 aggressive targets it had set itself to deliver by 2020. That's why, on Wednesday, April 25, 2011, Unilever decided to try an unprecedented social experiment: a 24-hour global, online dialogue called the Unilever Sustainable Living Lab. The invitation-only conference, hosted in a chatroom-style web platform, was structured around four topics, each representing a different component of the value chain: sustainable sourcing, sustainable production and distribution, consumer behavior change, and recycling and waste. Unilever said the lab was designed to "stimulate co-creation through conversation—for participants to learn from others, develop solutions, and share good practice." A total of 2,200 people from 77 countries joined the discussion. I was among those on the behavior change track, joining as an expert participant for an hour-long session.

It was a fast-paced hour of frantically typing out ideas and comments in an attempt to contribute while keeping pace with the other participants—a bit like a Twitter chat on steroids (before there were Twitter chats). In the spirit of multilateral sustainability, several of the other participants in the dialogue were my direct competitors, so I felt somewhat compelled to outdo them with the speed and relevance of my comments. It was also rather intimidating to be live-commenting, knowing that Paul Polman was dropping into different chats seemingly at random. (He commented on our track but not on anything I'd posted.) But it was exhilarating and exciting to see the collective brain coming together.

In 2014, Unilever moved to in-person formats with smaller groups, but the principle of the lab remained the same: crowdsourcing ideas from experts around Unilever's more intractable issues. I attended the New York event that year. Participants included the great and the good of the sustainable business world, characters who've peppered the pages of this book: Andrew Winston, Hunter Lovins, my colleague Carol Cone, Mindy Lubber of Ceres, and a carefully curated group of others. The mood at the event was collegial and collaborative. Being invited was something of a badge of honor; it felt good to have been included. It was also exciting to have the chance to be in a brainstorm with these characters. That's one of the reasons stakeholders are willing to give their time to efforts like these: It's a rare chance to see one another in action and to learn from people you respect as the best in your industry. It's unlike anything other companies have done.

In terms of breakthrough, business-building insights, what did the conference yield? People at Unilever told me the first Sustainable Living Lab gave them the impetus to expand their Enhancing Livelihoods program. That's the one that both Domestos and Lifebuoy, which have since transformed their approaches and become two of Unilever's fastest growing brands, sit under.

And top-line growth is not the only way these efforts contributed business value. For a company taking such risks, the strategy is smart, quite aside from any innovation ideas it might yield. When you have a cadre of naysayers ready to pounce at the first whiff of failure, you can create a force field around you with a network of interested parties you've anointed as your inner circle, invited to fully understand the complexities of the issues you're facing and encouraged to invest emotionally and intellectually in your success. It's one of the most effective forms of stakeholder engagement I've seen. Look: Here I am telling this story in my book as an example of industry best practice months (even years, in the case of the Sustainable Living Lab) later.

Unilever has also launched an Open Innovation portal, where it outlines detailed requests for help in approximately 10 key areas where it has struggled, such as how to cut the weight, quantity, and waste of product packaging; effective, odorless, eco-friendly cleansing agents for fats; and technology or devices to (you guessed it) encourage people to take shorter showers. At launch, commentators were surprised at how much information Unilever was giving away. But it worked. Today, Unilever claims that 60 percent of its new product development work involves collaboration.

The Sustainable Living Lab, in-person event, and portal are all examples of the other form of collaboration Green Giants are experimenting with: Open Innovation. I deliberated over putting this section in Chapter 2, on innovation, but since none of the Disruptive

Innovations listed in that chapter resulted from Open Innovation, I decided to keep it here. It is still too experimental in nature to have resulted in a billion-dollar breakthrough. But as a behavior, it sends a strong signal to the world that Unilever gets it and is modern, entrepreneurial, humble, and curious.

GE is another Green Giant willing to admit it doesn't have all the answers, and it is experimenting with Open Innovation to try to get there. As it progressed with Ecomagination, GE encountered unexpected challenges in its energy business. In the cleantech space, much of the innovation was happening outside of GE's walls and at a pace a large company was not structured to keep. Moreover, because so many solutions were in early stages, it was unclear which would succeed, creating a need to spread investments across a diverse portfolio of bets. GE knew there were start-ups out there that would be great complements to its core business and help it scale, but it needed a new way to engage.

The idea of an Open Innovation challenge was born. GE partnered with venture capital firms Emerald Technology Ventures, Foundation Capital, Kleiner Perkins Caufield & Byers, and RockPort Capital, which was in itself a mold-breaking move. Acknowledging that their external expertise would be valuable to GE in this unfamiliar space was the first part of opening up. The combined group then launched the Ecomagination Challenge, an open-source call for "ideas to update the existing power grid through 21st century technologies." Winning entrants would earn a portion of the $200 million total in investments to help them bring their ideas to market.

The idea to proceed was not easy. There were some at GE who thought the $200 million would be better used to support additional internal research. Others were concerned about giving the VC community access to GE's IP. The VCs too were wary. They realized that having a major player like GE in the market could help the speed of growing new ideas and therefore the speed to recognize revenue. But they needed to make sure agreements would not limit their options.

When the Ecomagination Challenge launched on July 14, 2010, GE had no way to gauge how many entries might be received, nor whether the effort would succeed.[30] The company need not have worried. Entries began pouring in from all over the world, even before the announcement was complete. Entrepreneurs, inventors, academics, and governments applied. In 10 weeks, the challenge had attracted more than 70,000 participants from 150 countries, making it one of the world's largest Open Innovation contests to date.

The awards were judged by GE executives, the VC firms, and other subject matter experts. The general public too was invited to vote, although the professional judges had the final say. The discussions were revealing for the judges. GE recognized that most of the entries were significantly earlier stage than the Round 2 investments it usually participates in, and that many of the ventures were tiny compared to its own nearly $40 billion energy business. It was hard to see how GE could mesh with them. The VC community and GE learned that their criteria for investment differed, and one VC firm wanted to invest in a start-up that GE viewed as a competitor.

Some of the ideas submitted were obvious candidates for investment, like the Irish business FMC-Tech, which provides utilities with real-time information on their grids, including power outages and power line capacity ratings, serving as a "central nervous system" for the grid. GE could see applications to its Smart Grid Delivery Optimization service, and it awarded FMC-Tech $55 million and support from GE's teams.[31]

Other ideas were a little more out there, like Solar Roadways, the brainchild of a couple from Idaho, Scott and Julie Brusaw. Solar

Roadways makes a system of hexagonal-shaped solar panels, which are designed to replace asphalt on roads across the country, turning the highway infrastructure into a giant solar-power–generating network. The Brusaws claim their panels "can withstand 250,000 pound trucks . . . can be installed on roads, parking lots, driveways, sidewalks, bike paths, playgrounds . . . include heating elements to stay snow/ice free, LEDs to make road lines and signage, and attached Cable Corridor to store and treat stormwater and provide a 'home' for power and data cables." This system got the people's vote, qualifying it for a $50,000 "community award," but the idea ultimately didn't secure further awards in the professional judging rounds.

The idea for the Ecomagination Challenge was always that it would be more than a one-time-only contest: GE was sourcing businesses to invest in that could ultimately enhance its core energy business. So how did it play out, specifically with FMC-Tech and Solar Roadways?

FMC-Tech went from strength to strength after receiving the Ecomagination award, and the synergies with GE's portfolio were a no-brainer. GE acquired the company later in 2011 in order to integrate its online power management into GE's portfolio.

Solar Roadways, on the other hand, is still on the journey to viability. In late 2014, it was close to completing its second phase of funding from the U.S. Federal Highway Administration to build a prototype parking lot and was getting ready to build it. The company had raised more than $2 million in an Indiegogo crowdsourcing campaign, thanks in part to its in-your-face "Solar Freaking Roadways" video, which racked up more than 18 million views on YouTube. (My mother-in-law emailed the video to me in June, so clearly it had gone viral.)

The Ecomagination Challenge was a valuable experiment that helped GE build its presence in the cleantech space and attract some important collaborators. But GE acknowledged that, as most large companies have found, meshing with start-ups was hard. In the end, as with the Unilever Sustainable Living Lab, the exercise may have contributed more in terms of reputation, learning, and relationship building than revenue growth, but as a demonstration of a new GE to the world, it was powerful. Actions speak louder than words, and as an engagement strategy, it was significant and far-reaching.

Open Innovation is an idea still in the beta stage, but as the business world shifts to transparency and collaboration as a way of working, it is likely here to stay.

How to Do It
Getting collaboration right is about deploying it strategically, not universally. When work is precompetitive, where you suspect others are grappling with the same issues (as Walmart did in recycling and apparel), and where there is little to be gained from trying to change a system single-handedly, it may be time for multilateral sustainability. Whether you need to join an existing entity or spearhead the formation of a new one depends on the maturity of the issue. Either way, a neutral and credible third party is an essential ingredient. And embrace the different perspectives. As Walmart and Patagonia proved, sometimes the most unlikely bedfellows can make great allies.

Managing these initiatives can be cumbersome, so it's important to focus on the areas of greatest impact and deploy the right staff. Often groups want CEO involvement, but reserve him or her for a high-profile launch or top-tier media opportunity (like the Walmart summit meeting for the Closed Loop Fund). The rest of the time, the relationship should be handled by the executive with the most relevant subject matter expertise, who could be the head of procurement or the chief sustainability officer. It is important, though, to invest—whether time, money, IP, or expertise. These organizations are only as good as what you put in.

As for Open Innovation, more and more organizations are trying it on for size. The key is to identify specific areas where you need help; pilot in a low-profile way before going more public; issue tight briefs; and ask for ideas that are sufficiently mature as to mesh quickly within your organization. Obviously, the initiative will be only as good as the entries you get, so getting the word out to folks qualified to help you is also key. The Ecomagination Challenge, for example, was supported with a multimedia campaign, and because video submissions were included, it was inherently social. Unilever chose a more direct invitation, key opinion former, model for its Sustainable Living Labs. Both approaches worked. In addition, if you're large, enlist a third party to manage and screen applications; Unilever's program is implemented by yet2.com. And a prize is never a bad incentive. Indeed, there has been a resurgence of the prize in the past decade, with total current philanthropic prize monies estimated by McKinsey at between $1 billion and $2 billion.[32]

The New Behavioral Contract is a work in progress. Nobody has it all figured out. But as Green Giants and their ilk experiment with new ways of conducting their affairs, businesses that fail to take responsibility, embrace transparency, and open up to collaboration will increasingly seem out of touch. So go on, behave better. Your business will thank you for it.

Next Billions and the Green Giant Effect

In 2009, a young American designer named Yael Aflalo went to China on a sourcing trip for her fashion line, Reformation. At the time, Reformation had two stores, one in Los Angeles and one in New York, stocking mostly refurbished vintage clothes. The business was modest but stable.

On arriving in China, Aflalo was horrified by the pollution. "I went to a part of China where 80 percent of what they produce is fashion, and the pollution was on a level hard to ignore. An LA native, I'd been aware of environmental issues, but seeing it first hand, I became intimately aware of my part in the process as a designer and consumer of fashion," she said.

Aflalo returned to the United States and completely overhauled her business model. With an ambition to develop the first sustainable fast fashion label—to "make killer clothes that don't kill the environment," as the company's Facebook page puts it—she began working only with sustainable fabrics, vintage fabrics, or surplus fabric from fashion houses that had over-ordered. She moved her business into a former LA bakery large enough to allow all design and manufacturing to be done on site by LA natives who earn a living wage and health benefits. As the Reformation website puts it, "We don't have to worry about where or how our clothes are manufactured. Literally we just walk a few feet and see the clothes being made by our own team."[1] The building was given a green retrofit; it recycles gray water, features energy-efficient fixtures, and is powered by 100 percent renewable energy.

Today, Aflalo's website invites customers to "Join the Reformation," and the company's slogan, which graces the entrance of the Soho, New York store, is "Change the world without changing your style." Her clientele includes trendsetting megastar Rihanna, pop princess Taylor Swift, and supermodel Karlie Kloss, all of whom are regularly snapped by paparazzi emerging from her Soho store, bags in hand. It doesn't hurt that Aflalo herself is tall, willowy, and porcelain-skinned, with high cheekbones. Her personal brand is irreverent—iconoclastic, even. Most important, though, are the clothes. They completely subvert the hemp-and-Birkenstock stereotype of sustainable fashion. Instead, they are well-cut, trendy, sexy, and affordable. They're what every hip, bicoastal 20-something woman about town wants to be seen wearing. In 2013, Reformation's revenue was $9 million. In 2014, it topped $25 million.

Okay, so $25 million is a drop in the bucket compared to the Green Giants' revenues. Even with 150 percent growth in a single year, Reformation has a long way to go to reach the billion-dollar benchmark. But the ingredients of success are there:

- Aflalo's Iconoclastic Leadership, spawned by a personal conversion

- A Disruptive Innovation that overturns the rules of the fast fashion category (there was some debate that such a thing was possible, since "sustainable fast fashion" seems like an oxymoron)

- A purpose to change the world and inspire a generation of fashionistas to do it with her

- Sustainability built into her business, not bolted on

- Appeal to the people from whom the mainstream take their fashion cues

- Good behavior, including building transparency into every corner of her business

Reformation is one of a growing collection of brands in the fashion category built upon Green Giant principles. Others include Everlane (whose tagline is "Radical Transparency: Know your factories. Know your costs. Always ask why."), founded by a former venture capitalist and committed to a transparent, ethical supply chain and low mark-ups; Zady, an e-commerce site stocking ethical, sustainable, chic fashion that landed on the *Fast Company* most innovative list of retailers in 2014; and Master & Muse, conceived and curated by supermodel Amber Valletta. For a book about giants, these brands are small. But they are growing fast. They are the Next Billions, and there are examples like them bubbling up across the economy.

Chipotle-lovers are now able to satisfy the taste for sustainable, healthy food the burrito chain helped cultivate at an expanding list of Chipotle wannabes. By late 2014, ethical East Coast salad shop sweetgreen had turned eating your vegetables into a 27-store, $50 million business with a $57.5 million round of funding in hand to fuel an expansion to the West Coast. Sweetgreen works extensively with local farmers, many of whom now grow produce especially for the chain, which aims to be "delicious, healthy, and transparent." Among its backers is Steve Case, former CEO of AOL, who believes sweetgreen "does have the potential some day to be the Chipotle of healthier options."[2]

Similarly, Dig Inn is fast becoming one of the largest buyers of local produce in New York. Founded by former private equity hotshot Adam Eskin in 2011, the chain had 2014 revenue of $30 million from seven New York City locations and has ambitious plans to expand beyond New York. Eskin says he's confident Dig Inn can make it to $1 billion[3] off its diet of organic roasted beets, Sicilian-roasted cauliflower, and wild salmon. According to BuzzFeed, Dig Inn "wants to be the Chipotle of farm-to-table dining." Are you seeing a theme here? When imitators are aiming to be "the Chipotle of . . . ," you know you've created a new paradigm.

Then there's the influence Chipotle has exerted over the industry at large. Panera Bread is making major strides to ensure that its supply chain is sustainable and socially responsible. First, the company has four Panera Cares cafes, where customers who can afford to are asked to pay the suggested donation listed, which covers the retail price of the food in addition to operating costs. Meanwhile, those who cannot afford the suggested donation can eat for free if they volunteer for one hour per week. Second, Panera launched a campaign in 2013 with the slogan "Live consciously. Eat deliciously." The ads touted Panera's commitment to antibiotic-free chicken and donating bread to the hungry. Now, investors are asking if Panera will catch up to Chipotle.

Similarly, McDonald's launched a major transparency offensive in 2014 called "Our Food. Your Questions," sharing the ingredient list of each of its menu items online and inviting customers to submit their questions on Twitter. It also introduced its farmers to the public in a major ad campaign.

This is the Green Giant Effect. Ideas pioneered by the Green Giants, ideas that once seemed niche, have become so popular that they've changed expectations of entire industries and are becoming the new normal. The incumbents are forced to follow the Green Giants' lead.

The Green Giant Effect is alive and well in the auto world. Tesla's competitors, which had been eating its zero-tailpipe-emissions dust, began 2015 with a show of EV and hybrid strength at the Detroit auto show. Top billing went to the BMW i8 hybrid. One reviewer described it as "more like driving in a video game than driving a car: silent, smooth, otherworldly . . . one day, all cars will be like this."[4] Naturally, the media is replete with Tesla versus BMW i8 comparisons. As to whether the i8 will become "the Model S killer," for now, the jury is out. But it's clear that in the new Green Giant world order, the start-up has become the incumbent, while the legacy player is playing catch-up.

Nissan also showcased a new Leaf model that will get 200 miles on a full charge.[5] As we saw in Chapter 5, Nissan's Leaf division is well on track to become a Green Giant; indeed, if units sold were the metric, the Leaf would beat Tesla several times over. It is by far the world's best-selling plug-in car.[6] GM, too, redoubled its EV efforts with its new model Volt and the newly launched Bolt, a $30,000 concept car slated for launch in 2017.

At the time of this writing, low prices at the gas pump were raising questions about the continued pace of EV adoption, but the consensus from Detroit seemed to be that 10 years hence, that debate will be over and the EVs will have won.[7] The Green Giant Effect will see gasoline vehicles consigned to the scrap heap of history and EVs sold as standard.

The Green Giant Effect extends beyond the verticals the Green Giants themselves inhabit. Airbnb—a leading light in the sharing economy movement beloved by sustainability advocates because it makes better use of existing resources rather than exploiting new ones—has undergone hockey-stick growth since its founding in 2008. The company, which enables anyone to post a room or apartment online for others to rent, is governed by the purpose "to create a global marketplace for space." It's a purpose that has seen the start-up, cofounded by three school friends now in their early 30s, grow to more than 1 million listings worldwide, which means it offers more lodging than any hotel chain in the world. Airbnb achieved a valuation of $13 billion in 2014,[8] which put its value above that of Hyatt Hotels or Wyndham Worldwide. Its founders are now worth $1.5 billion each, and while Airbnb's revenues are unknown, it is hotly tipped to reach $1 billion ere long. Airbnb is the second most highly valued tech firm after Uber, which would have qualified as a Next Billion if it weren't for serious, serial transgressions of the behavioral contract in 2014. (Uber has been accused of having failed to take seriously the safety of female passengers and expressing misogyny in comments by its executives.[9]) An Airbnb IPO is hotly anticipated.

In eyewear, Warby Parker is the Next Billion to watch, having built a business that donates a pair of specs to someone in need for every pair that's purchased. Warby Parker has raised more than $115 million from investors since its founding and was valued at $500 million in its most recent round of funding in December 2013. It follows the model popularized by TOMS, a brand that began with buy-one, give-one shoes in 2006 and is expanding into do-gooding coffee and beyond. TOMS sold a stake to Bain Capital in 2014, a deal that valued the company at $625 million.

Then there's the Honest Company, founded by Hollywood actress Jessica Alba in 2011. What could be more Green Giant-esque than calling your product "honest"? Honest offers groovy young moms eco- and baby-friendly diapers with hipster-genic designs like skull-and-crossbones and moustache prints, as well as laundry, cleaning, and personal care products. Alba founded it when she was expecting her first child and couldn't find products that were both cool and safe. In 2014, Honest was reported to have $150 million in revenue and a reported $1 billion valuation. *Inc.* magazine ran a 2014 story titled "How Jessica Alba Proved Her Doubters Wrong."[10] A contrarian Iconoclastic Leader in the making.

In baby food, organic brands like Ella's Kitchen and Plum Organics have taken over the baby food displays at Babies "R" Us with their pop-art pouches and six-figure revenues. Juice brands like Blue-Print and Organic Avenue are popping up in the best retail locations across Manhattan. And even the media is getting in on the act with Jeff Skoll's Participant Media offshoot Pivot TV, committed to bringing content that promotes social values to the airwaves and encouraging viewers to get involved with everything from jobs for veterans to marine habitats. The list goes on. Across the economy, companies built in the image of the Green Giants are flourishing, a new generation of businesses for a new era.

Change is afoot. You can feel it. As I write this, world leaders and CEOs are in Davos debating how business can transform society, end economic inequality, and lift millions out of poverty. Among young entrepreneurs, the race is on to be the Chipotle of X or the Warby Parker of Y. 2015 is set to be a pivotal year. The public and private sectors are gearing up to agree on a new set of sustainable development goals that will set the global agenda on issues as diverse as poverty eradication, sustainable development financing, gender equality, and climate change. The United Nations has made an unprecedented appeal to the private sector to engage in the process. In December 2015, world leaders are scheduled to convene in Paris to seek agreement on an ambitious and binding global climate agreement. This offers unprecedented opportunities for business to lead the debate for change.

The Green Giants prove the revenue opportunity is there. The Next Billions show this isn't just a story about a handful of businesses, cherry-picked to prove a point. This is a new way, a new paradigm for business. And the model is replicable.

So, now you know how to build a billion-dollar business with sustainability or social good at its core. You have the blueprint for success.

Better go build the next Green Giant—before someone else does.

Methodology for Research Cited in Chapter 1

To conduct research for this book, Jason Denner of the consulting group POINT380 developed a pair trade analysis methodology that enabled us to compare the stock market performance of publicly traded Green Giants (IKEA is the only privately held Green Giant company) to a set of comparison companies between the close of trading on June 29, 2010 to March 2, 2015 (beginning with the first trading day after Tesla's IPO, the most recently listed Green Giant). The comparison companies were selected to represent a major, publicly traded competitor that closely resembles each Green Giant company, with the exception that it has not built a billion-dollar, sustainable, or socially responsible product or line of business (e.g., P&G in the case of Unilever, Hypermarcas for Natura). Company performance was measured based on the annualized holding period returns of common stocks, adjusted for splits and dividends. Even when the Green Giant case was based upon a line of business rather than the total institution (e.g., GE Ecomagination), the overall performance of the corporation was used for the analysis. Performance data were based on stock prices published by major exchanges in the countries in which the Green Giants were listed (see below.) All closing stock prices were converted to U.S. dollars at the prevailing exchange rates on the date used for the analysis. The source for all stock price data was Yahoo! Finance and for currency exchange Oanda.com, and all datasets were downloaded on March, 3 2015. For the comparison list:

Green Giant	Comparison Company (Ticker)
Natura (NATU3.SA)	Hypermarcas (HYPE3.SA)
Tesla (TSLA)	BMW (BMW.DE)
Toyota (TM)	Nissan (NISANY)
Whole Foods (WFM)	Kroger (KR)
Unilever (UL)	P&G (PG)
Nike (NKE)	Adidas (ADS.DE)
GE (GE)	Siemens (SIE.DE)
Chipotle (CMG)	McDonald's (MCD)

This research is based on POINT380 proprietary research and analysis of global markets and investing. The information and/or analysis contained in this material have been compiled or arrived at from sources believed to be reliable; however, POINT380 does not make any representation as to their accuracy or completeness and does not accept liability for any loss arising from the use hereof. The reader should not assume that any investments in sectors and markets identified or described were or will be profitable. Investing entails risks, including possible loss of principal. The use of tools cannot guarantee performance. Past performance is no guarantee of future results. Market indexes are used only as context reflecting general market results during the period.

ENDNOTES

Introduction

1. http://finance.yahoo.com/q?s=CMG.
2. http://www.nasdaq.com/symbol/cmg/revenue-eps;http://www.statista.com/chart/2623/tim=hortons=makes=almost=three=times=as much=money=as=burger=kiing/.
3. http://newhope360.com/whole-foods-2014-earnings.
4. 10. http://markets.ft.com/research/Markets/Tearsheets/Forecasts?s=NATU3:SAO 7.41 billion Brazilian Real, exchange rate calculated February 27, 2015.
5. http://quotes.wsj.com/TSLA/financials.
6. IKEA 2014 Sustainability Report. Figure of 1.015 billion Euros, at exchange rate calculated on February 27, 2015.
7. "Nike CEO Hints at Flyknit's *Potential,*" *Portland Business Journal*, December 21, 2012. Estimated figure. Nike does not report on Flyknit as a category, and does not repeat on revenue figures for individual product lines.
8. The estimated annualized total figure of $15.442 billion is based on the following calculation of global sales for the first half of 2014: Prius C, $19,080 MSRP x sales of 150,000 = $2.862 billion; Prius, $24,200 MSRP x sales of 128,940 = $3.120 billion; Prius V, $26,750 MSRP x sales of 65,000 = $1.738 billion. When doubled for a full-year figure, this is approximately $15.442 billion. Based on http://www.greencarreports.com/news/1094125_toyota-continues-to-dominate-global-hybrid-sales-no-surprise-there.
9. See Daniel C. Esty and Andrew S. Winston, *Green to Gold: How Smart Companies Use Environmental Strategy to Innovate, Create Value, and Build Competitive Advantage* (Hoboken, N.J.: Wiley, 2009); L. Hunter Lovins and Boyd Cohen, *The Way Out: Kick-Starting Capitalism to Save Our Economic Ass* (New York: Hill and Wang, 2012).

259

10. http://www.natcapsolutions.org/businesscasereports.pdf.

11. http://www.natcapsolutions.org/business-case/GoldmanSachs Report_v2007.pdf.

12. *Climate Action and Profitability*; CDP S&P 500 Climate Change Report 2014. https://www.cdp.net/CDPResults/CDP-SP500-leaders-report-2014.pdf.

13. http://www.vanityfair.com/politics/features/2006/07/generalelectric 200607#.

14. http://www.reuters.com/article/2008/02/22/idUSN22372976.

15. http://thinkprogress.org/climate/2012/04/17/465678/former-gm-executive-bob-lutz-slams-the-gops-pure-fiction-knee-jerk-hatred-of-electric-cars/.

16. http://www.businesswire.com/news/home/20140630006140/en/GE-Releases-2013-Progress-Sustainability-Commitments#.VPfR4bPF-pc.

17. http://fortune.com/fortune500/peabody-energy-corporation-365/.

18. See the Appendix for research methodology.

19. Difference in average annualized holding period return of stocks, adjusted for splits and reinvested dividends, evaluated at close of trading on June 29, 2010 to March 2, 2015.

20. Computed as the net appreciation of equal investments in each publicly traded company (i.e., $125 invested in each of eight companies in each portfolio), adjusted for splits and dividends, evaluated at close of trading on June 29, 2010 to March 2, 2015.

21. Average annualized holding period return of stocks, adjusted for splits but not including dividends, as compared to the S&P500 index, evaluated at close of trading on June 29, 2010 to March 2, 2015.

22. Total growth of stock prices, adjusted for splits and dividends, evaluated at close of trading on June 29, 2010 to March 2, 2015.

23. http://www.environmentalleader.com/2013/05/09/global-green-trade-to-reach-2-2-trillion-by-2020/.

Chapter 1

1. http://www.esquire.com/features/most-inspiring-ceo-1012-steve-ells#slide-12.

2. Author interview with Chris Arnold, April 15, 2014.

3. http://www.nasdaq.com/symbol/cmg/revenue-eps.

4. http://seekingalpha.com/article/2167643-weighing-the-pros-and-cons-of-chipotle-mexican-grill?isDirectRoadblock=true&uprof=82.

5. http://www.forbes.com/2009/02/05/unilever-earnings-update-markets-equity-0205_consumers_guidance25.html.

6. http://www.unilever.com/sustainable-living-2014/our-approach-to-sustainability/unilever-sustainable-living-plan-summary/.

7. http://fortune.com/2013/05/23/unilevers-ceo-has-a-green-thumb/.

8. http://www.economist.com/news/business/21567062-pursuit-shareholder-value-attracting-criticismnot-all-it-foolish-taking-long.

9. http://www.managementtoday.co.uk/features/1055793/MT-Interview-Paul-Polman-Unilever/.

10. http://www.globescan.com/news-and-analysis/press-releases/press-releases-2014/310-global-experts-rank-unilever-number-one-for-sustainability-leadership-in-new-survey.html.

11. http://www.mckinsey.com/insights/sustainability/business_society_and_the_future_of_capitalism.

12. https://www.linkedin.com/indemand/global/2014.

13. https://hbr.org/2012/06/captain-planet.

14. Peter Andrews and Fiona Wood, *Uberpreneurs: How to Create Innovative Global Businesses and Transform Human Societies* (New York: Palgrave Macmillan, 2014).

15. http://www.theguardian.com/sustainable-business/epiphany-transform-corporate-sustainability.

16. http://www.vanityfair.com/politics/features/2006/07/generalelectric 200607#.

17. Ibid.

18. Author interview with Gary Sheffer, May 8, 2014.

19. Ibid.

20. Ibid.

21. http://www.businessweek.com/stories/2008-03-04/the-issue-immelts-unpopular-ideabusinessweek-business-news-stock-market-and-financial-advice.

22. Ibid.

23. Ibid.

24. GE.com.

25. http://www.vanityfair.com/politics/features/2006/07/generalelectric 200607#.

26. GE.com.

27. https://www.crunchbase.com/organization/tesla-motors/funding-rounds.

28. http://www.theguardian.com/theobserver/2014/may/25/elon-musk-entrepreneur-observer-profile.

29. http://www.teslanews.net/model-s.html.

30. http://topgear.wikia.com/wiki/Tesla_Roadster.

31. http://www.newyorker.com/magazine/2009/08/24/plugged-in.

32. http://www.nytimes.com/2010/07/25/business/25elon.html?pagewanted=all.

33. http://www.fastcompany.com/1662643/tesla-only-sells-10-cars-week-still-has-plans-build-cabriolet-van-and-suv.

34. http://www.wired.com/2012/10/romney-tesla-loser/.

35. http://www.telegraph.co.uk/motoring/motoringvideo/11301983/Tesla-Model-S-the-most-important-car-of-the-last-20-years.html.

36. http://247wallst.com/autos/2014/09/01/can-tesla-be-more-valuable-than-gm/.

37. http://www.forbes.com/profile/elon-musk/.

38. http://blogs.wsj.com/corporate-intelligence/2013/04/30/fords-former-bolshevik-says-hats-off-to-tesla/.

39. http://www.greenbiz.com/blog/2012/02/06/how-she-leads-hannah-jones-nike.

40. http://www.ssireview.org/articles/entry/15_minutes_with_hannah_jones.

41. http://www.nikeresponsibility.com/timeline/.

42. http://www.bloomberg.com/news/2012-05-03/nike-raises-factory-labor-and-sustainability-standards.html.

43. http://www.nytimes.com/2014/04/28/opinion/one-year-after-rana-plaza.html?_r=0.

44. http://www.wsj.com/articles/SB10001424052702303873604579493502231397942.

45. http://money.cnn.com/galleries/2007/biz2/0705/gallery.contrarians.biz2/3.html.

46. Author interview with Gary Sheffer, May 8, 2014.

47. https://hbr.org/2012/06/captain-planet.

Chapter 2

1. http://insideevs.com/gm-ceo-assembles-task-force-to-analyze-the-disruptive-threat-from-tesla/.

2. http://www.fastcompany.com/most-innovative-companies/2013/nike.

3. http://theweek.com/articles/477805/nikes-flyknit-sneaker-thats-knit-like-sock.

4. http://www.popsugar.com/fitness/photo-gallery/21859651/image/21859688/Nike-FlyKnit.

5. http://money.cnn.com/2006/02/17/news/companies/mostadmired_fortune_toyota/.

6. https://alumni.stanford.edu/get/page/magazine/article/?article_id=31675

7. Robert G. Eccles and George Serafeim, "The Performance Frontier: Innovating for a Sustainable Strategy," *Harvard Business Review*, May 2013.

8. http://www.usatoday.com/story/money/cars/2014/03/02/tesla-stock/5908695/.

9. http://business.time.com/2013/08/29/fast-food-companies-can-afford-to-pay-their-workers-more/.

10. http://finance.yahoo.com/blogs/the-exchange/fast-food-chains-aren-t-rich-protesters-think-192549497.html.

11. Author email interview with Sally Uren, January 2015.

12. http://www.oxforddictionaries.com/us/definition/american_english/greenwash.

13. http://www.forbes.com/sites/joannmuller/2013/05/16/teslas-elon-musk-is-no-dummy/.

14. https://www.fundable.com/learn/startup-stories/chipotle.

15. http://www.huffingtonpost.com/2013/07/12/steve-ells-chipotle-20th-anniversary_n_3583927.html.

16. http://www.wsj.com/articles/SB113829672351557263.

17. http://www.bloomberg.com/bw/articles/2013-10-03/chipotle-the-one-that-got-away-from-mcdonalds.

18. *The Climate Has Changed: Why Bold, Low Carbon Action Makes Good Business Sense*, We Mean Business, September 2014.

19. http://alumni.stanford.edu/get/page/magazine/article/?article_id=31675.

20. http://money.cnn.com/2006/02/17/news/companies/mostadmired_fortune_toyota/.

21. Author interview with Jessamyn Rodriguez, January 2015.

22. "Taking on Tesla: Big Auto's First Steps to Dominating Electric," Shai Agassi, Linked In, August 21, 2013.

23. http://www.adweek.com/news/advertising-branding/patagonia-taking-provocative-anti-growth-position-152782.

24. http://analystreports.som.yale.edu/reports/BrandedApparel2012.pdf.

25. Liz Welch, "The Way I Work: Yvon Chouinard, Patagonia," *Inc Magazine* March 12, 2013.

26. Drake Baer, "How Patagonia's New CEO Is Increasing Profits While Trying to Save the World," *Fast Company*, February 28, 2014.

27. "Hybrid Sales Still Climbing," *Green Car Reports*, April 2, 2013.

Chapter 3

1. http://www.missionstatements.com/fortune_500_mission_statements.html.

2. *Putting Purpose into Marketing*, World Federation of Advertisers and Edelman, March 7, 2013; http://www.wfanet.org/en/global-news/brands-will-increasingly-need-purpose-say-worldu2019s-biggest-marketers?p=32.

3. Milton Friedman, "The Social Responsibility of Business Is to Increase its Profits," *New York Times Magazine*, September 13, 1970.

4. http://www.brookings.edu/~/media/research/files/papers/2011/7/19%20corporation%20west/0719_corporation_west.pdf.

5. bteam.org.

6. http://www.bcorporation.net/.

7. http://www.theguardian.com/sustainable-business/2015/jan/23/benefit-corporations-bcorps-business-social-responsibility.

8. http://www.conservativeblog.org/amyridenour/2011/3/10/spot-the-bias-in-ny-times-global-warming-hearing-story.html.

9. http://www.conservativeblog.org/amyridenour/2014/7/20/correcting-the-record-on-yet-another-idiotic-article-miscove.html.

10. http://www.nationalcenter.org/PR-GE_Climate_Change_022114.html.

11. http://www.theguardian.com/sustainable-business/sustainability-key-corporate-success.

12. *The GS Sustain Focus List*, Goldman Sachs Group Inc., June 22, 2007; http://www.natcapsolutions.org/business-case/GoldmanSachsReport_v2007.pdf.

13. *From the Stockholder to the Stakeholder: How Sustainability Can Drive Financial Outperformance* (University of Oxford and Arabesque Asset Management, 2014).

14. http://www.natcapsolutions.org/businesscasereports.pdf.

15. http://www.consumerreports.org/cro/news/2012/03/bad-karma-our-fisker-karma-plug-in-hybrid-breaks-down/index.htm.

16. http://www.automobilemag.com/features/news/1208_q_and_a_elon_musk_ceo_tesla/involvement.html.

17. Ibid.

18. http://www.mckinsey.com/features/capitalism/paul_polman.

19. http://www.mercurynews.com/business/ci_25010333/coast-coast-tesla-model-s.

20. http://www.businessweek.com/articles/2014-06-19/why-teslas-elon-musk-doubed-down-on-solar-with-solarcity-deal.

21. http://www.fool.com/investing/general/2014/10/30/tesla-motors-incs-secret-growth-weapon-hint-its-no.aspx.

22. http://www.fastcompany.com/3035975/generation-flux/find-your-mission.

23. Author interview with Gary Sheffer, May 8, 2014.

24. http://www.fastcoexist.com/3037823/millennials-will-become-the-majority-in-the-workforce-in-2015-is-your-company-ready.

25. https://netimpact.org/sites/default/files/documents/business-as-unusual-2014.pdf.

26. Edelman brandshare survey, 2014.

27. https://www.scribd.com/doc/90411623/Executive-Summary-2012-Edelman-goodpurpose-Study.

28. http://purpose.edelman.com/slides/introducing-goodpurpose-2012/.

29. http://www.havasmedia.com/meaningful-brands.

30. http://archive.fortune.com/magazines/fortune/fortune_archive/1999/11/22/269126/index.htm.

31. http://www.ft.com/intl/cms/s/0/294ff1f2-0f27-11de-ba10-0000779fd2ac.html?siteedition=intl#axzz3MYzB6tfa.

Chapter 4

1. Robert G. Eccles and George Serafeim, "The Performance Frontier: Innovating for a Sustainable Strategy," *Harvard Business Review*, May 2013.

2. http://www.pginvestor.com/GenPage.aspx?IID=4004124&GKP=208821.

3. http://www.unilever.com/aboutus/introductiontounilever/ourmission/.

4. http://www.fool.com/investing/general/2013/02/06/procter-gamble-on-track-or-adrift.aspx.

5. http://www.economist.com/node/13648978.

6. http://qz.com/284142/we-have-yet-seen-peak-chipotle/.

7. Research conducted for this book by Jason Denner at POINT380.

8. Lynn S. Paine, Nien-hê Hsieh, and Lara Adamsons, "Governance and Sustainabillty at Nike (A)," Harvard Business School Case 313-146, June 2013.

9. This section draws heavily on the case cited in Note 8.

10. Ibid.

11. Author interview with Lynn S. Paine, March 5th 2015.

12. Ibid.

13. Lynn S. Paine, "Sustainability in the Boardroom," *Harvard Business Review*, July–August, 2014; https://hbr.org/2014/07/sustainability-in-the-board-room.

14. http://www.managementexchange.com/story/innovation-in-well-being.

15. Author email interview with Andrew Winston, January 2015.

16. *The Climate Has Changed: Why Bold, Low Carbon Action Makes Good Business Sense*, We Mean Business, September 2014.

17. Author email interview with Jessica Sobel, January 2015.

18. Author interview with Deb Frodl, March 2014.

19. Paine, "Sustainability in the Boardroom," *Harvard Business Review*, July 2014.

20. Harry Bradford, "Chipotle Salary Cn Top $95,000 Annually," *Huffington Post*, February 1, 2013; http://www.glassdoor.com/Salary/McDonald-s-General-Manager-Salaries-E432_D_KO11,26.htm.

21. http://www.restfinance.com/Restaurant-Finance-Across-America/May-2014/A-Look-At-Chipotles-Efficiency/.

22. Rupinder Singh, "Weighing the Pros and Cons of Chipotle Mexican Grill, *Seeking Alpha*, April 27, 2014.

23. http://seekingalpha.com/article/2327525-chipotle-mexican-grills-cmg-ceo-steve-ells-on-q2-2014-results-earnings-call-transcript?part=single.

24. Author interview with Chris Arnold, April 15, 2014.

25. http://www.autoblog.com/2012/04/06/lithium-ion-battery-costs-will-still-be-about-400-kwh-by-2020/.

26. http://www.greencarreports.com/news/1089545_2014-nissan-leaf-electric-car-84-mile-range-aroundview-standard.

27. http://www.greencarreports.com/news/1084682_what-goes-into-a-tesla-model-s-battery--and-what-it-may-cost.

28. http://www.spacex.com/about.

29. *Gaining Ground: Corporate Progress on the Ceres Roadmap for Sustainability*, Ceres and Sustainalytics, 2014.

30. http://sustainability.thomsonreuters.com/2013/04/11/executive-perspective-global-reporting-initiatives-chief-executive-ernst-ligteringen/.

31. http://www.theguardian.com/sustainable-business/stock-exchanges-fail-hold-account-sustainability.

32. http://www.fm-magazine.com/feature/depth/jean-marc-hu%C3%ABt#.

33. Research conducted for this book by Jason Denner at POINT380.

34. http://www.unilever.com/investorrelations/annual_reports/Annual ReportandAccounts2013/index.aspx.

35. Robert G. Eccles, George Serafeim, and James Heffernan, "Natura Cosméticos, S.A." Harvard Business School Case 412-052, November 2011. (Revised June 2013.)

36. Ibid.

37. https://hbr.org/2012/06/captain-planet.

38. http://www.cgma.org/magazine/features/pages/20137408.aspx?Test CookiesEnabled=redirect.

39. http://www.unilever.com/aboutus/foundation/aboutfoundation/index.aspx.

40. http://www.triplepundit.com/2014/10/speaking-unspeakable-business-case-embracing-taboos/.

Chapter 5

1. http://www.wri.org/blog/2010/04/otarian-restaurant-new-york-city-uses-wri%E2%80%99s-greenhouse-gas-protocol.

2. http://www.nytimes.com/2010/06/09/dining/09dinbriefs-2.html.

3. http://www.express.co.uk/life-style/health/517246/Vegetarians-are-on-the-increase-in-Britain.

4. http://opinionator.blogs.nytimes.com/2012/01/10/were-eating-less-meat-why/.

5. http://www.grubstreet.com/2011/08/generally_when_were_angry_with.html.

6. http://www.eater.com/2014/10/20/7024161/chipotle-will-open-more-than-200-new-locations-in-2015.

7. Author interview with Chris Arnold, April 15, 2014.

8. http://www.westerncity.com/Western-City/September-2009/The-Co-Benefits-of-Sustainability-Strategies/.

9. http://www.smh.com.au/business/the-ammonia-and-acrimony-remain-20110128-1a8bc.html#ixzz3O0ihioPg.

10. Author interview with Chris Arnold, April 15, 2014.

11. http://www.bizjournals.com/denver/news/2014/07/21/chipotles-record-sales-26-profit-jump-fuel-after.html?page=all.

12. From Unilever research on the Walmart shopper, conducted in 2010.

13. http://www.wsj.com/articles/SB10001424052702304655304579548343382157608.

14. http://www.wnyc.org/story/what-planet-whole-foods-cheaper-option/.

15. http://www.kiplinger.com/article/spending/T050-C011-S001-best-things-to-buy-at-whole-foods.html.

16. http://media.wholefoodsmarket.com/press/values-matter-brand-campaign.

17. http://www.slate.com/blogs/moneybox/2014/11/05/whole_foods_q4_2014_results_values_matter_might_be_working_for_the_organic.html.

18. http://www.forbes.com/sites/greatspeculations/2014/10/20/chipotles-earning-preview-increasing-customer-count-new-store-openings-to-drive-

sales/; http://www.forbes.com/sites/greatspeculations/2014/06/23/how-the-fast-casual-segment-is-gaining-market-share-in-the-restaurant-industry/.

19. http://insideevs.com/tesla-announces-500month-model-s-leasing/.

20. "The Seven Sins of Greenwashing," TerraChoice, 2009.

Chapter 6

1. http://magazine.good.is/articles/apple-s-brand-at-stake-as-customers-demand-better-labor-practices.

2. Bob Baum, "Study Shows Wages for Nike Workers in Vietnam, Indonesia More than Adequate," *The Columbian*, October 17, 1997.

3. http://www.nytimes.com/1998/05/13/business/international-business-nike-pledges-to-end-child-labor-and-apply-us-rules-abroad.html.

4. https://hbr.org/2014/07/a-conversation-with-jill-ker-conway.

5. http://www.businessinsider.com/how-nike-solved-its-sweatshop-problem-2013-5.

6. http://www.theguardian.com/sustainable-business/nike-supply-chain-measures-up.

7. http://www.greenbiz.com/blog/2012/05/07/nike-sustainability-goals-supply-chain.

8. Edelman Trust Barometer, 2014; http://www.edelman.com/insights/intellectual-property/2014-edelman-trust-barometer/trust-around-the-world/.

9. Edelman brandshare survey, 2014.

10. Global Trends, *Corporate Clout 2013: Time for Responsible Capitalism*; http://www.globaltrends.com/?Itemid=87.

11. http://www.fm-magazine.com/feature/depth/jean-marc-hu%C3%ABt.

12. GlobeScan Radar research, 2011.

13. http://newyork.walmartcommunity.com/unilever-and-walmart-in-joint-water-saving-campaign/.

14. http://www.reuters.com/article/2009/12/11/unilever-idUSGEE5BA0Z320091211.

15. http://www.facing-finance.org/en/2014/06/investors-call-on-all-palm-oil-producers-to-cease-deforestation-development-on-peat-lands-and-violations-of-human-rights/.

16. Edelman brandshare survey, 2014.

17. http://www.nytimes.com/2014/10/16/business/whole-foods-to-rate-its-produce-and-flowers-for-environmental-impact.html?smprod=nytcore-iphone&smid=nytcore-iphone-share.

18. http://www.ecolabelindex.com/.

19. https://www.globalreporting.org/resourcelibrary/carrots-and-sticks.pdf.

20. http://www.ecova.com/news-media/ecova-insights-newsletter/commercial-industrial/issue-4/cdp-reporting.aspx.

21. http://trendwatching.com/trends/10trends2013/?fullfrontal.

22. http://www.unilever.com/images/slp_Unilever-Sustainable-Living-Plan-2013_tcm13-388693.pdf.

23. https://econsultancy.com/blog/8638-bad-reviews-improve-conversion-by-67.

24. http://www.closedloopfund.com/page/why-the-closed-loop-fund.

25. http://www.closedloopfund.com/page/about.

26. http://www.politico.com/arena/bio/hannah_jones_.html.

27. http://www.patagonia.com/us/patagonia.go?assetid=2047.

28. http://www.wsj.com/news/interactive/STYLE0726?ref=SB1000087239 63904435709045775476106349453308.

29. http://www.triplepundit.com/2014/02/higg-2-0-index-journey-industry-wide-sustainable-apparel-standard/.

30. http://cmr.berkeley.edu/BHCS_award_2012_2_ecomagination_5672.pdf.

31. http://www.greentechmedia.com/articles/read/ge-announces-ecomagination-challenge-winners.

32. http://mckinseyonsociety.com/capturing-the-promise-of-philanthropic-prizes/.

Conclusion

1. https://www.thereformation.com/about-us.

2. http://www.entrepreneur.com/article/230233.

3. http://www.buzzfeed.com/sapna/dig-inn-follows-sweetgreen-chipotle-path-as-food#.uaxz09KdeK.

4. http://www.theguardian.com/technology/2015/jan/17/bmw-i8-car-review-zoe-williams?CMP=share_btn_link.

5. http://oilprice.com/Latest-Energy-News/World-News/Amazing-Green-Cars-at-the-2015-Detroit-Auto-Show.html.

6. http://www.greencarreports.com/news/1094705_plug-in-electric-car-sales-in-sept-leaf-up-again-volt-down.

7. http://oilprice.com/Latest-Energy-News/World-News/Amazing-Green-Cars-at-the-2015-Detroit-Auto-Show.html.

8. http://www.wsj.com/articles/airbnb-mulls-employee-stock-sale-at-13-billion-valuation-1414100930.

9. http://www.institutionalinvestor.com/inside-edge/3402854/uber-silicon-valley-and-sexism.html.

10. http://www.inc.com/magazine/201411/lindsay-blakely/how-jessica-alba-proved-her-doubters-were-wrong.html.

INDEX